D1481007

INSTITUTIONAL DEVELOPMENT

Institutional Development

A Third World City Management Perspective

Ronald McGill
Management Adviser
Civil Service Reform Programme, Tanzania

Withdrawn
IOWA STATE UNIVERSITY
of Science and Technology
LIBRARY

First published in Great Britain 1996 by
MACMILLAN PRESS LTD
Houndmills, Basingstoke, Hampshire RG21 6XS
and London
Companies and representatives
throughout the world

A catalogue record for this book is available
from the British Library.

ISBN 0–333–65413–7

First published in the United States of America 1996 by
ST. MARTIN'S PRESS, INC.,
Scholarly and Reference Division,
175 Fifth Avenue,
New York, N.Y. 10010

ISBN 0–312–15819–X

Library of Congress Cataloging-in-Publication Data
McGill, Ronald.
Institutional development : a third world city management
perspective / Ronald McGill.
p.   cm.
Includes bibliographical references and index.
ISBN 0–312–15819–X (cloth)
1. Urbanization—Developing countries.   2. Municipal government by
city manager—Developing countries.   I. Title.
JS384.D4M33   1996
352'.0009172'4—dc20   96–2598
                                                                                    CIP

© Ronald McGill 1996
Foreword © George L. Gattoni 1996

All rights reserved. No reproduction, copy or transmission of
this publication may be made without written permission.

No paragraph of this publication may be reproduced, copied or
transmitted save with written permission or in accordance with
the provisions of the Copyright, Designs and Patents Act 1988,
or under the terms of any licence permitting limited copying
issued by the Copyright Licensing Agency, 90 Tottenham Court
Road, London W1P 9HE.

Any person who does any unauthorised act in relation to this
publication may be liable to criminal prosecution and civil
claims for damages.

10   9   8   7   6   5   4   3   2   1
05   04   03   02   01   00   99   98   97   96

Printed in Great Britain by
The Ipswich Book Company Ltd
Ipswich, Suffolk

To Karen

Contents

List of Tables and Figures

Tables

Figures

Foreword

The unprecedented rate of urbanisation in developing nations has created massive new tasks for national and local policy-makers and administrators. In the developing world, the management of urban areas is failing. Local authorities and their urban managers are besieged with the tremendous challenge to fill the gaps in services, keep pace with the needs of growing populations and tackle problems never seen before. The third world's cities and towns are most difficult to administer, for it is only recently that local institutions were called upon to take over increasingly complex responsibilities, with meagre resources. Development agencies like the World Bank, UNDP and so on, in seeking to help countries deal with the impact of urbanisation, are confronted with implementation constraints termed 'weak municipalities' or 'lack of institutional capacity'. However, it is more difficult and daunting to develop strong and effective institutions than to install infrastructure. Nevertheless, years of experience in supporting urban development has proved that without a strong local institutional base to manage today's cities, urbanisation is not sustainable.

International development agencies are focusing on promoting the decentralisation of government authority as a critical element in managing urban growth. However, effective decentralisation depends on local institutions with a greater capacity and vision to handle wider responsibilities. Local (and national) institutions must evolve and restructure to eliminate bottlenecks and adapt to new roles. The key to sustainable urbanisation rests with institutions that can facilitate and motivate, so that the creative and economic energies of city dwellers can be productively employed.

In this timely book Ron McGill rightly aims at the relationship between institutional development and city management in developing countries. Its focus on developing management structures and planning expertise is vital to the future of cities. Dr McGill is eminently qualified to make these proposals for organisational strengthening and building a planning capability. This is by virtue of his rich experience in not only successfully managing an African capital city but also in developing an urban management capability for that country's urban sector generally. He presents us with a set of valuable principles that are not only a guide to institutional development but also a much needed starting point for helping to meet the urban challenge of the future. This work will no doubt be a basic instrument for policy-makers, practitioners and development agencies promoting sound urban institutions.

GEORGE L. GATTONI
Principal Urban Planner
Economic Development Institute
The World Bank

Preface

This book owes its genesis to my former colleagues in the Malawi local government service. My ideas about urban management in developing countries, having languished over the previous decade, were not only formalised but also tested in Malawi's urban sector. People who contributed to the test were Francis Mfune, Chief Executive of Lilongwe City Council; my first direct counterpart. Donny Alufandika, Chief Executive of Blantyre City Council, Nicholas Ngwira, Chief Executive of Mzuzu City Council and Fred Baluwa, Chief Executive of Zomba Municipal Council, became arms length counterparts as my work moved from a specific executive to a general advisory role. We had some rigorous debates. The particular pleasures were the two training workshops at the beautiful Lake Malawi. The first, in 1992, concentrated on the general urban management process.[1] The second, in 1993, looked at assessing urban management performance.[2] The conclusions from both workshops found their way into practice.

Particular discussion took place on the dilemma between the desire for urban development and the lack of financial capacity. Lilongwe's City Planner, Aggrey Kawonga, and City Treasurer, San Kumwenda, represented both sides of the debate. They gradually came to understand the urban management perspective of urban and council performance as one holistic entity.

This book makes observations about the constraining and therefore frustrating environment within which local government sometimes has to operate. This inevitably means the 'parent' ministry (of local government). In truth, this constraint is often a product of the contextual regulations and not the people who inhabit the ministry. In this regard, special mention should be made of Brian Phangapanga, Secretary for Local Government during the second half of my time in Malawi. He often produced calm counsel under difficult circumstances. Paul Lungu, Chief Local Government Officer and recently promoted to the role of Local Government Commissioner, offered some timely advice during my work there. Martin Phiri, the former Secretary for Local Government, should also be acknowledged as the person who influenced my original appointment to Malawi.

The early days of work in Malawi were coloured by discussions with World Bank personnel. They were laying the foundations for the

Local Government Development Project. Roberto Chavez, George Gattoni and Anders Zeijlon were key personalities in this debate.

The practical side of this book had to be tested by a more academic consideration. Inevitably therefore, the text was framed after a year of full-time academic research. This was in the Department of Human Resource Management at Strathclyde University in Glasgow, under the supervision of D.C. Pitt, Professor of Organisational Analysis and Dean of the Strathclyde Business School.

Finally, it was my wife Karen who persuaded me that we should both give up our respective urban development posts in Britain in order to take up the challenges presented to me in Malawi. I was nervous about such a dramatic step into an unknown future. This book is ultimately a testimony to her underlying strength in these matters. It is also a tribute to her continuing endurance. By the time this text was being finalised, we were contending with the increasing demands of not only our young son Jamie, but also our twin baby daughters, Rhona and Kirsty. As this preface is concluded, Karen is showing her mettle again; this time, helping me to embrace new challenges in Tanzania, is our second son, Roddy. With a partner like that, how can one fail?

Dar es Salaam   RONALD McGILL
Tanzania

Introduction

This book seeks to identify some general principles to guide the institutional development (ID) process, in relation to third world city management. It does so by reviewing the theoretical perspectives for ID, the function and form of third world city management.

The practice looks at two related cases of ID. The first concerns the process of organisational restructuring and strengthening. It seeks to highlight the importance of an organisation's relationship with its development environment. The second focuses on building a policy and planning capability. It seeks to highlight the notion of sustainability in ID.

The synthesising chapters seek to offer some operational guidelines. These are aimed at practitioners, in their quest to strengthen local institutions in order to meet the monumental challenges of rapid urbanisation in developing countries.

There is no doubt that ID is current practice in multilateral and bilateral donor agencies. For example, the World Bank has recently published some interesting research on the subject. Similarly, Britain's Overseas Development Administration has recently increased its ID activity throughout its geographical domains.

There is also little doubt in this author's opinion that the parameters to govern ID practice have still to be generally agreed. This volume attempts to make a contribution to that end. The contribution is presented in six parts.

Part I explores the characteristics of institutional development (ID). It does so in the knowledge of the literature's suggestion that there is no standard model for third world ID. Chapter 1 attempts to define the concept of ID. Chapter 2 assesses the nature of its application in the third world. The Summary to Part I identifies the key characteristics of institutional development. An initial conceptual framework is introduced.

Part II explores the characteristics of the function of city management. It does so in the knowledge of the literature's suggestion that there is no accepted model of third world city management. Chapter 3 attempts to identify the planning perspectives on the third world city. Chapter 4 assesses the scope of its intervention in third world cities. The Summary to Part II identifies the key characteristics of the city management function in the third world. An initial conceptual framework is introduced.

Part III explores the characteristics of the form of city management. It does so in the knowledge of the literature's suggestion that there is no standard organisational arrangement for third world city management. Chapter 5 identifies some organisational dilemmas. Chapter 6 assesses the structuring criteria for organising city management. The Summary to Part III identifies the key characteristics of the city management form in the third world. An initial conceptual framework is introduced.

Part IV seeks to explore the first of two important aspects of the institutional development process. Ultimately, it focuses on the importance of the organisation–environment relationship. Chapter 7 looks at a case of project development in organisational restructuring and strengthening. Chapter 8 reviews the ID performance of the case. The Summary to Part IV identifies the key characteristics of this practice.

Part V seeks to explore the second of two important aspects of the institutional development process. Ultimately, it focuses on the importance of testing sustainability. Chapter 9 looks at a case of project development in a policy and planning capability. Chapter 10 reviews the ID performance of the case. The Summary to Part V identifies the key characteristics of this ID practice.

Finally, Part VI synthesises the two stages of the institutional development process. Chapter 11 offers a structure to ID. Chapter 12 identifies the institutional development imperatives for third world city management.

There is also a short concluding chapter.

The theoretical material is taken from a wide range of literature. To maintain the currency of the debate, the majority of the cited texts cover the decade 1984 to 1994.

The case material is recorded in some detail. This is in order to convey the intensely practical and time-consuming nature of the process. Despite this, certain patterns and operational principles do emerge. The practice took place in the five-year period 1989 to 1993.

In essence, this book seeks to achieve five things. First, it attempts to offer conceptual frameworks, for institutional development, the city management function and the city management form. Secondly, it attempts to highlight the fundamental importance of the organisation–environment relationship in institutional development. Thirdly, it attempts to present a practical framework for testing the sustainability of ID; in this case, the transfer of an urban management capability to counterpart urban chief executives in Malawi. Fourthly, it attempts to offer operating checklists for both the institutional development process and the preparation of integrated development strategies. Finally, it seeks to highlight the institutional development imperatives for third world city management.

Part I

Institutional Development (ID)

Part I explores the characteristics of institutional development (ID). It does so in the knowledge of the literature's suggestion that there is no standard model for third world ID. Chapter 1 attempts to define the concept of ID. Chapter 2 assesses the nature of its application in the third world. The Summary to Part I identifies the key characteristics of institutional development. An initial conceptual framework is introduced.

1 Defining Institutional Development (ID)

There is no standard definition of institutional development (ID) in the third world literature. Blase (1986) has suggested that 'while a single, all-purpose definition of the institution would be convenient, it does not exist and the literature is not mature enough for its formulation at this time'.[1] Others concur with this view: 'A variety of terms is used to describe [institutional development] ... These expressions are ... still relatively ill defined. Clarity of definition will help to ensure common interpretation and usage.'[2]

This chapter therefore seeks to identify the essential characteristics of ID. It considers three topics:

- INSTITUTIONS
- DEVELOPMENT
- INSTITUTIONAL DEVELOPMENT.

INSTITUTIONS

Under the heading of institutions, three ideas are considered: institutions and development; institutions and values; institutions being political.

Institutions and development

It has been argued that 'institutional weakness ... constitutes a roadblock to development in developing countries. This institutional weakness is reputed to be most severe in Sub-Saharan Africa where the third UN Development Decade, the 1980s, has been written off as a lost decade'.[3] This seems to be a travesty of human endeavour. For example, in Mozambique, 'three essential institutional issues have continued to plague the [development] system; poor donor co-ordination, an inability to provide an efficient and effective allocation of resources, and a difficulty in reducing unit costs'.[4] In this case, it was the recipient government that was institutionally weak.

3

The pivotal role of institutions is central to the debate on development.

> Institutions are central to sustainable and beneficial economic growth.
> They create the policies, mobilize and manage the resources, and
> deliver the services which stimulate and sustain development. Growth
> and prosperity are unlikely to be maintained if the institutions which
> guide them are dysfunctional.[5]

Here, institutions seem to be the essential filter of, and guide to, the
development process.

It is argued that 'over 70 per cent of the world's population lives in
developing countries that face challenging administrative problems in
trying to survive'.[6] The challenge is clear enough. What matters at
this time is an agreement on the nature of an institution, as the instrument of development.

The whole basis of institutions in the development process has been
questioned. The effect has been to highlight their importance. 'A seg-
ment of the central literature addresses the question of why institutions should be considered with regard to the development process.'[7]
The concept is developed that the institutions play a strategic role when
the focus is on development rather than growth. The implication is
that growth is a private sector dominated activity; if growth exists, no
intervention is required. In contrast, development is a qualitative, public sector oriented function. It is embarked upon in order to encourage
development (defined in the next section) to take place.

There is an argument that institutions play a pivotal role in the development process, especially in urban development.

> The impact of programmes aimed at providing urban shelter, ser-
> vices and infrastructure depends upon the quality of institutions re-
> sponsible for planning and implementing these projects. The
> institutional machinery provides the channel through which the ur-
> ban sector issues and priorities are articulated, projects are planned
> and implemented and inter-sectoral complementarity is accomplished.
> It serves as the most critical intervening factor through which econ-
> omic resources and human skills are utilised for, among other things,
> promoting urban development.[8]

The same point is reinforced by Shabbir Cheema in a later volume.[9]

In summary, it is clear that institutions play a pivotal role in the
development process.

Institutions and values

One can take a very practical approach to the question of what constitutes an institution. An argument given in Uphoff (1986) suggests that the terms institution and organisation are used interchangeably. According to this, three categories are commonly recognised:

- organisations that are not institutions;
- institutions that are not organisations; and
- organisations that are institutions (and vice versa).

The argument goes on to suggest that, from the law, a new legal firm is an organisation, the law is an institution and the court is both.[10] Such conceptual semantics seem academic at this stage.

In theorising about institutions, an attempt has been made to offer some functional definitions, to lay the parameters for subsequent analysis. The suggestion is first, that organisations are internally cohesive; secondly, organisations are called into existence by virtue of their instrumental capacities; thirdly, that they are essentially hierarchical and, finally, that their preoccupation is to institute organisational arrangements to accomplish their stated objectives.[11] On the face of it, this seems a fairly standard classification.

Others are more circumspect. 'Clearly, enough variation in the connotation of the term institution exists to require careful reading to determine the meaning each author attaches to it ... At best, several common threads run through some of the literature. One such is value'.[12]

Uphoff (1986) concurs with this view. 'Both role-oriented and rule-oriented approaches to institutional analysis encompass consideration of people's values and social norms. Institutions are inextricably bound up with normative considerations, which is why they cannot be constructed mechanically like a hydro-electric dam or a trunk road.'[13] The argument continues that to institutionalise is to infuse with a value beyond the technical requirements of the task in hand. This suggests that an institution is an organisation that is valued by persons over and above the direct and immediate benefits they derive from it.

This point is echoed in Adamolekun (1990): 'I want to argue that to build institutional capacity for development ... it is essential to pay attention to the values that underpin the institutions being developed or strengthened.'[14]

The Inter-University Research Programme in Institution Building (IRPIB) offers a view concerning the conceptual difference between an organisation and an institution: ' ... the IRPIB school of thought, more than other authors, has developed the concept that values represent important dimensions of institutions.'[15] In turn, this acknowledges the earlier writing of Esman and Bruhns, who suggest that

> an organisation is primarily a technical instrument, a means to reach certain objectives, but never an end in itself ... The institutional approach emphasises not only the instrumental characteristics; nor is the focus of the analysis primarily on the structural, functional and behavioral elements which are internal to the organisational system ... In institutional analysis, we are concerned with purposes and values which extend beyond the immediate task at hand ...[16]

The same point is made elsewhere:

> The terms 'institution' and 'organisation' have agreed meanings in the applied social sciences. Any college is an organisation, since it involves the conscious planning of work through the formal allocation of roles and tasks, governed by the hierarchical structuring of authority. Superimposed on colleges, however, is a set of distinctive values and interests which express important professional and social concerns regarding education in general and further education in particular. It is this feature which makes the term 'institution' also appropriate.[17]

Taking this notion of value as a unifying theme in the concept of an institution, its translation into policy is not hard to construct. Such a notion is fundamental in relation to local government, the institutional focus of this volume.

One piece of analysis is based on the proposition that councils are arenas in which 'allocations of valued resources are made'. They go on to highlight various identities for local government. These concern the council as:

- a legal entity
- a representative body
- a service body
- an agency for other government bodies
- a place where people work
- a body with a history
- a local body.[18]

Such a range of classifications is not immediately relevant. It merely suggests a number of institutional and organisational attributes. However, it also alludes to a conceptual difficulty. When someone talks about local government they may construe this in terms of a legal entity. The recipient may filter the message from the standpoint of a place of work. A unifying message is required. One such brings the argument back to the idea of inherent value.

In summary, it is suggested that institutions are not only instruments for action but also that they have an inherent value beyond this mere instrumentality.

Institutions being political

Colebatch and Degeling (1986) have suggested that institutions present three levels of analysis. First . . .

> organising is inherently a political process; it entails and reproduces relationships of power and advantage. For this reason, analysis should focus on what it is that people are doing as they structure their relationships with others, the meanings and interests which are embodied in their actions, the social practices through which they are expressed and how some of the meanings and interests embodied in action have come to be institutionalised. It follows therefore that policy and organisation are not separate phenomena . . .[19]

Secondly, the authors note 'how the study of organisations focused on subjects who were both conscious and articulate about what they and others were doing as they acted to structure and contest their relations with others'.[20] Finally, the authors attest that 'the study of policy and organisations is not separate from the activity of organising, but engaged and implicated; both in the way that these activities come to be construed and in the outcomes that they produce'.[21]

Brown (1989) agrees with this political perspective, which plays down the role of cultural and social predispositions and focuses attention on the crucial influence of the political environment in organisational analysis.[22] However, this still does not satisfactorily define what an institution is.

Uphoff (1986) advances some thoughts on the question of definition:

> One way of thinking about the extent to which an organisation qualifies

as an institution is to ask whether, if it were to disappear, people in the community, not just members or direct beneficiaries, would want it back and to what extent people would act or sacrifice to preserve the institution in question. Whether an organisation has become institutionalised depends on peoples' evaluations of it – whether it is seen as having acquired value beyond direct instrumental considerations.[23]

In practical terms, an example might be where an organisation, such as India's propensity to establish urban development corporations, has established itself as a natural inheritor of roles and responsibilities formerly conducted by various tiers of local government in the same location. If the answer is yes, the development corporation has become institutionalised. If not, it has merely remained an organisation, liable to major restructuring or liquidation. It could be argued that this is the political dimension to institutional analysis.

In summary, it is suggested that institutions are political (i.e. policy) entities.

A general summary to this first section may propose that, in terms of characteristics, institutions play a pivotal role in the development process. Despite this, there is no standard definition of an institution in the literature. An institution is seen to have three characteristics. It is an instrument for action. It has inherent value to its recipients, beyond its mere instrumentality. It is a political (i.e. a policy) entity. The essential point to grasp is that institutions are fundamental to the development process.

The next section looks at the concept of development.

DEVELOPMENT

Under the heading of development, three ideas are considered: development organisation; development rationalism; development for liberation.

Development organisation

Blunt (1990) has suggested that 'the ruling paradigm of modern management thinking is contingency theory; the idea that there is no best way to manage or to organise'.[24] He then offers an alternative view. 'A contingency approach must be built around a core of organisational values and imperatives. In this view, the key values espoused by a critical mass of organisation members provide a necessary foundation for the harnessing of organisational imperatives and variables'. These core values and imperatives concern the organisation's functional alignment, co-ordination and control, and accountability and role relationships.[25] Planning and communication,[26] performance and reward[27] and effective leadership[28] are the remaining items in the analytical checklist.

Werlin (1991b) offers a more cautious approach to the current confusion in development administration literature, which may suggest a solution. 'There is no best way of organising . . . no best policy, approach or technology . . . We suggest what might be called a "political software" approach, referring to the quality of human relationships essential for organisations [political hardware] to effectively carry out whatever policies, programmes or techniques they attempt.' In so doing, this argument draws on the example of the various United States local government systems. 'There is no evidence that any of the major forms of local government . . . works better than the others. Each succeeds to the extent that it maintains a high quality of political relationships.'[29]

This view unwittingly reflects ideas presented earlier. The case is presented by Honandle (1992) in the context of strengthening institutions. 'The capacity building emphasis can be distinguished from the earlier emphasis on institutional building by its use of an existing organisational base as opposed to the introduction of a new enclave. In turn, this requires a greater understanding and use of the social networks and organisational resources which extend outside the public sector.'[30] That is to say, the 'political software' will increasingly dominate the process of institution building. 'Thus, political and sustainability considerations will receive more attention . . . and surpass narrow technical and project approaches to return on investments.'[31] In this sense, political is taken to mean the ordering of relationships; in other words, which organisational component is considered more senior than the other. The issue of sustainability is another matter entirely, and it is reviewed in Chapter 10.

The case is reinforced by Adamolekun (1990): 'The central argument . . . can be summed up as an advocacy for building institutional capacity for development on the foundation of democratic values. It is also an assertion of the supremacy of values over techniques.'[32] This is clear. Various techniques merely assist in the production of outputs. It is the value attached to those outputs and their sustainability, both as an output and an impact, that is of paramount concern in the development process.

In summary, it is suggested that a development organisation is concerned with the nature of political relationships.

Development rationalism

The dominance of techniques in development administration was at one point dangerously pervasive.

> The key to prosperity was thought to be foreign aid, with the necessary transfer of economic and technical expertise, instrumentalised through a revamped administrative system. Apparently, all that was thought to be necessary to bring this instant miracle was an interplay of two processes. One was the diffusion of technical know-how with suitable economic planning; and the other was the absorption of these external inputs by the recipient nations, through a development administration. Development administration was supposed to be based on professionally-oriented, technically competent, politically and ideologically-neutral bureaucratic machinery.[33]

Clearly, this is not the case.

> Development administration cannot be divorced from a political economy and a theory of development. The core assumption here is the identity between development and modernisation, the latter understood as Westernisation. The function of development administration was chiefly that of midwife for Western development – creating stable and orderly change . . .[34]

This argument centres on development administration as an instrument of change. As such, it harks back to the Weberian concept of bureaucracy.

> All these presuppositions spelled out basically a Weberian model of bureaucratic administration. The great insistence of the dominant literature on the causal link between bureaucracy and development was indeed overemphasised . . .[35]

The argument continues that

> the central issue of development administration is then no longer manageability of the administrative structure. It is a more fundamental incompatibility between bureaucracy as a form of insti-

tutionalised society and development, defined as quality of life for the population.[36]

Development administration is therefore being suggested as no longer the rational instrument for transferring Westernisation *per se* on the host government and its population. Instead, it should be seen as the process of self-determination where the host government is seeking a locally defined answer to the development problems it faces.

The democratic values argument advanced by Adamolekun (1990)[37] reflects the philosophical dichotomy between the technical rationalists (techniques and procedures) and the critical theorists (values and liberation). To refute the Weberian analysis, two views of society are offered.

> One of these is called the sociology of regulation [where] society [is] regarded as a stable, well integrated social structure, bearing the stamp of elements and functions which help to hold society together and to avoid conflicts. It is assumed that there is a basic consensus with regard to the dominant values. The other view is called the sociology of radical change. This is characterised by the emphasis on the process and change aspect of society rather than its stability. Society is regarded as being affected by opposition and conflicts of interest between different social groups and classes, by the domination of different groups or classes over each other, as well as of different contradictory values.[38]

In summary, it is suggested that development negates the rationalist construction and recognises the political nature of the process.

Development for liberation

In this political context, there are four components to a critical organisational theory that are directly applicable to development administration.

- In organisations, there is a state of tension between technological rationality and the negation of that rationality.[39]
- The dominance of technological rationality over the operational process corresponds to the interests of the predominating social strata.[40]
- An organisational practice built around the dominance of technological rationality calls for a highly developed ideology which is

capable of covering the contradictions and the criticisms caused by technical rationality.[41]

- An organisational practice which corresponds to the mental make-up of human beings as well as to the interests of the popular majority must break with the supremacy of the technological rationality.[42]

This critical perception of organisations reinforces a concept of development that is politically- and value-laden, that is not dominated by technical instruments, that seeks to address real needs as opposed to ensuring organisational survival through the merits of its technology and therefore, its rationality.

The argument is carried forward by Werlin (1991b). 'The alternative to systems theory (and other rational constructs) is political elasticity theory. This theory suggests that you, as the manager, cannot afford to take for granted what Weberian and scientific management theorists often did, that followers will automatically or unquestionably respond to directions . . .' Later in the same work, he adds

organisational theorists, in trying to exclude politics from administration, end up dehumanising their subject with mechanistic or biological metaphors. The failure to recognise the political nature of administration stems from a failure to understand the multidimensional nature of politics. On the one side of it, there is the struggle for competitive advantage; on the other, there is a struggle for consensus and the needs of the polis [the community].[43]

Honandle (1982) restates the argument. The need for that consensus must have an ultimate test in the idea of sustainability in development.

Development is concerned with inducing activity which leads to self-sustaining dynamics that improve human well-being. Since development administration emphasises the design, organisation and management of such activity, the sustainability of the strategic interventions must occupy a prominent position in the field.[44]

All development should seek to improve the human condition for the masses. In order to be successful, all development should be sustainable and, ultimately, be liable to self-development.

This analysis is supported elsewhere.

The previous two development decades emphasised modernisation through the transfer of technology (both ideas and tools) assisted by foreign aid. The third development decade, if it is going to be relevant, must change its focus and strategy to include such key goals as self-reliance, human needs, social justice and the removal of poverty. Development administration must provide the initiative for the achievement of these core objectives, effectively and forcibly. The challenge before the international bodies and the aid-giving agencies will be to make a difficult but not impossible mid-course correction in their approaches.[45]

Such a change in direction has to be induced from two sources. First, there will have to be a growing acceptance of the human as opposed to the technical view of development, by the donor community. Secondly, 'each country will have to innovate its own strategy of development . . . by charting its own [development] theories and methods'.[46]

Brown (1989) has suggested that: 'If the study of public sector management issues in the Third World is to advance, then there is a need for a radical reorientation of approach, with less emphasis on assumed optimal performance criteria and more upon how the relevant organisations actually perform . . . In short, what I am advocating is a behavioral rather than an idealistic approach to Third World management.'[47] This behavioral approach suggests a concern to understand the specific activities within an organisation; the idea of identifying units of analysis. This is a matter which will be re-examined later.

One contribution from the recipient's perspective is offered where

> . . . we are concerned not to define an organisational culture which is more nearly right for developing countries but to develop another cultural model which contributes to the participants' understanding of their organisations and the diverse forces operating within them.[48]

It is the 'participants' understanding' that is vital to the concept. Development is, or should be, about self-understanding and, ultimately, self-determination. It should not be about a pattern of organisational behaviour, imposed from external sources.

This argument can be illustrated by suggesting that African governments should

> shift their emphasis from control and regulation to a catalytic or supportive role in development. In practice, this means that government

agencies should be involved less in planning ... It can best help the citizenry by creating and maintaining the physical and legal infrastructure necessary to launch and sustain development.[49]

In this context, there are two tiers of self-determination. First is national government in relation to the international community. Then there is local government, and its supporting citizens, in relation to national government.

This two-tier concept is very important. The international community, through multilateral and bilateral donor agencies, negotiate and sign contracts with national governments. In the legal sense, they do not deal with local government. The catalytic role in development is therefore a two-tier process.

In summary, it is apparent that development suggests a process of exploration rather than imposition.

A general summary of this second section suggests that development is seen to have four features. It is concerned with the nature of political relationships. It negates the rationalist construction. It recognises the political nature of the process. It suggests exploration rather than imposition. In essence, development is a political process, dominated by policy concerns and human needs.

The next section combines the ideas of institutions and development.

INSTITUTIONAL DEVELOPMENT

Under institutional development, four ideas are considered: the components of ID; learning through ID; ID for sustainability; the scope of ID.

Components of ID

Hirschmann (1993) states that in ID

the first problem in the relationship between policy reform and institutional development relates to the interconnection between institutions and culture ... The second area of concern relates to the speed of change ... The third problem relates to politics and institutions, for institutional development is inherently as political as it is technical in nature.[50]

Israel (1987) considers the question more pragmatically, suggesting that ID 'refers to the process of improving the ability of institutions to make effective use of human and financial resources available (variously defined as) institution building, public sector management, public administration and so on.'[51] Here, it is contended that the flaw, even in recent practice, is that for 'most development strategies, the emphasis is still on planning and appraisal but not on implementation; on investments and policies but not on operations.'[52]

In another contribution to the debate, Buyck (1991) has said that 'ID is the creation or reinforcement of the capacity of an organisation to generate, allocate and use human and financial resources effectively to attain development objectives, public or private. It includes not only the building and strengthening of institutions but also their retrenchment or liquidation in the pursuit of institutional, sectoral, or government-wide rationalisation of expenditure'. The suggestion is that, operationally, 'ID is typically aimed at improving and strengthening:

- internal organisational structures
- management systems, including monitoring and evaluation
- financial management (budgeting, accounting, auditing procedures) and planning systems
- personnel management, staff development and training
- inter-institutional relationships
- institutional structures of subsectors or sectors
- legal framework
- government regulations and procedures'.[53]

Others present a similar ID checklist in the context of defining ID. For example, 'ID implies more than the mere strengthening of organisations that will facilitate project implementation and completion. [It means] strengthening:

- legal and para-legal systems
- the internal organisation and distribution of functions
- physical and financial capacity for project implementation
- personnel policies and reward systems
- competency and skills levels in the institutional environment'.[54]

Paul (1990a) also presents an operational checklist for ID. It covers an analysis of:

- manpower inadequacies, including skills
- co-ordination problems
- gaps in planning, monitoring and evaluation systems
- weak local capacity
- need to restructure or decentralise organisations
- problems of financial management (cost recovery and support systems, budgetary controls)
- constraints on compensation and incentive structures
- lack of attention to demand for project services
- autonomy issues.[55]

UNDP (1991) suggests that institutional-building strategies tackle key functions through standard interventions, as follows.

On functions:
- applied analytical capabilities
- planning and programme design capacities
- management and implementation capacities
- monitoring and evaluation capacities.

On interventions:
- changing management strategy
- improving efficiency and effectiveness of management processes
- changing systems and structures
- matching missions to environmental demands
- changing management structures.[56]

There is yet another contribution to the definition in Horberry and Le Marchant (1991).

The main objective [of ID] is to create or strengthen the capacity to manage ... programmes – developing structures which strengthen the responsibility for the environment, and which provides incentives for individual and collective action ... It requires a long term view [as opposed to merely policy formulation] ... It must be tailored to suit the local political, economic and cultural conditions. Suitability to the local situation is especially important in developing countries where institutions are unique, complex and deeply traditional ...[57]

The suggestion is that no ID model can be imposed. It must be discerned through negotiation and planning. As far as possible, it should get the client participants into a position of being able to construct their own ID programmes.

There are other opinions on the institutional building process. 'A variety of definitions of institution building can be found in the literature.' The most frequently encountered one is that used by the IRPIB scholars. According to one of them, ID is 'the planning, structuring and guidance of new or reconstituted organisations which (a) embody changes in values, functions, physical and/or social technologies, (b) establish, foster and protect normative relationships and action patterns, and (c) attain support and complementarity in the environment'.[58] In simpler terms, the suggested ID process concerns the instruments, standards and objects of performance.

The institutional variables concern 'leadership,[59] doctrine,[60] programme,[61] resources and internal structure'.[62] These are related to the internal structure and processes of the organisation. What is equally fundamental to institutional development is the institution's relationship with its environment. Under linkages and transactions, it is argued that 'because the basic purpose of the institution is to induce change in its environment, linkages and transactions take on a particular importance, and indeed, the conscious thrust towards the environment has given the institutional building perspective a distinctive appeal'.[63] This is very important and is a practical theme for Parts IV and V of this text.

In reviewing recent World Bank practice, an author suggests that the Bank 'concentrates on factors internal to the organisation at the expense of external environmental factors . . .'[64] It is concluded that institutional analysis and ID which are broader in scope (i.e. to include the organisation's development environment) will improve project design and implementation.

In summary, institutional development is seen as having an internal concern with its organisation and an external concern with its development environment.

Learning through ID

The institution–environment relationship centres on the premise that some feedback exists, which allows the organisation to respond (or to learn) accordingly. In the words of Blase (1986), 'one element of systems analysis that tends to be common . . . and is applicable for institution building, is feedback.'[65] Introducing a 'learning through feedback' system presupposes an important change of emphasis in development administration. 'Much of the early literature on institution building emphasised a social engineering, implying a top-down approach to institutional development. Recent literature . . . indicates the need for much more emphasis on a participative, bottom-up approach.'[66]

Uphoff (1986) develops this argument at some length.

Recent years have seen an evaluation in thinking about planning and implementing development projects. The previously dominant conception was essentially a blueprint approach. This assumes that all problems and goals can be identified and agreed upon clearly enough for precise interventions to be specified and carried out according to a comprehensive and detailed plan. This approach is sequential, with experts called upon to design a programme and with less qualified or less capable persons then doing the implementation . . . What has emerged as an alternative to the blueprint approach is what Korton describes as the learning process approach, sometimes referred to simply as the process approach. This can be categorised as inductive planning, to emphasise the value of formulating hypotheses about what will probably work with continual assessment and revision of the strategy. All development initiatives [are] real world experiments.[67]

What is being advocated here is an iterative approach to development administration.

An iterative approach to development administration, which supports the learning process, is dependent on human capacity. This suggests that

although institutional development seems to refer to things – to structures, procedures and abstract performance capabilities – it should always call to mind people, their skills, motivation and personal efficacy. When one talks of building or strengthening institutions, it is necessary to figure out how the talents and energies in the relevant population can be enlisted, upgraded and committed on a regular basis to these institutions' operations and improvements. Thus, supporting ID requires particular attention to the human aspects of institutional capacity.[68]

This exploratory model with the human emphasis to ID is suggested as the means to build capacity in the institutional administration of development. However, that capacity depends on sustainability.

In summary, it is suggested that institutional development is an exploratory process, to be explored through client institutions.

ID for sustainability

The World Bank is at pains to recognise the problem of bottlenecks in the administration of development projects. This has become a primary concern of the World Bank's public sector management unit . . . 'because of its recognition that nearly half of Bank projects (two-thirds in Africa) have a low probability of successfully continuing after the Bank terminates funding'.[69] Ultimately, institutional development (ID) will open up these bottlenecks and ensure some measure of sustainability.

The World Bank is a frequent producer of analyses of its own performance. One piece, concerning civil service reform, focuses on sustainability. It has been suggested, by Nunberg and Nellis (1990), that 'most Bank activities have concentrated on short-term cost containment measures. More emphasis must be given to longer term management issues, if sustained improvement is to take place'.[70] Later, they suggest that 'underlying the longer term approach is the recognition that shorter term measures must be supported by institutionalised systems that can sustain ongoing reforms'.[71] In order to achieve this, they advocate 'adequate preparation, detailed diagnosis, appropriate technology, sensitively delivered; these are the building blocks of success'.[72]

Gray *et al.* (1990) suggest that 'policy changes that ignore the institutional underpinnings are unlikely to last and may even have pervasive outcomes'.[73] Later, they add, 'it is no accident that projects in certain sectors tend to have better ID treatment than projects in other sectors. Energy and infrastructure projects tend to be more self-contained, and the institutional issues tend to be more standard from country to country'.[74]

There has been an attempt, by Churchill (1991), to build standard lessons for ID, citing development work in the energy sector. These lessons highlight: ID as a political activity;[75] ID as a process;[76] the need to account for external factors;[77] that results are important;[78] that specific impacts must be carefully targeted;[79] that any political risks must be widely spread;[80] that all financial issues must be resolved from the start;[81] that early major impact is important – learning by doing is more important than following pre-conceived and detailed plans.[82] In summary, it is suggested that 'these eight rules are largely common sense. Finally, all this recognises the essentially political nature of the process and that it requires the continuous consultation and participation of those affected'.[83]

Paul (1990a) suggests that 'the task ahead is not to broaden but to deepen the process of ID work ... by shifting the focus more towards sustainability, by allocating adequate resources to support more relevant upstream diagnostic work, and upgrading the quality of the staff who work on ID issues'.[84] Such work is time-consuming. Though time-consuming, in a later paper it is suggested that

> ID achievement and project sustainability [continuation of benefits beyond the project period] are also positively correlated ... Of 41 projects with substantial ID achievement, 40 were judged as likely to be sustainable. On the other hand, of the 46 projects with negligible ID achievement, 33 were unlikely to be sustainable.[85]

Sustainability is obviously influenced by several factors, but ID is certainly an important one among them.

The point is sharpened by stressing the need for the wider internal and external approach to ID in order to help achieve a higher prospect of ID sustainability.[86] This is another very important point, and provides the practical theme for Parts IV and V of this book.

In 1988, OECD contributed to the debate by not only stressing the importance of sustainability, but also the factors on which success depend.[87] Unfortunately, 'on neither of these issues is their unanimity among the scholars or the practitioners, nor is there agreement that the impact of each of the factors may be different in different institutional experiences'.[88] It was suggested that OECD singled out government policy, financial allocation, management, organisational structure and local participation, and external economic and political factors (among others) as the most relevant factors.

Gray *et al.* (1990) argued that 'good ID work takes an in-depth knowledge and careful negotiation with many people, all of which takes time. Projects with thorny institutional issues should not be rushed to the [World Bank] board (for approval) ... Unfortunately, we were repeatedly told that no incentives exist in the World Bank for good supervision – that the incentives stopped once the project was taken to the board. Responsibility for project outcomes appears to be very weak'.[89] The World Bank's logic seems to fall into the traditional trap of seeing the ID project's implementation as being determined by its plan (its preparation phase). The increasing reality is that implementation should be part of the exploratory nature of ID.

The World Bank has now recognised this important shift of emphasis and has incorporated it in its new operations declaration. It will 'redirect the Bank's international incentives, toward a better balance between approving new operations and ensuring the success of those in progress'.[90] Later, it will 'enhance the role of operations evaluation, and focus the evaluation of completed operations on whether the benefits are sustainable'.[91] This is a very important change of policy.

UNDP has also lamented its own weakness in institutional development. 'In many of [its] projects, the institutional strengthening components were either largely ignored or dealt with superficially. It was often assumed that achieving the technical objectives of a project would automatically lead to greater institutional capability... In practice, institutional capacity-building remains a "black box" of UNDP project design.'[92] As recently as 1989, such an admission from a multilateral donor agency illustrates the infancy of the institutional development concept in third world practice.

In summary, institutional development must have a central concern for ensuring sustainability of the increased institutional capacity. Only then can ID be regarded as a success.

Scope of ID

Paul (1990a) argues that 'the basic objectives of ID are three-fold:

- to facilitate the project implementation process;
- to contribute to the sustainability of the project (the contribution of benefits beyond the project period);
- to support the development of sector or subsector level institutions and linkages among them, even if these are not directly relevant to the project.'[93]

The first objective is a short-term issue; the second and third objectives look beyond the project to sustainability and other creative and mutually supporting relationships.

To highlight this distinction between the short and longer term, a telling point is made in relation to the World Bank's municipal development programme.

In current theory, institutional development has a precise meaning.

It refers to that point where an organisation can be seen to be of value beyond its immediate outputs. It develops an intrinsic value in the community at large, beyond its mere instrumentalities ... A test would be the raising of the profile of municipal governments in the [East Africa] region to the point where the mass of informed (but not necessarily educated) population identified municipal government as being an external economy; a mechanism that turns resources (institutional capacity) into affordable infrastructure and services for the masses.[94]

The short term is the immediate process of change – the instrumentalities of ID. The longer term is the impact of sustained change, in terms of a lasting benefit to the community.

In the case of local government, it is suggested by Blunt and Collins (1994) that 'four areas have emerged [from ID practice] as common targets of [World] Bank efforts to strengthen local authorities'. These are recurrent resource mobilisation, financial management, the efficiency of line agencies and the financing of municipal infrastructure.[95] More generally, others suggest that 'institution building can be used to help government organisations understand clearly the purposes they are supposed to fulfil and the means for their attainment'.[96]

The basic components of institutional development in the Bank's sector adjustment operations consist of:

- organisational restructuring and strengthening;
- building a policy and planning capability;
- regulatory and procedural reform.[97]

This text looks at the practice of the first two items, in Parts IV and V. That practice will highlight the frustrations caused by the supervising environment and, therefore, the need to tackle regulatory and procedural reform.

In summary, it is clear that institutional development concerns interventions in organisational structures, their processes and their regulatory environment.

A general summary of this third section emphasises that institutional development (ID) is seen as making the best use of an institution's human and financial resources. It is an exploratory process, to be performed through the client institution. It seeks to strengthen institutions both as an internal entity and as an external impact mechanism. The iterative model of the process seeks to avoid the blueprint approach and embrace a learning concept. Sustainability is a central issue. The process concerns interventions in organisational structures, their processes and their regulatory environment.

Thus, at the end of this chapter, three key characteristics can be discerned that identify the specific nature of institutional development. These are:

1. That 'value' distinguishes an institution from an organisation; 'We are concerned with purposes and values which extend beyond the immediate task in hand'.[98]
2. That 'sustainability' must be the test of development; 'Development is concerned with inducing activity which leads to self-sustaining dynamics that improves human well being'.[99]
3. That 'exploration' is the key to contemporary institutional development practice; 'All development initiatives are real world experiments'.[100]

It is now necessary to review the application of institutional development (ID) in the third world.

2 Applying ID in the Third World

There is no standard set of principles or techniques for applying ID in the third world. Buyck (1991) suggests that 'the state of the art and the lessons of experience are only slowly emerging, especially in areas like public sector management'.[1] An operational framework must be established. This second chapter therefore seeks to identify the operational parameters of institutional development. It considers three topics:

- PROJECTS
- TECHNICAL ASSISTANCE
- TRAINING.

PROJECTS

Under the heading of projects, three ideas are reviewed: projects as imposition; factors for success; projects for impact.

Projects as imposition

The classic model of the project is that of a cycle, running from inception, through to completion and evaluation. The project cycle is frequently cited.[2]

Honandle and Rosengard (1983) have argued that

> projects are discrete activities aimed at specific objectives with earmarked budgets and limited time frames. This is in contrast to programmes which have more nebulous objectives and occupy a more permanent status in an institutional setting. Projects are also more likely to be targeted on specific geographic areas and aimed at particular beneficiary groups.[3]

At present, the project is the standard instrument for ID in practice. Rondinelli (1983) comments:

as projects have become more prominent channels for international assistance, and as managerial arrangements for implementing development policies, they have also come under increasing criticism by development theorists and practitioners who argue that they have not achieved their objectives and, indeed, have inhibited social learning and institution building in developing countries.[4]

The inference from both quotations is that the project approach is mechanistic; that they lack the vital exploratory component. Projects are often criticised because they are 'planned and managed ineffectively . . . [they are] complex, mechanistic and inflexible . . . instruments of control rather than facilitation . . . [and] often contribute little to building administrative capacity'.[5] In this sense, projects are seen as an imposition from external sources and not as a form of self-determination with external support.

Some principles to guide a more enlightened approach to ID have been offered. An important contribution has been made by Hulme (1992):

Aid donors must eschew their preference for organisational blueprints and recognise the contingent nature of reforms. [They must] recognise that many public sector organisations have only a small controlled decision making space and thus pay more attention to influenceable decision-making opportunities. [They must] acknowledge that machine model approaches are likely to reinforce the negative aspects of hierarchical control in bureaucracies. [Finally, they must] pay much more attention to organisational sustainability in terms of finance and strategic management capacity.[6]

One phrase to highlight is the necessity to 'eschew [the] preference for organisational blueprints'. There is no single model and no single standard solution.

The negative aspects of the blueprint approach are reinforced by Brinkerhoff and Ingle (1989). 'The dominant mode of development management consists of following a set of prescribed steps beginning with problem specification and concluding with post-project evaluation. While the exact number of steps and the terminology varies among donor and development country agencies, the basic elements of the model are the same.'[7]

Further criticism of the blueprint approach comes from Dichter (1989).

Blueprint management is the term recently and negatively used to categorise the approach of the large bilateral and multilateral aid agencies. As its name implies, it suggests management by a preconceived, ordered plan. Borrowed from the world of engineering, it is an approach that defines a problem, cites objectives, chooses solutions, puts together resources, implements the plan and evaluates the results. It is hierarchical in structure and works from the top down. [The opposing perspective is] people centred management, or the learning process approach to development management.[8]

In summary, it is apparent that the traditional project approach has two flaws: it is a blueprint (or mechanistic) construction and it is a hierarchical (and deductive) method.

Factors for success

It is clear from the evidence that learning is a factor for success.

This learning process has been described and contrasted to the blueprint approach in the development literature ... The blueprint model follows the approach to project design used in engineering. While blueprints work well with the construction of defined materials into pre-determined forms (dams, bridges or buildings), they are far less suited to the indefinite matter which makes up human society.[9]

Baldwin (1990) concurs with this view. 'The term "learning process" can be used to summarise this bottom-up approach which can be contrasted with the [failed] "blueprint" approach.' In the article, a table is presented to show the contrast between the two approaches, using the checklist of the development process, from initiation to evaluation.[10]

The World Bank (1983) offers an analysis of the importance of learning. 'The implied rejection of blueprints in tackling the complexities of development is not a counsel of despair. The chief lesson to be drawn from the experience is the importance of building into every strategy and programme an effective learning process.'[11]

In order to suggest an alternative direction, some authors attempt to identify the ingredients of success in the application of ID. One group tries in the context of local government.

Identifying successful local government projects or initiatives is notoriously difficult. The first is the choice of criteria for determining effectiveness which are applicable to all projects which are capable of measurement. The second is that, frequently, a judgement must be made to determine whether the magnitude of the effects achieved constitute success.[12]

According to them, three factors contribute to project success. The first is support in the project environment. This includes the political environment,[13] local leadership and a history of self-reliance.[14] The second is the basic character of the project. This includes beneficiary involvement, the utilisation of local resources,[15] organisational culture[16] and the scale of the project.[17] The third is the organisation and management of the project. This includes the clarity of project goals,[18] flexibility and responsiveness, autonomy and accountability,[19] a learning process, leadership and human resource development.[20]

A similar task is performed by Kaul (1988) in attempting to identify the common factors of successful development projects. There must be clear project goals.[21] There must be strong project leadership.[22] There must be clear involvement with the project beneficiaries.[23] There must be reasonable autonomy in project management.[24] Lines of accountability must be clear.[25] Explicit feedback mechanisms must be built in.[26] Finally, there must be strong staff motivation and development.[27]

Israel (1987) argues in a similar manner. 'The so-called standard explanations [of success], those derived from the evaluation studies, can be divided into six groups.'[28] These are the exogenous factors,[29] outstanding individuals,[30] effective planning and implementation,[31] the effective application of management techniques,[32] adequate relative prices (for trading entities), as well as sufficient political commitment.[34] Of all these items, the idea of commitment seems paramount. 'The firm commitment of a country is an essential ingredient in the success of an ID programme. Conversely, lack of commitment is the main cause of failure . . .'[35] While all these factors are important, they reinforce the dominance of the project as the instrument of ID.

The debate is carried forward by Shabbir Cheema (1987).

Projects are, and will continue in the foreseeable future as, the main instrument of development policy and international assistance. Yet, the project approach to development assistance could have negative implications for institution-building due, in some cases, to its short time horizon, tight schedules, fragmentation of local institutions and its limitations in ensuring self-sustaining results. It is imperative, therefore, to redefine the project cycle in order to incorporate the above and other related concerns in the process of planning, implementing and evaluating urban development projects.[36]

The criticism of the project approach centres on the notions of specificity and mechanistic processes. Others warn against excessive projectisation but throw caution against its total abandonment. 'Much of the criticism aimed at projects is really focused on poor use of the approach rather than the approach itself. Thus care must be taken not to throw the baby out with the bathwater.'[37]

However, the criticism of the mechanistic nature of the process has led some authors to propose a clear and exploratory alternative. Brinkerhoff and Ingle suggest that

> There are several variants. However, all share a number of key features; flexibility and incremental adaption, continuous information gathering at the micro-level, experimentation, and iterative learning. The process model starts from the assumption that not enough is known in the pre-implementation stage, about what will be successful, to specify all details in advance. Design and implementation are merged in that the project is modified and adapted as knowledge is acquired about the specific environment. Each design iteration represents an experimental solution . . .[38]

The learning process is advocated.

In summary, it is clear that the exploratory, iterative (or learning) approach and environmental factors are keys to project success.

Projects for impact

From an urban management perspective, UNDP presents a shift of emphasis towards the idea of having relevant impact.

> The primary objectives of UNDP programmes and projects in the urban sector should be refocused from solving specific technical problems to strengthening the institutional capacity of the public and private organisations in developing countries to address urbanisation issues . . . [it] must shift from a project-based to a programme based approach to providing assistance. The essential characteristic of a programme approach are linkages with ongoing activities of the host government; emphasis on replication and sustainability of activities; focus on procedures and systems to incorporate policy

concerns into operational activities; emphasis on achieving specific sectoral and intersectoral development objectives including mechanisms to do that; and complementarity with other bilateral and multilateral technical activities in the country.[39]

The nature of this development management is expanded upon in an article by Dichter (1989).

The issue of management for development can therefore be dealt with in an unadorned and straightforward fashion. Whether the management approach is people-centred or blueprint becomes far less important than whether the efforts engaged in move towards their goals. Is the management able? Are the basic functions provided for? Keeping these plainer sorts of questions in mind will help to avoid the tendency towards overzealous promotion of even more heavily value-laden agendas.[40]

The argument is a contention that, ultimately, it is the output of the process that should be the determining factor.

The stress on the effectiveness of a project is reinforced by Kinder (1988):

Much of the work on ID in the Third World has concentrated on improving organisational efficiency to the exclusion of issues relating to institutional effectiveness. Questions about the organisation's aims and objectives, its outputs, its customers and their needs, the quality of the product/service and the organisation's responsiveness to changes in its environment have rarely been posed, let alone answered. Even when dealing with efficiency, the emphasis has often been restricted to narrow issues of labour productivity rather than dealing with how to improve total productivity; that is the combined effect of improving the performance of people, capital and materials.[41]

This is introducing a holistic perspective to the notion of ID. It is therefore emphasising the importance of dealing with both the internal concerns of the organisation and the organisation's impact on its environment – that is, its external concerns.

An example from education stresses this holism. It is argued that a college has to be 'developed' in relation to the needs of the student learning programme. Thus, all organisational structures and management systems are determined by the needs of the college's development environment. This is referred to as 'curriculum-led institutional development'.[42] That is, the development environment determines the ID needs. In the trading sector, the market determines everything. In public administration, ID can too often be concerned with organisational strengthening and restructuring, in ignorance of the institution's relationship with its environment; an argument explored in Chapter 7.

In summary, it is apparent that projects should focus on both the organisation and its impact on its development environment.

As a general summary to this section, the project approach is seen to have two flaws. It is a blueprint (or mechanistic) construction. It is a hierarchical (and deductive) method. In its place, the exploratory, iterative (or learning) model is advocated. It focuses on both the organisation and its impact in the environment. This is seen to be a central platform for any meaningful intervention in third world development.

TECHNICAL ASSISTANCE (TA)

Under the heading of technical assistance, three ideas are considered: TA characteristics; TA opportunities; factors for success.

TA characteristics

It has been argued that 'technical assistance is first of all purposive . . . [it] is co-operative . . . and (perhaps most important of all), technical assistance involves an international transfer of knowledge'.[43]

Israel (1987) suggests that

> techniques for ID include quantitative, systems and social science. The first includes network and critical path analysis, programming and financial analysis. The second includes analysing organisational structures and procedures, manpower and organisational planning, job description and job evaluation. The third includes the study of structures, procedures and management decisions from a behavioral point of view.[44]

The point here is that these techniques are all part of the analytical armoury that precedes skills transfer through technical assistance.

There is a very critical view of the traditional approach to technical assistance (TA) in the development process, advanced by Blase (1986).

> The role of a donor truly interested in fostering institutions that will serve as 'engines' of the development process is a most challenging task ... The capital assistance process format does not fit institution building situations well. The rush to obligate technical assistance funds results in, for example, the technical assistance personnel arriving on the scene, with counterpart personnel hardly knowing they are coming, much less agreeing to the objectives some high-level administrator in their institution agreed to.[45]

Similarly, Buyck (1991) laments the continued domination of technical assistance in development projects in Africa.[46] Buyck stresses that, of all the regions, Africa continues to rely most heavily on long-term advisers (due to pervasive institutional weaknesses).[47] Later,

> ID related technical assistance is much more difficult to design and deliver than investment-related TA because of the nature of institutional development. In the words of one colleague, the ID process is long, iterative, complex, non-linear, sensitive and unpredictable and requires behavioral changes. As a result:
>
> • the need for ID-related TA may be less clearly perceived by governments, and more easily resented ...
> • efficient delivery of ID does not guarantee long lasting impact.[48]

This second point is very important. The output of ID is within a controlled environment, especially where resident advisers are involved. The outputs are identified through the organisational activities that are to be strengthened. The necessary skills transfer is part of this identification. The impacts are determined when these skills are turned into processes that have a discernible effect on the institution's performance.

The methods for assessing ID performance are in their infancy. However, two authors make an admirable attempt at offering a structure to help in that assessment. First, they make the important distinction between outputs, which the project is intended to produce, and impacts, which it is hoped will occur as a result of the project. They go on to stress that 'success is significantly affected by the characteristics of the target population and by the political and economic context within which the project is implemented'. The concept that is not touched is that of sustainability.[49]

In summary, it is suggested that TA has been associated with a traditional project approach to ID.

TA opportunities

It is argued that there are two continuing weaknesses in technical assistance for ID.

> There are few best practitioners. Finding the right person is a challenging assignment. For ID and capacity building, technical and substantive knowledge is not sufficient. A proven ability to coach, work in a team, good knowledge of the local environment and culture, adaptability, and a track record of demonstrated successful experience are also required. There are not many people on the market who meet these demands. [Secondly], much more work is also needed to quantify achievement indicators and tools to measure performance.[50]

It is important to understand the intellectual infancy of ID; that is, there is a lack of a generally accepted, or cohesive, pattern of intervention in ID through technical assistance.

Thus, in the process of ID planning, it is suggested that 'clients, planners, administrators and technical staff are involved in an iterative process in which programmes evolve within the framework provided by the open system components of mobilisation, organisation, training, resource provision and system management. To this extent, the open systems approach is the antithesis of the prescriptive formula, as each policy implementation situation has to be related to its particular context. This approach is an acknowledgement of the sociopolitical and economic diversity of Third World countries'.[51] TA should therefore be conceived as part of an open-ended learning process, and not as a mere component of a traditional, mechanistic development project.

In order to ensure success, the approach to ID (whether or not through technical assistance) must settle on some tangible units of analysis. Otherwise, ID will too often be just an ephemeral concept, divorced from a practitioner's reality. This idea is presented by Wunsch (1991a).

> In this analytical strategy, the key features of given goods or services and their production processes are the level of analysis; and the individuals taking or not taking actions to produce these goods or services are the unit of analysis. Organisational arrangements, among other factors, become variables important in predicting/explaining why certain outcomes are reached or not.[52]

There is a less specific view, expounded by Israel (1987), that still seeks to identify a unit of analysis. 'The appropriate unit of analysis for institutional effectiveness is an activity within an organisation.'[53] By inference and practical logic, an activity involves the deployment of human and financial (including material) resources to achieve some unit of organisational output. The unit of organisational analysis is an important concept, both in terms of understanding performance and its related budgeting.

Israel goes on to identify the thought processes in ID analysis.

ID programmes themselves are designed with a great sense of totality, which makes it easy to commit the sin of comprehensiveness. Programmes begin with a complete analysis of the institution involved, and the solutions proposed represent a package of actions which, if successful, would create strong institutions.

The argument is that such a comprehensive approach does not work.

The principles of selectivity ... should be applied to ID which, by definition, is a low specificity activity. A comprehensive attack on all the problems faced by an institution cannot hope to achieve final results in a specified time. In sum, comprehensiveness in scope and in time should be abandoned in ID efforts, and a partial, cumulative and highly focused approach pursued.

This is interpreted as a morphological approach. In essence, one does not proceed with item B until item A has been achieved. '[Thus] if there is one message from the book, it is that the development process for most countries will continue to be a slow, painstaking process, perhaps slower and more painstaking than is generally acknowledged.'[54]

In summary, it is apparent that TA is now seen as moving away from project-based technical assistance to a more exploratory and participatory mode of project formulation and implementation. Functional analysis is also seen to be important.

Factors for success

The nature of ID can be painstaking. This highlights the effort required for success: '... change cannot be planned or executed rapidly. It takes time to understand an existing situation, and even longer to bring about the often fundamental changes in attitudes and practices which are necessary for meaningful improvement.'[55] This alludes to the essential characteristic that distinguishes an organisation from an institution. Intervention in organisations is concerned with the instrumentalities of organisational performance. Intervention in institutions is concerned with instrumentalities and their over-riding attributes of policy and value, both to participants (internal) and their beneficiaries (external).

The ingredients for good contemporary ID practice have been recorded. The challenge, as elucidated by Buyck (1991), is to design a project that

> (1) responds to genuine needs of the recipients; (2) is adaptable to the recipients absorptive capacity; and (3) is designed for flexible, effective implementation. First, thorough institutional analysis is necessary, including an assessment of country commitment. Secondly, to generate commitment and put it to the test, the design process must be conducted in a participatory fashion, with government taking the lead in defining priority needs, objectives, terms of reference and work programmes. Finally, to make implementation manageable . . . the project should be simple:
>
> - with clearly defined goals
> - few components
> - as few implementing agencies as possible
> - inputs should be adapted to local needs and capabilities
> - a series of verifiable performance indicators should be defined.[56]

The contention is that ID is an amorphous and sometimes intangible process.

Because of its lack of specificity in contrast to engineering-based projects, ID often fails. While the previous paragraphs suggest a method to achieve success, another author warns against conventional technical inputs to ID.

It is stated by Buyck (1991) that

> the most widely practised ID method is the one proven to be a disappointment to all parties concerned: long term adviser cum counterpart training on the job (i.e. the standard form of technical assistance). The disappointment stems from two factors: national staff may have problems of motivation and incentives, and experts rarely can successfully combine the assignment of implementing/doing with training, since both tasks require different skills and dispositions. More promising for successful TA delivery of ID technical assistance is

the integration of short-term consultants and long-term technical assistants with national agency staff.[57]

This highlights the essential components of ID practice, in terms of skills transfer, through occasional consultants, resident advisers and training.

From a different perspective, the Asian Development Bank looks at the question of staffing projects and the problem of skills transfer. One way to ensure project success is 'to use as many counterparts as possible from the [parent] agency. This develops a sense of ownership of the project... Both the government and the international agency should be realistic in planning the project, its budget and its staffing'.[58] The key questions are: What are the roles for expert advisers, and counterparts? What will be the government input? Will there be TOR flexibility for shortfalls in support? Will there be a full-time host project manager? Will there be time for technology transfer? Will there be time for advisers to assist counterparts?

In the final analysis, ID is concerned with training people to be able to think through problems to solutions and implementation. To this end, a telling point has been made. 'Technical assistance is becoming less the transmission of well-codified techniques... and rather more the transfer of technical innovation, research results, policy reconsiderations and concerns less easily defined.'[59] Organisational structures, their attendant processes and the financial resources are merely instruments to that end.

In summary, it is clear that there is a trend away from long-term technical assistance towards more intensive, short-term counterpart training.

As a general summary to this section: technical assistance has been associated with a traditional project approach to ID. TA for ID is now seen as moving away from project-based technical assistance towards a more exploratory and participatory mode of project formation and implementation. The unit of analysis must be clearly established in any TA intervention. There is a trend away from long-term technical assistance towards more intensive, short-term counterpart training. This elevates training from an appendage of project work in ID, to a central and practically focused activity. In essence, technical assistance is moving towards a more exploratory and participatory mode of project formulation and implementation.

The role of training, in the context of local government strengthening for urban management performance, is explored below.

TRAINING

Under the heading of training, two ideas are considered: training for urban management; training in practice.

Training for urban management

In 1989, the World Bank published its seminal tract on Sub-Saharan Africa.[60] It advocated the need for a sustained increase in capacity to perform. From the urban perspective, five elements were considered: urbanisation; efficient cities; sustainability; improved infrastructure; and strengthening local government. Of these, the last is the most immediately relevant.

It suggests that 'in most countries, urban growth has far outstripped planning and administrative capacity at both central and local levels. The task of meeting mounting infrastructure needs has increasingly fallen on local governments. This is as it should be. Although weak and underfunded, local governments are best suited to meet the needs of local communities ... Developing competent and responsive local governments is central to capacity building'.[61]

UNCHS highlights that challenge in relation to training. 'The complex issues involved in human settlements development call for considerable training. The spectrum of such training should be very wide, reflecting the breadth and scope of human settlements policies and ranging from technical skills to operate services, to the formulation of policy and programmes at the highest levels of administration. What is important, however, is for training to be practically oriented ...'[62]

Conyers and Kaul (1990a) highlight a concern with 'two main issues: firstly, the training of change agents at the project level ... and secondly, the implications of a people centred local development approach for the development of manpower within these agencies.' Their initial conclusion is that training 'should be based on learning by doing. The aim is not to produce highly qualified professionals but to create people who are able to work effectively with local communities. The main skills needed include those related to consciousness-raising, and participatory modes of planning'.[63]

In reviewing human resources development for human settlement policies, a simple but effective statement from Laquian (1979) suggests that 'One of the best ways of learning how to do something is by actually doing it'.[64]

A ladder or morphology of skills levels is introduced to highlight the scope of the training challenge. This is in the context of a comprehensive approach to training for human settlements. Six levels are introduced to illustrate the stages of capacity building through training:

Level 1	Knowledge of facts.
Level 2	Understanding and application of principles.
Level 3	Ability to execute simple skills, observe and do routine problem-solving.
Level 4	Ability to display skills of social co-operation and professional attitudes.
Level 5	Ability to evaluate urban environmental design and appropriate production and construction procedures.
Level 6	Ability to solve non-routine problems and take professional decisions.[65]

The challenge of strengthening human capacity in the field of urban management is in order to strengthen the urban management system itself. Not only is one attempting 'to reshape the municipal administrative structure' but also to recognise that 'greater effort is needed from every national government and from every municipality in the Third World than has been available in the past, if we are to see a change from the present directions towards urban involution to one of positive and progressive urbanisation'.[66]

The point is reinforced with the suggested focus for a human resource development programme. 'It should encompass a full range of teaching, research, publication, apprenticeships, collaborative projects and consultancies, formal and informal dialogue and associations'.[67]

The scope of education for human settlements, 'education for habitat', has been defined by Blair (1985):

Education for habitat is broadly concerned with the concept and promotion of the comprehensive integration and implementation of human settlements planning and development. Integration, as used here, refers to a comprehensive planning process that embraces a broad range of physical, social, economic and environmental factors and issues. It is a process rather than a one-off master plan approach . . .[68]

The need for adequate training for urban management is stressed.

The provision of urban shelter, services and infrastructure requires adequate training of three groups of managers: (a) concerned government leaders and civil servants from the national and local governments . . . (b) leadership and staff of non-government organisations, and (c) formal and informal community leaders. These groups have different roles and functions and the content and methodology of their training would therefore be different . . . Among the priorities of training in the urban sector are: (a) operations and maintenance of municipal services and facilities, (b) public works and construction management, (c) planning and implementing slum upgrading, sites and services and low-cost sanitation projects, (d) project planning and design, (e) project management . . . (f) city level and corporate planning, (g) community organisation . . . (h) resource mobilisation, financial management and cost recovery, (i) land acquisition . . . and (j) budgeting and personnel management.[69]

This is a comprehensive list. It illustrates the wide-ranging nature of urban management. However, in order to encourage a measure of success, some authors advocate the training for urban management within a very practical context.

A number of factors contribute to effective urban management training. Gunesekera (1988) suggests that:

The training needs to be aimed at a closely defined constituency. It should be part of a system development package that allows for organisational involvement in the training . . . The courses should have a significant practical component [and] should have some clear practical application.[70]

The practical component and application of training should not be lost sight of.

In training for urban management, according to Kopardekar (1989), 'it is important that training programmes are organised in the context of the overall urban management problem, and to achieve the desired objectives of development in the particular situation in the country'.[71] Training should therefore have a practical, problem-solving, focus. If one was taking this to an ID conclusion, one could draw upon an analysis where a training institute approach could be instilled in an organisation (ideally), training for and implementing urban management. Thus, from Sanwal (1990), 'in training institutes, goals evolve as spiral iterations rather than in a linear fashion'.[72] That is, the whole training ethos is not only exploratory rather than prescriptive but also, the exploration is built into the organisation's operational culture.

The need for training to be a central component of technical assistance for ID is reinforced in Mattingly (1989). 'Training as an institution building function has received relatively little support in practice. Training, as an implementation tool, could be more successful.'[73] Later, 'it appears that the immediate purpose of training ... lies beyond the achievement of learning and the production of able staff. It aims to produce policy actions during the training event. The training is not seen as a prelude to but as an act of implementation'.[74]

The practice of the World Bank's municipal development programme (MDP) in Eastern and Southern Africa confirms the idea of 'producing policy actions during the training event'. What MDP classified as training was, in fact, a series of policy outputs: action plan; strategic plan; training plan ...[75]

The Nairobi Group cites the following practical components to training:

- Determine the goals and objectives of local authorities ... local communities ... and public policies (that determine contextual strategy).
- Determine the functions that must be carried out ... to achieve these goals.
- Isolate the specific tasks which must be undertaken to implement the functions.
- Identify the skills required to carry out these tasks.
- Analyse the existing skills of the officials and community members responsible for carrying out given tasks.
- Compare the required skill profile with the existing skill profiles to identify, gaps overlaps and mismatches.
- Prioritise training modules suitable to fill gaps and to raise skills to desired levels.[76]

This represents the other side of the practical nature of training – from policy outputs to skills gap filling.

In summary, it is clear that training is moving away from a general strengthening perspective, to a specifically focused, implementation oriented activity.

Training in practice

Two specific cases of training for urban management can be cited. In 1985, the Indonesian government embarked on an ambitious new Integrated Urban Infrastructure Development Programme (IUIDP). This programme not only follows a basic needs approach but has, as its major objective, the increase of the role of the provincial and local governments. IUIDP has an associated training programme.

> The training programme concentrates on the ability of such staff to develop a consistent set of IUIDP proposals which integrate urban development policies and strategic planning, formulate infrastructure investment programmes and define financial and institutional resources for implementing, operating and maintaining infrastructure.[77]

The IUIDP training programme is a set of inter-connecting modules. There are four courses for local government. These are strategic urban planning, followed by IUIDP programming followed by implementation and supervision, followed by operation and maintenance. The strategic urban planning and implementation/supervision modules are supplemented by one on thematic map preparation. The IUIDP programming module is supplemented by two; on institutional planning and financial planning. The provincial government has two training modules. The first is on programme/project appraisal. This feeds into the IUIDP programming course. The second is on monitoring and implementation. This feeds into the implementation/supervision course.[78] To see such a clearly structured training programme is very encouraging.

More recently, another comprehensive programme for the strengthening of a developing country's urban management has been reported. Sri Lanka has a performance improvement programme (PIP) for its local government system. 'The rationale of PIP has been to concentrate on recovering lost ground before anything else, by bringing urban local authorities' essential management, financial and service delivery functions up to an acceptable standard. It has, accordingly, focused on four such activity areas, with training as a fifth activity supporting them'. The first area is general management; 'the introduction of a more managerial and systematic approach to running local authority affairs . . . Its objective is to eliminate budget deficits with realistic budgets, payments to all creditors, sound capital programmes and sound financial management and budgeting'. The second is resource mobilisation; its objectives include 'generating more local revenues by improving collections, raising levels of rates, taxes and fees to expenditure levels, and to ensure viability of water and electricity undertakings'. The third is a joint one of financial management, service delivery and maintenance systems. Its objective is 'to halt the deterioration of facilities and roads and drains, deliver a high standard of maintenance and emphasise maintenance over capital expenditure'. Finally comes training to support all the preceding performance objectives. Its objective is 'to achieve a significant increase in quantitative and qualitative delivery of training, mobilise training resources and institutions to support the performance improvement programme, and build training infrastructure in each local authority, including capacity for organisational change'.[79]

Both the preceding training programmes seek to strengthen the performance of their respective local governments. However, there is a fundamental difference in their perspectives. The first embraces the totality of the urban management system as an explicit and practical process. The second is more in the traditional mould of strengthening organisational and financial capacity to perform. The first approach is more likely to address the needs of institutional development for third world city management.

The importance of the integration of training to the host institution is apparent

> Much has been said about institutional development as a prerequisite to proper urban growth in the Third World. This discussion usually falls short in relation to planning ... Institution-building and institutional change aiming to go this much further, requires strategies to develop an appreciation of (1) the objectives of larger plans and (2) the benefits of actions taken in co-ordination and co-operation with others.[80]

The relationship between urban management and training is reinforced in Steinberg (1991):

> The formulation of this ... new urban management implies, in particular, a new emphasis on training of urban managers and administrators. This training needs to be closely oriented to strengthening local institutions which perform the management roles in the new operational programmes and projects.[81]

In order for this practical orientation to take place, relevant evaluation criteria should be built into each training programme, as suggested in Roberts (1990).

> Training evaluation usually includes two steps. The first is the judgement of participants, usually during the final phases of a training

course, as to whether the course has accomplished its purpose and whether they have learned something of value and relevance. The second is an assessment in the workplace . . . as to whether job performance has improved in a way that can be traced to the benefits of the training.[82]

It is suggested that this two-stage evaluation applies not only to training but also to the general task of skills transfer through technical assistance (whether from resident advisers or short-term consultants).

Finally, there is a disheartening assessment of planning education in less developed countries. At no time is the concept of urban management discussed. This is despite the fact that it distinguishes between 'technical and design' and 'policy and process' orientations to planning education. In the developing world, urban management is central to and not a potential adjunct of town planning.[83] This point should not obscure the generally positive direction being suggested in this text.

In summary, it is clear that innovative practice sees training as tied to practical organisational problem solving.

As a general summary to this third section: training is seen as an essential component in the ID process for third world city management. Its emphasis is being seen increasingly as moving away from a general strengthening perspective, to a specifically focused, implementation-oriented activity. Innovative practice therefore suggests training tied to practical problem-solving. The training should ideally be integrated with the host institution's perceptions of its need and desires. In essence, training is being increasingly viewed as a practical, task-oriented contribution to institutional development.

Thus, at the end of this chapter, another three key characteristics can be discerned that embellish the nature of institutional development in practice. These are:

4. The 'learning' approach is essential to institutional development; 'Each design iteration represents and experimental solution'.[84]
5. That 'function' must be identified for institutional development; 'The appropriate unit of analysis for institutional effectiveness is an activity within an organisation – that is, a specific function'.[85]
6. That 'training' must be practice- and implementation-oriented; 'The training is not seen as a prelude to but an act of implementation'.[86]

The next section summarises the arguments from Part I.

Summary to Part I

Two authors have sought to trace a general trend in the progress of development administration. Luke (1986) suggests that this trend is seeing development administration move away

> from an initial preoccupation with appropriate administrative theory for the developing world in the 1960's and early 1970's, to a practical concern with the implementation of development policy . . . with over 800 million people of the Third World living in absolute poverty, the instrumentalities of improving their life chances certainly demand more than casual attention.[1]

Esman (1988) offers a similar analysis.

> A number of common themes have emerged at the level of middle range theory at the critical interface between concepts and societal action. While they fall short of consensus, they nevertheless represent common ground which unites the interests of scholars and practitioners and provides the basis for informed dialogue and mutual criticism and learning . . . These themes represent a considerable departure from the dominant spirit of the 1960's.[2]

Together, Luke and Esman provide a much more mature and realistic orientation to the prospects for third world development and the functions of public administration.

The World Bank rounds off the argument: '. . . poor performance is a function of weak institutional capacity in the public sector; the best policies cannot be put into effect with a poor public administration. The conclusion?: institutional capacity matters; often crucially so.'[3]

Part I has analysed the process of institutional development (ID) in the third world. Chapter 1 looked at various ID perspectives. Chapter 2 considered various applications in developing countries. The urban management perspective was introduced. The underlying issues from both chapters are summarised as follows.

DEFINING INSTITUTIONAL DEVELOPMENT

Institutions

Institutions play a pivotal role in the development process; indeed, they are frequently cited as impediments to progress. Despite this, there is no standard definition of an institution in the literature. An institution is seen to have three characteristics. It is an instrument for action. It has inherent value to its recipients, beyond its mere instrumentalities. It is a political (i.e. a policy) entity. In essence, institutions are fundamental to the development process.

Development

Development is seen to have four concerns. It needs institutional capacity. It negates the rationalist construction. It recognises the political nature of the process, dominated by policy concerns and human needs. It suggests exploration rather than imposition. The idea of sustainability is introduced. In essence, development is a political process, dominated by policy concerns and human needs.

Institutional development

Institutional development (ID) is seen as making the best use of an institution's human and financial resources. It is an exploratory process, to be performed through the client institution. It seeks to strengthen institutions both as an internal entity and as an external impact mechanism. The iterative model of the process seeks to avoid the blueprint approach and embrace a learning concept. Sustainability is a central issue. The process concerns interventions in organisational structures, their processes and their regulatory environment. At this stage, there is no common agreement on the nature of institutional development. In essence, ID is seen as an exploratory, rather than a prescriptive process.

APPLYING ID IN THE THIRD WORLD

Projects

The project approach is seen to have two flaws. It is a blueprint (or mechanistic) construction. It is a hierarchical (and deductive) method.

In its place, the exploratory, iterative (or learning) model is advocated. This focuses on both the organisation and its impact in the environment, which is seen to be a central platform for any meaningful intervention in third world development. In essence, projects are seen as mechanistic, in the style of the blueprint approach to technical assistance.

Technical assistance (TA)

Technical assistance (TA) has been associated with a traditional project approach to ID. Technical assistance for ID is now seen as moving away from project-based technical assistance towards a more exploratory and participatory mode of project formation and implementation. The unit of analysis must be clearly established in any TA intervention. There is a trend away from long-term technical assistance towards more intensive, short-term counterpart training. It elevates training from an appendage of project work in ID, to a central practically focused activity. In essence, TA is moving towards a more exploratory and participatory mode of project formulation and implementation.

Training

Training for urban management is seen as an essential component in the ID process. Its emphasis is seen increasingly as moving away from a general strengthening perspective, to a specifically focused, implementation oriented activity. Innovative practice therefore suggests training tied to practical problem solving. The training should ideally be integrated with the host institution's perceptions of its need and desires. In essence, training is being increasingly viewed as a practical, task oriented contribution to institutional development.

Two sets of conclusions are therefore drawn from this analysis. The first concerns the general characteristics of institutional development. The second concerns the specific nature of the process. They are not mutually exclusive.

The *general characteristics* of the ID process are suggested to be as follows:

1. Institutions are fundamental to the development process; indeed, they are frequently cited as impediments to progress.
2. Development is a political process dominated by policy concerns and human needs.
3. ID is seen as an exploratory rather than a prescriptive process.

4. Projects are seen as mechanistic, in the style of the blueprint approach to technical assistance.
5. TA is moving towards a more exploratory and participatory mode of project formulation and implementation.
6. Training is being increasingly viewed as a practical, task oriented contribution to institutional development.

The *specific nature* of the ID process is suggested to involve the following arguments:

1. That 'value' distinguishes an institution from an organisation; 'We are concerned with purposes and values which extend beyond the immediate task in hand'.[4]
2. That 'sustainability' must be the test of development; 'Development is concerned with inducing activity which leads to self-sustaining dynamics that improves human well being'.[5]
3. That 'exploration' is the key to contemporary institutional development practice; 'All development initiatives are real world experiments'.[6]
4. That 'learning' is essential to institutional development; 'Each design iteration represents an experimental solution'.[7]
5. That 'function' must be identified for institutional development; 'The appropriate unit of analysis for institutional effectiveness is an activity within an organisation – that is, a specific function'.[8]
6. That 'training' must be practice and implementation oriented; 'The training is not seen as a prelude to but an act of implementation'.[9]

In conclusion, the importance of this analysis is two-fold. First, it offers a definition of an institution and secondly, it identifies an intervention process that seeks to guide patterns of (institutional development) thinking, without prescribing outcomes.

On the first point, there is a suggested test of the term 'institution'. Taking an excerpt from that quote (and reinforcing point 1, above):

Whether an organisation has become institutionalised depends on peoples' evaluations of it – whether it is seen as having acquired value beyond direct instrumental considerations.[10]

On the second point, what remains is the need to introduce an initial conceptual framework for the process of third world institutional development. The specific characteristics of training for urban management

Table 1.1   Variables for institutional development

SCOPE OF THE PROCESS	*Frequency*
Sustainability of ID	11
Iterative, learning and experimental ID	10
Value to the wider community	9
Political not technical rationality	6
Institutions; a pivotal role in development	5
Releasing local potential for self-help	2
Quality of relations (political software)	2
Strengthening human and financial resources	2
Structures, processes and outputs	2
MODES OF INTERVENTION	
Assessing the environment	5
Structure and organisation	3
Policy and management processes	3
Personnel and training	2
Finance	2
Legal framework and government regulations	2
Inter-institutional arrangements	2
Remuneration/incentives to performance	2
FACTORS FOR SUCCESS	
Project leadership and environmental support	7
Project clarity and clear goals	3
Beneficiary/counterpart involvement	3
Autonomy and accountability	2
Project scale/few components	2
Use of local resources	2

Note: The frequency denotes the number of times each variable is cited in Part I.

are excluded at this first stage, in order to retain an aggregate picture of the generic ID process. The suggested framework is in three parts:

- SCOPE OF THE PROCESS
- MODES OF INTERVENTION
- FACTORS FOR SUCCESS.

Under each, a number of variables are identified. They are ordered according to the frequency of the citations in this Part I. The conceptual framework is presented in Table 1.1. This will be returned to in Chapter 11.

Part II now analyses the function of third world city management.

Part II

City Management Function

Part II explores the characteristics of the function of city management. It does so in the knowledge of the literature's suggestion that there is no accepted model of third world city management. Chapter 3 attempts to identify the planning perspectives on the third world city. Chapter 4 assesses the scope of its intervention in third world cities. The Summary to Part II identifies the key characteristics of the city management function in the third world. An initial conceptual framework is introduced.

3 Planning Perspectives

UNCHS (1987c) suggests that 'there is no universal model for settlement management: development strategies and institutional arrangements for human settlements will respond to specific political structures and to changing needs and opportunities'.[1] This chapter and Chapter 4 look at various aspects of 'development strategies'. Part III analyses 'institutional arrangements'. This chapter therefore seeks to identify the salient themes in the move from traditional planning to contemporary management. It considers three topics:

- CITIES AND ECONOMIC GROWTH
- REQUIRED PLANNING RESPONSES
- FROM PLANNING TO INTEGRATED MANAGEMENT.

CITIES AND ECONOMIC GROWTH

Under the heading of cities and economic growth, two ideas are considered: a force for the good; new approaches.

A force for the good

There has been considerable debate over the past twenty years but especially since the Vancouver Human Settlements Conference of 1978 on the nature of public intervention in third world urban growth.[2]

Both UNCHS and other authors[3] suggest that the population of third world cities 'is already larger than the total population of Europe, North America and Japan combined. Current estimates suggest a total of 1.3 billion people, with the total growing by 50 million each year.' In this context, most third world nations are still urbanising; many continue to urbanise rapidly. The point is reinforced by Stren and McCarney, who highlight the extensive urbanisation process in developing countries, both current and projected to 2025.[4] The aggregate figures and annual growth rates are a sharp reminder of what urban management is having to contend with. If South America used to dominate the urban growth figures and Asia is currently wrestling with its mega-cities, Sub-Saharan

Africa is the last but seemingly inevitable global region for massive urban growth. This growth can be seen as both a problem and an opportunity.

Lee-Smith and Stren (1991) comment: 'History shows that cities, not national governments, are the powerhouses of economic development'.[5] The point is reinforced by Mills (1991). 'Cities are crucial for economic development. Their size and density permit economies of scale and scope that are prerequisites to growth ... The growth of urban areas makes efficient production possible and encourages the adoption of new technology.'[6]

The positive economic benefit of cities has been highlighted by a number of authors. Wegelin (1990) has argued that 'there is an increasing awareness that the positive economic functions which cities fulfil can be made more effective through appropriate investments in infrastructure, urban services and shelter improvements'.[7] UNCHS (1987b) expands the theme.

> Cities are not only here to stay but here to grow in size and expand in social and economic importance, as the developing countries move increasingly in the direction of urban based economies, dependent on cities and the services and goods only they can provide. Cities are creators of wealth. Cities are the location for and supporters of employment generating activities. Cities are the agents of the social change necessary for developing countries to move into the mainstream of international commerce and politics. However, as with all tools of production, cities require adequate capital investment, skilful operation, methodological maintenance and periodic improvement. This means giving due attention to the infrastructure networks, structures and services that allow the city to function.[8]

Stren (1993) again comments perceptively: 'The connection between economic activity and large cities can be demonstrated in the close correlation between national income levels and urbanisation.'[9] In essence, the higher the level of urbanisation, the higher the growth rates expected from that economy.

However, there is also a negative aspect to rapid urban development:

> although cities are the engines of economic development, failure to manage the impacts of rapid urbanisation is threatening human health, environmental quality and urban productivity. The immediate and most critical environmental problems facing the third world cities

[are] a lack of safe water, inadequate waste management and pollution control, accidents linked to congestion and crowding, occupation and degradation of sensitive lands, and the inter-relationships between these problems. Their cost falls most heavily on current generations, particularly the urban poor, who are most affected by poor health, lower productivity, reduced incomes and lowered quality of life.

Leitmann *et al.* (1992) go on to suggest that 'the challenge of rapid urbanisation will be to sustain economic growth while solving the associated environmental and social equity problems'.[10] This is the dilemma facing urbanists as they wrestle to harness the inevitable urban growth for the benefit of the mass of citizens. The outcome of this centralised growth pattern, apart from the dire environmental and public health consequences, is the concentration of national economic production in the largest cities. Others discuss this particular issue at some length.[11]

Contemporary policy makers are having to accept the need to harness the energies and opportunities of rapid urbanisation. 'It is now becoming more and more accepted that urbanisation is a force for the good in countries' economic development.' At the same time, the dangers of rapid growth to the urban inhabitants are repeated. 'There is an urgent need to improve the best of human, technical and other resources and to overcome or prevent the environmental and poverty problems associated with the concentration of economic and social activities in cities.'[12]

In summary, it is clear that third world cities are growing rapidly and should be seen as a force for economic and social development.

New approaches

In governmental terms, the consequence is that 'the rate of urban growth has outstripped management capacity, financial resources and even information on the urbanisation process itself. Perhaps most critically of all, the physical environment is suffering from gross misuse and an absence of long-term planning'.[13]

Additionally,

towns and cities have been looked at from different points of view. On the one hand, they are seen as generators of economic growth and are considered the strongholds of modern economic development and progress; on the other hand, they are also seen as social and cultural entities with particular characteristics and atmosphere. However, in recent years, what is most talked about is [neither] of these features but [rather] the abject levels of poverty and inhuman living conditions that a large number of city dwellers are subject to.[14]

It is the negative picture of social and environmental degradation that has to be addressed.

In whatever guise one conceives a suitable response to the third world urban challenge, 'there is a need to abandon Eurocentric value judgements in defining and solving (in this case) Africa's urban problems. New solutions based on concepts relevant to local situations must be bred. One way of doing this is to learn from what the urbanites are doing – and can do – for themselves to solve various problems and to see whether there is room for improvement'.[15] This point is reinforced by Knox and Masilela (1989). 'Research in Europe and North America has shown that urban planners in industrialised countries operate in a professional culture that is dominated by rationalistic, problem solving, technocratic and managerial orientations [whose] distinctive values . . . steer economic and social change along particular [Western] channels.'[16] Rogerson (1989a) is seeking lessons from both Asia and other parts of Africa, rather than the West, to help cope with the predicted urban explosion to come [in South Africa]. The lessons are being sought from countries similar to his own.[17]

For example, the most common practice in past years was to clear slums and squatter areas. There can be a locally determined and more enlightened view, as is suggested by Okpala (1987). 'Most prevailing ideas about slum and squatter settlements and the need for their wholesale clearance therefore need to be finally abandoned. Indeed, in the prevailing circumstances, it is difficult to imagine how urban human settlements development could by-pass the present conditions. Slums and squatter settlements are thus better viewed from more dynamic perspectives such as evolving communities and housing in process of improvement.'[18] The tenor of this approach to third world city growth is developed in Chapter 4.

Moving from a social to an economic perspective, the city as a 'tool of production' is a fundamental concept. It recognises the economic function of the city in national economic development. It also introduces the managerial approach to the city as a means of production. London University's Development Planning Unit published some pioneering work on this subject in 1975. Its central arguments 'spring from the managerial perception of the urban system as a complex productive unit which has the capacity for meeting the needs and aspirations of the majority of its inhabitants'.[19] In order to achieve this, the response to urban growth must have a particular set of characteristics.

The challenge is defined by Chandrasekhara (1989).

> Municipal management has to foresee the population growth and provide for it in advance and in anticipation . . . The procedures for planning, execution, budgeting, monitoring etc. currently available are thoroughly inadequate to handle this magnitude of problem. Therefore, municipal management has to devise new strategies, advance procedures anticipating growth and provide for the housing and proper living and working of the incoming population and to make it contribute to the city's revenues.

The responses must seek to enhance the economic production potential of the new urban population. Key concepts such as planning, execution, budgeting and monitoring are introduced, in the context of 'new strategies'.[20]

The analysis of Pernia (1991) suggests there are three topics to be considered. First, there is no clear understanding of a human settlements policy. 'One of the main problems is that it would have to be an overarching policy in the sense that, to be meaningful and effective, it would have to touch on virtually all aspects of economic and social life. This is necessitated by the very concept of human settlements as not simply housing or, for that matter, merely the physical structure of a city . . . but an integrated combination of all human activity processes and the physical structure that supports them'.[21]

Secondly, in order to start managing cities properly, there has to be some clear policy instrument and institutional arrangement to make the instrument effective. This is very difficult because of the overarching nature of human settlements policy. 'A ministry of human settlements once existed in the Philippines under the powerful First Lady of the previous regime. Yet, even with all her power, there was no functional human settlement policy as such but at best, fragments of a policy'.[22]

Thirdly, access to infrastructure plays a major role in the spatial pattern of urban development.

> Studies show that the availability of (or access to) infrastructure (power, transport, communications and water supply) and social

services (health and education) exerts a strong influence on the location of economic activity and population. By contrast, direct intervention measures, such as fiscal or financial incentives (subsidies, credit, etc.) or disincentives (bans, penalties, taxes, etc.) are often ineffective and very costly. [However], the critical issue is no longer just spatial balance per se but environmental redress and sustainable urbanisation.[23]

The importance of infrastructure, as a determinant of spatial pattern in urban growth, is introduced.

The general approach to be adopted here is well summarised by Rakodi (1987). 'The most crucial task of urban management in the cities of developing countries is to assist in the absorption of the rapidly growing population in such a way that basic needs are met and efficient and equitable use is made of urban land and other resources.'[24] The central idea is absorption: creating the conditions to allow urban immigrants to play a full and self-supporting role in the growth of the city. The wider notion concerns the management of the raw material necessary to sustain the insatiable appetite of the city as, arguably, the most complex of all tools of production.

In summary, it is suggested that any approach to confronting the urban challenge should seek to learn from third world practice and eschew wholesale acceptance of Western perceptions. Also, it is evident that the city as an economic production unit has some merit, when helping to understand the nature of the challenge.

As a general summary to this section; third world cities are growing and should be seen as a force for economic and social development. They already contribute disproportionately to gross domestic production. The idea of the city as an important economic production unit is introduced. The converse of this is the insanitary conditions, congestion, environmental degradation, poverty and disintegrating (or nonexistent) infrastructure and services which are created by rapid urban growth. Any approach to confronting this urban dilemma should seek to learn from third world practice and eschew the wholesale acceptance of Western perceptions. The question now is: what are the required planning responses to the third world urban challenge?

REQUIRED PLANNING RESPONSES

Under the heading of required planning responses, two ideas are considered: the master plan failure; a management approach.

The master plan failure

There is a central dilemma in traditional planning responses to third world cities. In the context of Madras, they suggest that 'until recently, the urban planning system was divorced from public investment and the budgetary and economic planning processes of the state and local government'.[25] That is, it was dominated by the master plan syndrome. The argument is echoed by Sinou (1988). 'The demographic explosion of third world cities (some attaining annual rates of up to 10%) also underlined the vain character of urban planning and methods modelled on cities with slow growth rates.'[26] This was epitomised by the master plan syndrome, modelled on the Western tradition.[27]

This critical discussion of the master plan syndrome is followed by Richardson (1993).

For example, several cities (e.g. Delhi, Madras, Karachi, Dhaka, and Jakarta) have periodically developed master plans that have included elements of a spatial strategy. Unfortunately, these plans have been almost useless. They usually involve wildly inaccurate population projections and land use zones that deviate, often dramatically, from reality. Invariably, they are too rigid and inflexible to accommodate readjustments as conditions change.[28]

Farvacque and McAuslan (1992) address the argument at some length.

Master plans take too long to prepare; they seldom offer guidance on the phasing and techniques of implementation; they seldom evaluate the costs of the development they propose or try to determine how they could be financed and pay little or no attention to the necessary resource allocation and financial feasibility of policies and programmes; master plans are seldom based on realistic appraisals of the city's economic potential or likely population growth; community leaders and implementation agencies are seldom meaningfully involved in the master planning process; master plans are infrequently updated and their static nature cannot keep up with the dynamic process of urban growth in the developing world. In the majority of cities with master plans, the supply of shelter for the low income population is built in spite of the master plan, not because of it. In brief, master planning and comprehensive planning techniques are primarily concerned with the product rather than the process and do not adequately address implementation issues, the increasing complexity of land markets, the role of the public sector versus private sector actions and the links between spatial and financial planning.[29]

Clarke (1992) adopts a similar line:

Traditional master plans have been mainly static in nature, attuned to a scenario of slow urban growth in which major investments in infrastructure, roads, services and other public investments could be carefully planned in the context of a finite long-term plan. Rapid population growth, lack of infrastructure and services, and shortages of funds and staff in the typical developing country city, require a more dynamic planning process in which priorities have to be continually assessed and re-assessed in the light of available resources ... Thus, the planning system needs to focus on short-term action planning.[30]

The argument is reinforced by UNCHS (1987c):

Initially, planning focused only on physical aspects of settlement development, indicating mainly desired land use distributions and transport networks. This type of [master] planning is known as indicative planning because although it could indicate the desired direction, it lacked control over the factors contributing to change ... While criticism of indicative planning continues, examples exist in many parts of the world of other planning devices which show promise of meeting real development needs ... Innovative planning can achieve development objectives, improve living conditions and efficiently deliver basic services. Planning can thus be seen as a management tool.[31]

Here, the explicit link between planning and urban management is made.

In summary, it is clear that master planning is a long-term activity, divorced from financing and not suitable for managing third world urban development.

A management approach

Turner (1992) concurs with the point made above. 'Planning, or urban management, should be incremental in nature, following a step-by step achievement of limited goals and objectives. Over-ambitious projects might have political value, but are unlikely to achieve significant change in the majority of cases.'[32] The idea of an iterative planning process (of assessing and re-assessing priorities and programmes) is introduced. Also, a link is implied between planning and urban management.

A more responsive, process-oriented approach to development planning has been argued for elsewhere. Davey (1983) states:

> A more flexible process of periodic rolling policy review has distinct theoretical merits; the only question is whether it can generate the same political interest and commitment at present associated with the fixed term comprehensive plan ... Planning needs to be firmly grounded in monitoring and evaluation of current activities and policies ... A link between planning and monitoring allows for incremental adjustments of policy which makes more use of practical experience and calls for less dramatic shifts in organisational behaviour ... A widely acknowledged weakness is the relation of planning to budgeting.[33]

McNeill (1983) also emphasises the need to shift from long-term physical planning to shorter-term, budget dominated investment planning.[34] The literature has also confirmed a relationship between urban planning and urban management: 'Planning should not exist as an isolated exercise but should form an integral part of urban management'.[35] In an expansion of the argument, Safier (1992) comments that planning should be 'a continuous and cyclical process which combines immediate, flexible and incremental action in response to felt needs; opportunistic openings often based on negotiation and compromise, but based on longer-term strategic directions ... [It should have] a pervasive concern with implementability.'[36] Thus, the idea of urban management is confirmed.

A major publication by Sivaramakrishnan and Green (1986) reinforces the argument:

> Metropolitan management must adopt fresh perspectives in planning and administering urban development ... This perception has encouraged a shift of emphasis from town planning as conventionally

understood (that is, the designing of comprehensive land-use plans) towards the initiation of wide-ranging and policy-oriented research and analysis requiring contrasting and changing clusters, patterns, and flows of activity, not necessarily focused on land uses. This differently oriented activity may, in fact, be concerned mainly with defining development problems and goals in the economic and social context; such activity includes the design and appraisal of related action projects and schemes and it extends to learning by assessing performance.[37]

It could therefore be suggested that the fledgling urban management tradition is moving towards an exploratory and iterative process.

Halla (1985) has posited that, if the urban planning intervention is to be relevant, it must be based on political economy.

A planning based on political economy puts forward the ordering, priorities, and fostering of the basic needs of society as the agenda for urban planning. This is because accomplishing such an agenda is positive in support of and in guidance of a directly promotional and entrepreneurial role for government and public sector action in urban affairs. By basic needs is meant the needs of society, such as:

- urban growth and economic conditions of society,
- distribution or sharing of income and public wealth,
- involvement of citizens in political and resource allocation processes (organisation, management and administration of society's activities), and
- safeguarding the physical and ecological environment of society.[38]

This view suggests that 'a planning based on political economy breeds a tradition which is concerned with analysing the extent of problems and needs in urban areas. Then, it works priorities and fosters the most pressing ones, in order to gain a capacity to deal with the rest.'[39] This is an important departure. Traditional urban planning (through the master plan) viewed its purpose in physical and land-use terms. The new urban management seeks a general 'political' understanding in order to identify in what areas to intervene.

Through such contributions, a general planning methodology appropriate to the developing world has been introduced. At this stage, only two of the ten stages need to be highlighted. These are (a) the 'translation of the spatial analysis into an investment plan that identifies the projects and programmes that will be needed to ameliorate major development problems, to strengthen and articulate the regional spatial structure and to integrate the various levels of settlement within it'; and (b) the 'integration of projects identified through spatial and economic analysis into co-ordinated investment packages for different locations within the region, and the combination of the investments into priority-ranked and appropriately sequenced investment budgets for the development of various towns and cities over a given time period'.[40] The point to highlight here is the direct link between the planning for cities and the investment required to make these plans work. The word 'integration' begins to appear as part of the planning concept. The next section of this volume will focus more closely on the fundamental shift of emphasis from general planning to integrated management.

The instrument for achieving such an urban management intervention is proposed by the UN. It suggests that

> for successful management, planning must be associated with programming and budgeting. The programming process involves all those interventions, public or private, that need to be undertaken in order to implement settlement plans. Feasibility of implementation should be assessed according to the investment capabilities of all the agents involved in the process.[41]

This is a key development. For the first time, an author recognises the fundamental importance of integrating all the players in the city building process. Yet, as recently as 1993, Davey was suggesting that 'the integration of physical and investment planning is rarely adequate, and an appropriate [planning] methodology has proved elusive'.[42]

In summary, it is apparent that planning interventions should be shorter term and tied to a management perspective. Thus, the management approach should be dominated by processes, involving programme and budgeting.

A general summary to this second section established that master planning is a long-term activity, divorced from the financing of its proposals. Planning interventions in future should be shorter term and tied to a management perspective. This urban management should be dominated by a concern for processes. The process should centre on the political economy of the city (e.g. poverty and wealth). The instrument of this intervention is an urban management process that incorporates planning, programming and budgeting. The section has also introduced the notion of integrating all the players and sectors into the planning and development process. The characteristics of this intervention and integration are explored in the next section.

FROM PLANNING TO INTEGRATED MANAGEMENT

Under the heading of 'from planning to integrated management', three ideas are considered: integration; the informal sector; the banking trap.

Integration

The concept of integrated urban management takes many forms. Espinoza (1985) suggests that 'a development plan is, by definition, an economic and social policy; it integrates goals, measures and resources in a logical way, and is the guiding principle for all actions undertaken by local, regional and central government bodies. The best government policy is a kind of integrated socioeconomic plan, whereby all levels of government can respond to national priorities and not to those of privileged power groups'.[43] De Albornoz (1985) reinforces the point by citing a country where local planning is seen as an integral part of the national planning process: 'Local government in Venezuela will be playing a leading role in integrated planning ... Within the 7th National Plan, in which local planning is regarded as an important element, municipal councils have been given the opportunity to play a leading role in administering local planning within an integrated process.'[44] Each of these authors focuses on the integration of policy.

Again drawing on Venezuelan experience, Illaramendi (1985) suggests that 'integral planning has three aspects:

- Inter-institutional co-ordination based on homogeneous, consistent and concerted multi-sectoral effort to solve the problems of depressed low income urban settlements,
- Direct community participation in diagnostic planning processes, and
- Practical projects supported through financial assistance from public and/or private organisations and the communities.

These aspects are dealt with through an integrated structure of programme implementation consisting of inter-related councils at national, regional, state, municipal and local levels.'[45] This takes the concept a useful step forward, by highlighting the linked role of organisations, the explicit role of the clients and the implementation of practical projects. The case of Botswana is also a useful illustration. Wallis (1987) suggests that Botswana

> has taken development planning considerably more seriously than most African countries. It is relatively successful because of (a) a strong political commitment to pragmatic planning and economic rationality and (b) the integration of planning, budgeting and economic policy formulation, under a powerful senior minister.[46]

The stress here is not only on an integrated planning system but also on the senior co-ordination of all its players.

The challenge can also be seen in terms of integrating the environmental dimension into the overall urban management process. Rees (1987) notes that: 'Pressing urban environmental problems make it imperative to implement policies oriented to environmental planning and management on an integrated basis rather than merely by sector. Only from an integrated, dynamic perspective may sound development be achieved.'[47]

A case of district planning with community participation in Peru is presented by Dawson (1992). 'The second project was the integrated district development plan. The project sought to develop a system whereby the [local] population could participate in the design of a district development plan . . . [The project included] providing training to local community leaders.'[48] This is an ideal approach to integrating the community, as clients, in the planning of their town. However, 'the main obstacle' to success was, perversely, the municipality, its mayor and the overriding political factionalism. This shows the importance of a supportive environment. A similar analysis for Panama is offered, showing the importance the supervising environment (central government) places on locally defined information for development.[49]

An ideal scenario is to see an integrated urban management process incorporating the community in its deliberations. The argument is taken, perhaps, to an idealised conclusion by Aina (1990):

> The bottom-up approach [to planning] is a more people centred approach since it involves the political mobilisation of ordinary people . . . In this context, participation is defined not only as involvement through consultations and elections, but rather, as the yielding of the direct control of decision-making in urban settlements to the communities who live in them.[50]

From a different perspective, it is noted that international donor agencies are broadening their perspective on the urban sector. For example the

> upgrading of housing stock, water systems, drainage, sewerage and also transportation components may comprise a single project. The citywide approach is frequently more the result of increased technical and financial assistance reflected in more project components than any strategic analysis of development trends, potentials and constraints.

However, within such an enforced necessity, opportunities present themselves. 'In order to achieve better integration and to identify the broad range of potential problems, the Asian Development Bank's recent attempts to study urban sectors and then to identify related projects within this sphere, appears to be both successful and well received.'[51] In this case, integration is seen to encompass both institutional involvement and sectoral proposals.

Using the Asian Development Bank's territorial focus, Jakarta offers a good example. Clarke (1985) examined the planning process in the Indonesian capital: 'Given the projected scale of growth in the city, the uncertainties over future changes . . . and the resource limitations, only general long term plans were developed for the metropolitan region . . . Given the evident fragmentation of decision making and the difficulties in project implementation for both levels of government, a more integrated approach was stressed through better co-ordination between the socioeconomic, financial, physical and institutional planning sectors.'[52] At this stage, the evidence suggests the need to view the urban challenge as a holistic concept. Each variable seems to be dependent and interacting at both a strategic and operational level.

A similar case covers the urban management of Manila. Five major problems were identified. There was sectoral isolation of planning and inadequate involvement of local governments;[53] inadequacies in methods of planning and weaknesses in the system of resource management[54] and finally, a bane of urban management in developing countries, institutional fragmentation. In order to overcome these problems, a planning system was devised 'involving an annual planning cycle of activities linked to the national budgeting system and its major output is a five-year rolling investment programme of projects, which are consistent with expected available funds and government priority'. In this case the stress is on integrating not only the agencies in the planning process but also planning with programming and budgeting. Others herald this approach as a model to be developed elsewhere.[55]

The point here is to identify the central role of the annual policy and budgetary cycle and the integration of all the funding players in the urban management process. Amos (1989) proposes that: 'At the municipal level, there should be for each urban area, an urban programme which identifies projects together with the appropriate resource allocations for capital investment, maintenance and operating costs. The programmes should be . . . regularly reviewed, revised as necessary and rolled forward annually . . . It should include all public sector expenditure.'[56] These proposals offer important structures. First, the annual programme and budget cycle is recognised. Secondly, the need to integrate all the players in the city building process (i.e. 'all public sector expenditure') is advocated.

It is argued by Davidson (1991) that 'urban management is about mobilising resources in a way that can achieve urban development objectives'.[57] Later, it is suggested that

integration is a much used word. Many projects include the word integrated in their titles, but actually, achieving integration is much more difficult . . . Integration is a benefit when $2 + 2 = 5$. Factors for effective integration include an integrated plan, a modest initial scale, integrated area based management and integrated finances.[58]

Elsewhere, in the work of Lee (1991),

it has been argued that urban development is not a sector like any other traditional sectors involved in the development of urban areas. The merit of urban development is the opportunity it affords to co-ordinate and integrate . . . various components on an area basis. An issue is whether such co-ordination and integration are possible and practical, and whether there is a limit to such endeavour. In the formulation of a programme and a project, however, it is not only functional linkages that matter but also institutional arrangements . . .[59]

In other words, whatever the institutions in the city-building process, they should have a common reference point (or strategy) for both planning and implementation. Thus, irrespective of organisation, all the players can then participate in the urban management process. The concept of inter-agency arrangements is explored in Chapter 6.

Combining urban management with integration, one can cite UNCHS. 'Efficient settlements do not only mean improved living conditions within the settlements themselves; they are also crucial to achieving national development goals.' This concept of 'efficiency can only be reached through the integration of physical planning and resource management in a continuous process'.[60] This relationship between planning and budgeting is fundamental to the concept of urban management. This has already been noted as a major weakness in traditional planning practice (see previous section).

In summary, it is clear that the shift from planning to urban management needs an integrated perspective. The need for a holistic view of urban management has also been introduced.

The informal sector

The poor must be absorbed into the informal labour market as a first step in the individual process of development. At the very least, urban management should also be addressing this question (as well as, for example, water infrastructure). Linn (1983) makes the point clearly:

> In attempting to improve urban management and administration, it is important to bear in mind not only the economic interests and needs of the modern sector. If one of the prime objectives of urban employment policy is to improve the absorption of low-skilled labour, then urban management must be geared also to provide the complementary public services required by activities using such labour, and to adjust its regulatory and taxing practices to minimise the compliance cost for the informal sector.[61]

The concept of integration as a need to establish mutually reinforcing policy mechanisms in the context of absorbing the inevitable growth in the urban population has been recorded by the Institute of Development Studies (1978):

> Effective measures to increase urban absorption must reinforce each other, so that their combined impact is greater than the sum of their individual contributions. For example, when adult education and primary schools increase practical skills which can be applied to house improvement and infrastructure projects, which are themselves designed to increase job opportunities and income, then there is a genuinely integrated approach at work.[62]

This contribution of the informal sector to the city-building process is another fundamental point in the development of an integrated urban management system.

The point is reinforced by Stren and McCarney (1992): 'Since the 1970's, the development literature has recognised the growing importance of the "informal sector", particularly in terms of employment, and particularly in urban areas.'[63] Elsewhere, Perlman (1993) has suggested that 'the informal sector in most third world cities absorbs nearly one-third of the economically active urban labour force, and this proportion has remained fairly constant across cities and throughout booms and recessions over the past quarter-century.'[64]

In a World Bank discussion paper, Bhadra and Brandao (1993) comment that 'many authors argue that the informal sector operates in an orderly and efficient manner and benefits the urban sector in developing countries'.[65] Furthermore, it is suggested by Shabbir Cheema (1993) that 'the main strength of the urban informal sector is its ability to generate employment opportunities.'[66]

However, this order, efficiency and resilience is despite, and not because of, the regulatory environment. A practical example illustrates the point.

Most new housing and most new neighbourhoods in third world cities are organised, planned and built outside the law. Most urban citizens have no choice but to build, buy or rent an illegal dwelling since they cannot afford the cheapest legal house or apartment. It is now common for 30 to 60 percent of an entire city's population to live in houses and neighbourhoods which have been developed illegally. In most cities, 75 to 90 percent of all new housing is built illegally.[67]

UNCHS concurs with this view: 'The private sector (formal and informal) finances most (80 to 90 percent) of the shelter component of human settlements. The informal component of this sector . . . finances 70 to 80 percent of the shelter output of the private sector . . . In Nigeria, Sri Lanka, Thailand and Tanzania, this figure is above 90 percent.'[68]

The point is reinforced by Jones and Satterthwaite (1989): 'To a large extent, the future city will be financed, built and shaped by people with low incomes. These people provide the cheap labour and cheap goods and services on which much of the city's economy depends. But they are excluded from legal land and housing markets . . . These are the people who will manage most new city developments.'[69] In other words, integrated urban management must embrace both institutional co-ordination and direct community participation. Indeed, a formal sector integrated urban management process without the informal sector's explicit (and some might argue) potentially dominant role, is virtually meaningless. This is especially so if the percentages of informal sector city building, quoted above, are correct.

Yet, the informal sector is a two-edged sword. Its resilience rests in its informality and lack of entry rules. 'The informal sector is most precious precisely because its rules are minimal. It has no wage regulations, no price controls, and no (or few) obstacles to the entry of new economic agents.' The implication is that this sector should be recognised for what it is; the single working mechanism for absorbing the majority of urban citizens into the urban system. 'On the other hand, the informal sector is no paradise'.[70] The challenge is to harness the informal sector's dynamism without stifling it.

The role of the informal sector is taken a step further by Montgomery (1988):

> As an intellectual or political challenge ... planning for urban development rivals those that occur at the national level ... Cities have much to do but they are not to be thought of as nations writ small. Their resources, in proportion to their functions, are minuscule ... Urban governments cannot duplicate the range of expertise of central governments. Thus the task of improving the administrative capacity of cities is not a scaled down replica of the problem of improving the administrative capacity of states. Most of all, it requires the effective use of resources outside the useful range of public administration.[71]

This includes a range of possible informal sector contributions to urban services.

Hardoy and Satterthwaite (1990) emphasise this point. 'The failure of government to support and help co-ordinate the actions of these people represents an enormous loss in what both government and these people can achieve'.[72] This is especially so, given the informal sector's acknowledged contribution to economic development. At this point, it is sobering to return to work produced by the IDS that is now almost two decades old. 'The role of the informal sector has been emphasised already. It is particularly important in city building, house construction and the commercial sphere'.[73] Of the three components, the idea of city building should be kept in mind.

In order to address this dichotomy of the formal and informal city, urban management must have the resilience to address a range of problems simultaneously. Thus, in the words of Sinou (1988),

> urban management cannot limit itself to simply administering daily matters, but must aim to restructure its intervention methods according to the context of third world cities. For instance, institutional actors and intervention schemes who focus on urban development based on Western practices (which concern a small part of the city's inhabitants only) should make room for new actors and intervention methods. Such a step implies a new way of conceiving the city, not primarily as a physical space to be reshaped by noticeable operations but as a social space understood from a development point of view.[74]

In summary, it is clear that the informal sector's contribution to the city-building process must be harnessed.

The banking trap

The difficulty is that the international donor community is increasingly viewing its urban interventions in financial terms only. Sinou (1988) suggests that

> this rethinking of urban management now implicitly tends towards a new definition of the city; a purely financial view where access to services (housing, water supply, electricity, sanitation) depends on the inhabitants' resources. The opposition between the white and indigenous city gives way to the opposition between the legal and real city, a heritage of traditional urbanism.[75]

It is this real or 'illegal' city that must be addressed.

Mabogunje (1992) concurs and presents the first significant indicator of the required international response.

> ... institutional radicalisation has to be extended over wider areas of societal activities. At present, most of these activities are described as 'informal'. Whether it is a societal adaptive process of making land available for urban housing, building houses, engaging in capitalist-type productive activities, running transportation services, establishing credit institutions, even of organising themselves – all have been dismissed sometimes not simply as 'informal' but

also as 'illegal'. A situation where the activities of the majority of the population in a society are so described and treated cavalierly, needs to be critically reviewed and revised [in the context of] urban land and urban management.[76]

Ayittey (1990) proposes that the direction of this radicalisation could be 'integrating the indigenous into development strategies ... if development is correctly understood to mean improving the existing ways of doing things to lift the masses out of poverty, then the focus ought to be on the indigenous and informal sector, because this is where the masses are located'.[77]

Furthermore, 'there is a danger that a third new concept might be introduced – that of the bankable versus the insolvent city, less easily identifiable for the boundaries are not necessarily spatial.' The first term designates the city that is built, equipped and managed with the help of bankable projects (in experts' terminology meaning those that can be financed by a bank). The second term covers that large incompressible portion of the urban population whose sole meagre resources go into food and day-to-day survival. 'This population of poor people ... can only find themselves even more excluded under this new form of reasoning.'[78]

If the banking argument has a negative connotation for the informal sector, it also does for the environment. It is suggested by Rees (1992) that:

Mainstream economists generally reject the concept of carrying capacity outright on the grounds that technology will continuously improve productivity, that manufactured capital can substitute for natural capital and that inter-regional trade will relieve any local constraints on growth ... By contrast, the ecological perspective shows carrying capacity as fundamental to demographic/resource analysis. It reveals relationships and dependencies that are invisible to conventional models – marginal prices and monetary analysis reveal nothing about the functional roles, remaining volumes, necessary quantities or absolute values of the declining stocks of natural capital. Global ecological change suggests that the productive capacity of some forms of natural capital has already been breached on the scale of the ecosphere. While economic analysis properly treats individual urban regions as open to exchange, it does not recognise that the ecosphere is materially closed and ultimately limiting.[79]

The point is echoed by Kolo (1991): 'The prime dilemma is in using the environment for development, or to fight poverty. The link between the environment and a region's development, measured by the standards of living and economic growth, is a complex one. People rely almost directly on the environment, using crude technology, for most of life's essentials – food, shelter, energy, employment, and so on.'[80] The financial model of the city is therefore a danger to both the real (informal) city and its capital (ecological) base. Taking just one small example, the primary source of energy for the majority of the inhabitants in Sub-Saharan Africa is wood. Open fires are used for cooking. The rate of deforestation is greatly in excess of the current and projected supply of fuelwood.

Tacconi and Tisdell (1993) express the view that 'a holistic concept of sustainable development has emerged in which economic, ecological, social and political factors need to be simultaneously considered'.[81] The environmental issue must be clearly addressed in any meaningful urban management process. The banking arguments need to be subsumed to a wider environmental perspective.

Johnson (1990) gives an indication of what is required:

As less developed countries continue to grow, more attention must be paid to their environmental aspects. The urban environment is important for it is home to millions of households, not to mention the basis for their economic existence. This environment's capacity to sustain social and economic activities is ultimately limited. Development impact exactions (DIA) linkage with the concept of urban carrying capacity is important for it offers a chance of integrating the planning, management, and financing of urban infrastructure and services in a manner which is responsive to both the limitations of the urban environment and the potential of urban economies.[82]

The environmental issue and the informal sector are linked by the failure of 'bankable' projects to incorporate, respectively, their constraining and contributing capacities. These key elements should be signposted, for any future concept of urban management.

In summary, it is suggested that the concept of bankable projects not only excludes the informal sector but that it also fails to embrace the question of environmental capacity.

As a general summary of this third section, the shift from planning to urban management suggests an integrated concept to the process. There is a need for a holistic perspective to urban intervention. The instrument of that intervention should embrace institutional arrangements and community involvement in order to develop practical projects. The informal sector's major contribution to city building must be harnessed. The danger is that the informal sector is (perhaps unwittingly) being excluded because of the notion of 'bankable' projects. The concept of bankable projects also fails to embrace the question of environmental capacity. At this stage, there is still no general model of urban management.

Thus, at the end of this chapter, three key characteristics can be discerned from the planning perspectives.

1. Cities are the powerhouse of economic development.
2. The planning response should focus on the political economy of the city.
3. The informal sector's contribution to the city-building process must be harnessed.

The next chapter looks at the scope of interventions in urban management.

4 Scope of Intervention

As recently as 1993, two authors were lamenting the state of urban management. Stren noted that: 'Since the mid-1980s, urban management as an integrating concept has been strangely bereft of substantive content and definition . . . The central core of meaning attached to the concept has been surprisingly elusive'.[1] Later, 'while comparative and conceptual work has taken place within the (UN Habitat – Urban Management) Programme sectors, the overall concept of urban management has not been addressed head on'.[2] Similarly, Davey suggested that 'the evolution of urban management is littered with attempts to develop an effective methodology for strategic planning and management at the metropolitan and municipal levels. The literature has uncovered few examples of good practice'.[3] This chapter seeks to identify the parameters of urban management. It therefore considers three topics:

- OPERATIONAL PARAMETERS
- INFRASTRUCTURE
- INSTITUTIONAL STRENGTHENING.

OPERATIONAL PARAMETERS

Under the heading of operational parameters, three ideas are considered: the nature of the process; practical concerns; a holistic concept.

Nature of the process

An attempt has been made to define urban management as a topic of study. It is argued by Williams (1978) that 'urban managerialism is not a theory nor even an agreed perspective. It is instead a framework for study'.[4] Williams goes on to define the nature of urban management as having 'a far more explicit concern with power relations, the nature of cities and their social and economic structure'.[5] The article then considers the players in the process.

There has been considerable debate as to whether urban managerialism should simply be concerned with the role of government officials (at both central and local levels) as mediators or whether it should encompass a whole range of actors in both public service and private enterprise who appear to act as controllers of resources sought by urban populations.[6]

Clearly, the control of resources is a fundamental condition of success. The range of actors is another question, addressed later in the text. It is therefore suggested that

urban managerialism provides a useful way of penetrating the complex relationships that structure urban areas. It penetrates this web at the point of contact between individual consumers and the allocators of scarce resources. Not only can the allocation process be exposed but also the reason for it can be pursued.[7]

On the face of it, this is a political interpretation, centred on Western cities. As Leonard (1982) comments: 'Whilst society's managers, it would seem, remain central to the urban problematic, the development of a political economy approach ... must remain one of the most pressing research tasks facing human geography.'[8] The allocation of resources presupposes that there are resources to disperse. As has already been seen, in the third world there are precious few resources to allocate. The informal sector's potential role in city building is therefore paramount. One thing that is right is the idea that urban management should encompass a whole range of actors in both public and private enterprise.

Thus, in the words of Sharma (1989),

in very simple terms, urban management can be described as the set of activities which together shape and guide the social, physical and economic development of urban areas. The main concerns of urban management, then, would be intervention in these areas to promote economic development and well being, and to ensure necessary provision of essential services.[9]

The promotion of economic development and essential services seems reasonable enough, but only if considered as an early step in the analysis. A similar view is offered by Rakodi (1991):

Urban management aims to ensure that the components of the system are managed so that they make possible the daily functioning of a city which will both facilitate and encourage economic activity of all kinds and enable residents to meet their basic needs for shelter, access to utilities and services, and income generating opportunities.[10]

New directions in urban management 'are based on the belief that urban management should be concerned with the incremental, routine provision and maintenance of essential public works and services as much as with innovative planning and the execution of development projects'.[11] They are suggesting both an operational and strategic concern for the specifics of urban management.

This point is highlighted by Marbach (1986):

Concepts of urban government have changed radically over the past 50 years. In the past, urban authorities were expected to manage day-to-day urban affairs competently and provide a minimum of services, such as street lighting, water supply and refuse collection. Nowadays, a city is required to plan for the development of fast growing communities, stimulate or control growth and change, look after the housing, health, education, employment and welfare of the ever increasing numbers of the urban poor. Financially, it is no longer enough for a local authority to be a good housekeeper and accountant. It must plan and carry out major financial operations on its own account or on behalf of the controlling central or national government.[12]

Urban management has clearly moved from the routine to a complex set of activities, incorporating both operational and strategic activities.

Ramachandran (1993) proposes 'a rigorous conceptual definition of urban management'.[13] Later, 'in the establishment of a broad-based framework for city-wide strategic planning, five key areas are considered . . . These are land, infrastructure and services, transport, finance and organisational performance'.[14] This seems to go only part of the way to establishing a full understanding. Taking just one example, the term municipal management, the title and central focus of the paper, is suggested to embrace the urban management process. The flaw in that suggestion is equating municipal to a governing organisation only.[15] In contrast urban management is (or should be) concerned with the development of the city and its governing (municipal) organisation.

In summary, it is clear that urban management must have a central concern for resource allocation across the spectrum of interventions in urban development.

Practical concerns

The Indonesian experience is cited to identify the key operational concerns of its urban management process. These are 'drinking water, sewerage and human waste, solid waste, drainage and flood control, urban roads, housing, serviced land provision and spatial urban planning'. In this practice, urban management is concerned with the infrastructure and related service provision that is fundamental to life (water), public health (sanitation and waste management), economic development (roads), shelter (housing), and general infrastructure (serviced land) and their inter-relationships (spatial planning).[16]

A similar checklist is offered by Cotton and Franceys (1988) where 'primary infrastructure provides only the most basic of services . . .'. The list reads 'ground preparation, drainage, access, water, sanitation, solid waste, power and community.'[17] A similar but more qualitatively assessed checklist of urban infrastructure provision comes from Richardson (1993). It reviews housing, water, sewerage and drainage, power, health, education, transport and environmental protection.[18] The authors immediately above see the concept as the provision of infrastructure and services, but only one includes the spatial component.[19]

The municipal government's role can be taken a stage further.

> The quality of management by the urban authorities may have an important effect on whether and how a city grows . . . Among the elements of urban management at issue here are: the provision of adequate public utilities for industry and commerce; the existence of a well functioning transport system for the speedy distribution of goods and services; availability of serviced land for new industrial developments; adequate public marketing facilities, both wholesale and retail; a good communications system (telephones and postal); and a public administration that minimises efficiency losses and compliance costs for regulations and taxes.[20]

Here, the ideal policy and practical outputs of urban management are seen as external economies (roads) to the development of the city. Conversely, the failure of urban management to provide these outputs becomes an external diseconomy (no roads).

One of the World Bank's most recent reviews of the infrastructure needs of a major community (though not an urban centre) concerned the occupied West Bank of the River Jordan. Here, the infrastructure checklist follows the standard items of water, waste management, electricity, roads, education, health and, additionally, telephones.[21]

Chandrasekhara (1989) has noted that

> the municipal bodies have become helpless spectators of a large scale expansion of built up areas and of activities in their respective jurisdictions and are unable to meet, even partly, the new demands and are unsuccessfully struggling to maintain the existing level of services. Thus improving municipal management will have not only to upgrade the capability of the municipality to manage efficiently the day-to-day services, but also to enable them to meet the growing demands [of the future].[22]

In order to achieve this, he goes on to define the basic components of a municipal management system.

- Development promotion,
- Services planning, development and management,
- Resource mobilisation, and
- Training and capability improvement.[23]

According to UNDP, 'urban management must do more to mobilise urban wealth for the benefit of the community as a whole, to maintain and develop the infrastructure and services networks necessary for urban activities and to care for the growing numbers of the urban poor'. In its view, there are four critical issues to be addressed. These are:

- Decentralising power and resources from central government to municipalities,
- Mobilise municipal revenue through local sources with the active participation of the private sector and community organisations,
- Emphasise enabling strategies for shelter and infrastructure, with special assistance targeted to weaker groups, and
- Improving the quality of the urban environment, especially for the vast majority of the urban poor in slums and squatter settlements.[24]

Again, the focus of urban management is well stated but seems to be locked in a traditional perception of government's sole function in the process. This must be guarded against. Amos (1989) comments that:

> Urban management is the responsibility of municipal government
> and urban management is concerned with all aspects of urban de-
> velopment, both public and private. It is in no way confined to the
> services operated by the municipal authority ... Good urban man-
> agement depends on the power to co-ordinate the activities of a variety
> of agencies at national and local levels.[25]

This is very important. It brings back the notion of integrating the whole
urban management process. The topic is returned to later in the text.

Concerning the more strategic perspective, Thomson (1989) suggests
'that effective urban management is essential for the alleviation of
poverty'. Its range of activities should therefore include 'strategic planning ... policy on land tenure ... regulation of economic activities ...
and implementation of infrastructure and services'.[26]

Elsewhere, Stren (1991) argues that 'while there is no single definition of urban management, it encompasses at least four different elements. These are a concern:

- To situate urban development projects in the context of city-wide
  and institutional considerations;
- To pay more attention to sources of local finance for a more decentralised municipal government;
- To look at alternative means of organising and financing urban
  services such as water supply, public transport, electricity, sani-
  tary services and waste disposal; and
- To seek and promote local community participatory sources of
  support for urban services and infrastructure.'[27]

This is very good. It takes a wider view by linking urban and institutional considerations. It identifies the role of a decentralised municipal government. Financing infrastructure is an obvious concern. The
role of the informal sector is alluded to through the notion of participation. This argument seems to incorporate the political concept of
urban management with the practical concerns for infrastructure provision.

A similar perspective is offered by Amos (1989).

> The central concern of urban management is ... the manipulation
> or regulation of those parts of the economic, social and physical
> environment necessary to ensure an adequate provision of essential

services and to promote economic development and human well-being. The essential components of an urban management system are:

- An effective network of communication and co-operation between the relevant agencies;
- A strategy which provides common purposes for the agencies; and
- A programme of action and resource provision to ensure implementation of the strategy.

What makes the task of urban management both complex and difficult is the fact that the three essential components each have to be effective on more than one plane.[28]

In contrast, this view is promoting a process of action. Ideally, the former's perception should be combined with the latter's.

In summary, it is suggested that urban management should support economic development through various levels of policy and practical intervention.

A holistic concept

This wider view reflects an opinion present elsewhere. For example, in Churchill (1985)

The term 'urban management' is beginning to take on a new richer meaning. It no longer refers only to the systems of control but, rather, to sets of behavioral relationships, the process through which the myriad activities of the inhabitants interact with each other and with the governance of the city. The objectives of urban management are clear: to improve both the efficiency of the way in which people go about their daily business and the equity with which the gains from these activities are distributed ... More often than not, however, the inefficiencies of the city, whether in housing or transport, inevitably are borne on the back of the poor.[29]

The efficiency concept is, even now, well understood in practice. The question of equity, the gains from public interventions, is a much more nebulous concept to grasp.

Another perspective is offered in the work of Richardson (1993). This presents three tests of urban management success. 'The ability of metropolitan managers to implement a declared spatial strategy may be regarded as a reasonable test of managerial efficiency'.[30] 'Another reasonable test of the effectiveness of metropolitan management in cities of developing countries is the ability to deliver basic urban services and trunk infrastructure to a rapidly growing urban population'.[31] 'The other key managerial problem with urban service delivery is the simple one of operations and maintenance'.[32]

The argument is expanded in Clarke (1991). 'The typical city administration in a developing country is faced with the twin tasks of (1) promoting economic growth so as to raise living standards and (2) trying to improve the delivery of infrastructure and services so as to avoid permanent damage to environmental resources in and around the urban area.'[33] It goes on to recognise that there is a 'growing realisation that urban interventions should address the management of processes and that urbanisation itself does not proceed by fits and starts in neat packages'.[34] Then he makes a telling point in relation to integration. 'It is necessary to define urban management needs for any country over time. An integrated view of urban management encourages spatial integration, institutional co-ordination, pooling of resources and the interchange of information so as to facilitate beneficial exchanges'.[35] The holistic notion of urban management presents itself through such analysis.

What a strategy must not do, as part of the urban management process, is become dominated by short-termism. As Lea and Courtney (1985) discuss:

> Since the 1960s, a new project-oriented approach has emerged, which emphasises short term activities, uses budgets to ensure financial feasibility, and de-emphasises physical [land-use] planning, and includes a wider range of socio-economic policies. The new paradigm appears to have accelerated the rate of project implementation, but it has also produced the quick fix mentality . . .[36]

Later, the two authors note how the Kampung improvement programme in Jakarta

> failed to integrate the physical infrastructure programme with socio-economic policies designed to enhance employment through support for small businesses and non-formal education. In addition, institutional linkages and design have paid scant attention to the local organisations that must implement the projects.[37]

This illustrates the need for urban management to encompass the whole process of city building, maintenance and renewal. It also highlights the importance of both city and (its governing) institution building.

Such a need is endorsed by UNDP.

> One of the most important lessons learnt from the distant and recent past is the failure of outdated models and practices of physical planning as well as of isolated projects and initiatives in providing an answer to the vast and pressing needs of rapidly forming urban centres in the developing world. Urban management can be the answer to this challenge, provided that it develops, both in concept and in practice, as a holistic approach.[38]

This approach is very encouraging.

It is also reflected by other writers who are central to the urban management debate, such as Shabbir Cheema.

> Because policies and programmes to control rural-to-urban migration and the diffusion of urban population have not been successful, there is an increasing recognition that the growth of cities is inevitable and that the solutions to urban problems depend heavily on effective urban management. Urban management is a holistic concept. It is aimed at strengthening the capacity of government and non-government organisations to identify policy and programme alternatives and to implement them with optimal results. The challenge of urban management is thus to respond effectively to the problems and issues of individual cities in order to enable them to perform their functions.[39]

It goes on to identify 'basic urban services and infrastructure as an important issue facing all developing cities'.

Others constantly reinforce the idea that intervention in the urban system has to be both holistic and integrated. The text has eight authors. It may be coincidental, but the phrase 'holistic' is mentioned eight times, as follows.

1. Urban policy must be treated holistically (in terms of sectors, and in terms of the relationship between the urban and rural environments).[40]
2. The 'urban development approach' ... recognises the diversity of the urban experience and the many ways in which different

sectoral policies affect the urban areas. Such an approach is both holistic and multidisciplinary.[41]

3. The need for a holistic approach ... Approaches to the environmental challenge involve, first and foremost, a higher level of inter-sectoral cooperation.[42]

4. As urban life is dynamic and multidimensional, so the approach to the study of cities must reflect this diversity. The essence of the holistic approach ... is to recognise the interconnectedness of all sectors and locations ...[43]

5. Any strategy or approach which attempts to bring some coherence into the urban policy field is often called an urban development approach ... Ideally, such an approach should be holistic (recognising the complex interactions of elements which make a city 'work').[44]

6. A holistic approach is now essential [because] all human activities are closely linked, as the urban systems concept itself implies.[45]

7. A holistic approach, for example ... [requires] explicit linkages between policies involving the formal and informal sectors of the economy.[46]

8. Waste in the urban economy is a good example of the importance of viewing urban problems in an integrated and spatially coherent manner. The term waste economy is itself a holistic concept ...[47]

It is clear that the holistic approach to urban management is now regarded as central to its success as both a process and a structure.

In summary, it is apparent that there is a basic requirement for urban management to embrace all the players in the city building process. It should therefore be seen as a holistic concept.

As a general summary to this section, it is suggested that urban management must have a central concern for resource allocation across the spectrum of interventions in urban development. The interventions should support economic development through the provision of infrastructure and services. The role of municipal government is seen as crucial to this function. The output of urban management is seen as an external economy, to support the development of the city. The process of urban management encompasses both strategic and operational thinking. The process should embrace all the players in the city-building process. It should be seen as a holistic concept. The next section looks more closely at the output of this urban management.

INFRASTRUCTURE

Under the heading of infrastructure, three ideas are considered: supporting economic development; examples of the challenge; experience.

Supporting economic development

Infrastructure is the key to economic growth. Its provision is therefore a central output of any relevant urban management process. This is the general focus of current World Bank urban development work. One of its officials has suggested that

> urban areas are the focal point for economic activity. Efficient urban services are needed to support manufacturing and to nurture the growth of small enterprises and domestic markets. They require a strong underpinning of infrastructure and public services – from transportation to sanitation, shelter to schooling – and an urban management structure, capable of providing that essential support. This will require an effective local government administration that has the fiscal autonomy and decision making authority . . . to manage urban growth and to harness the resources needed to equip fast-expanding towns and cities.[48]

Right away, the original idea of cities as engines of economic growth is seen as requiring the nurturing support of decent infrastructure and service provision.

More recently, the World Bank has formalised this view. 'Urban economic activity depends heavily on infrastructure such as power, roads and water supply. Similarly, the health of urban populations (as well as urban economic activity) . . . is dependent on sanitation and clean water'.[49] Later in the same document, 'an inadequate supply of urban services constrains the growth of productivity of business enterprises and urban households and, hence, the contribution of cities to economic development'.[50] This line of argument has been taken to a succinct and perfect conclusion by Mabogunje (1993). 'The acid test of efficiency in the management of cities is the state of infrastructural provision.'[51]

The fundamental importance of infrastructure and services provision is clear. As Rondinelli (1990a) states: 'In the future, continued economic growth and social progress will depend primarily on the efficiency with which a country's system of cities transforms resources in new ways to replace imports and generate exports over long periods of time'.[52] In turn, 'the economic growth of cities will depend on the availability of urban services, facilities and infrastructure that support urban enterprises ... The location of investments in services and infrastructure strongly influence the pattern of urbanisation in developing countries and the pace and pattern of economic development within cities.'[53] Here, the author is confirming two important points. Firstly, the role of infrastructure in supporting economic development. Secondly, the role of infrastructure in influencing the spatial pattern of development. This spatial aspect must not be overlooked.

The importance of infrastructure to economic and, thus, urban development, is fundamental. 'The provision of infrastructure is a key input into efficient urbanisation. It is required by both enterprises and households.'[54] Three levels of infrastructure provision are then identified: national infrastructure networks; urban infrastructure networks; and neighbourhood infrastructure (i.e. sites and services for housing, commerce, industry, institutions and so on). Of these, urban network infrastructure (water, sanitation, solid waste, electricity, telecommunications, roads and transit systems) is crucial. 'The configuration of the network has much to do with the determination of the urban patterns.'[55] This obviously concerns the urban network. The site-specific locations are also important for urban development.

The argument is developed by Hardoy and Satterthwaite (1987) in relation to housing locations. 'All residential areas require three kinds of public intervention:

- Provision and maintenance of infrastructure – piped water of drinking quality, sewers or other ways to dispose of human wastes, storm and surface water drainage, paved roads and electricity.
- Provision of basic services – household waste collection, public transport and, if sewers are not provided, tankers to empty latrines, septic tanks or other containers for human waste.
- Encouragement and support for people to maintain, upgrade and extend their housing.'[56]

In both the network and site-specific cases, the challenge for urban management to provide infrastructure and services is clear. Then others can build the houses, factories and shops.

The point is reinforced by Cains (1988):

The public sector cannot afford to meet the shelter needs of the poor by direct government involvement in the construction of completed housing. The role of government has now been identified explicitly as that of an indirect promoter of housing development (to support self-help initiatives, for instance on slum upgrading projects).[57]

This is encouraging. It indicates a readiness to accept the vast building potential of the informal sector.

In summary, it is apparent that the provision of infrastructure and services is a key to urban economic development and helps to influence spatial patterns.

Examples of the challenge

There is a focused urban basic services programme (UBSP). The UBSP, as examined by Gnaneshwar (1990),

> centres on water, health, education, nutrition, environmental improvement, economic activities for women, recreation and shelter. All these services are to be provided to the target group with the active participation of private and public agencies. Cost-effectiveness and indigenous technology are emphasised. The utmost attention is paid to the well being of women and children on the assumption that their development ultimately leads to the development of the whole community.[58]

The need for the poor to have access to basic services is both obvious and fundamental to life.

Cheetham (1991) has suggested that 'about 350 million people live in absolute poverty. A much larger number has inadequate access to basic services ... More than forty percent of the urban population (of 2 billion) have inadequate sanitation'.[59] Apart from being deplorable, this indicates the enormity of the challenge facing urban management in the third world.

At the most basic level, the first concern simply has to be for the provision of clean water. As Roth (1987) states: 'Half of the infants that die in the world each year die from water-borne diseases. Eighty percent of all diseases in the world are water related. Half of all hospital beds in the world are occupied by people with water-borne diseases.'[60]

Later, Roth emphasises that:

a regular supply of drinkable water is essential for survival, and yet more than half of all persons in developing countries live without an adequate supply of drinkable water; about three quarters are without any kind of sanitation facility; and because water in some areas is remote as well as polluted, tens of millions of women and children spend as much as three or more hours daily fetching polluted water.

The final distortion of this situation is that in many countries 'rich people receive subsidised piped services and the poor pay for expensive services from vendors'.[61] This is, of course, a travesty. It highlights the fundamental need for clean water and the central role of women in its collection; for the vast majority, from communal standpipes or wells.

A first target for any meaningful urban management process is to tackle the supply and disposal of water and related sanitation. Other infrastructure issues relate to housing (the predominant land-use in all cities) and its supporting arterial (or trunk) infrastructure. The point is highlighted by Cohen (1988):

> It must be remembered that more than ninety percent of the shelter constructed each year throughout the world does not involve public agencies . . . trunk infrastructure is [therefore] essential to the success of community improvement and shelter upgrading. Without the extension of trunk networks, it is impossible to serve efficiently newly developed land. The efficient management and financing of these services is crucial to the success of housing programmes.[62]

For whatever infrastructure and services are provided, there is a need to understand their cost and impact in the community. This offers one way of determining how best to deploy limited resources. The question is addressed in some detail by Mills and Becker (1986). 'First, what kinds of service provision should have highest priority when both efficiency and equity considerations are taken into account? Secondly, what investments have the largest benefits relative to costs, and what investments best meet the needs of low income groups?'[63] One way to answer the question would be to focus first on water and sanitation. Water is fundamental to life. Sanitation is the key to basic public health.

The focus on low income groups has become an increasing concern in urban management, as is shown by the following extract from Rondinelli (1988b):

One of the most crucial challenges facing developing countries over the next decade will be meeting the growing demand for basic social services, infrastructure and public facilities in cities . . . Most studies of the problem indicate that government capacity to meet this growing need for urban services is limited and that political commitment to coping with problems of inadequate distribution and inequitable access is still somewhat weak. Municipal governments have neither the financial resources nor the administrative capacity to extend services rapidly to the poorest neighbourhoods.[64]

A similar conclusion is reached by Stren and McCarney (1992): 'An important dimension of urban poverty in third world cities is the decline – or at least the ineffective delivery – of urban services and infrastructure. As populations grow, and as available resources have declined, public services and infrastructure are being degraded to a point where cities are seriously losing their capacity to operate productively.'[65] The challenge for urban management is clear.

It is a challenge expressed by Lee (1987):

[The] continued upgrading or expansion of urban infrastructure and services is needed not only to reduce existing deficiencies but also to meet the growing need of rapidly expanding urban areas. Particularly essential in an integrated project framework are water, sewerage, drainage, solid waste management, roads, electricity and other essential services e.g. schools, health facilities and public markets . . . All segments of urban populations can benefit from improved infrastructure, but low income groups would be major beneficiaries of improved services, whether from better drainage or increased water supply, because low income areas are least adequately served.[66]

Planning for the provision and maintenance of infrastructure and services, as both a determinant of spatial development and as a claim on limited finances, is a rare topic in the literature. As seen above, many authors talk about cities, planning, management, infrastructure and integration. However, very few attempt to articulate an operational model of the practice of urban management. Those that come closest seem to cite experiences in South-east Asia. For example, Rogerson (1989b) suggests that in Seoul, a number of innovative experiments have been undertaken to mobilise community resources in the delivery of essential urban services to the poor through a bottom-up, decentralised and participatory approach. These attempts are viewed favourably as providing potential lessons for service delivery to the poor in other cities of the developing world, especially South Africa, with its prospect of major urban development in the context of its new majority government.[67]

In summary, it is suggested that the fundamental need for water is often overlooked, when evidenced by its associated diseases. It is also clear that the financing of infrastructure remains a perennial concern.

Experience

It is possible to review the best cases in Asia. The Philippines introduced a programme for essential municipal infrastructure, utilities, maintenance and engineering development (PREMIUMED) in 1984 as a specific strategy to promote self-reliant local governments. It has the following objectives:

- To reduce the gap between the delivery of and the need for urban infrastructure, utilities and services in relation to rapid urban population growth.
- To strengthen/improve the financial/revenue base of local governments, particularly the urban centres.
- To strengthen the technical and administrative capability of local government in planning, programming and management of projects and to upgrade its capability to maintain infrastructure, utilities and facilities.[68]

In Thailand, the main focus was to ensure that the development of the Bangkok Metropolitan Region (BMR) would adequately support the objectives of the plan which, in its economic growth strategy, relies heavily on industrial and service sector growth. In that context, an urban management strategy was adopted with the following features:

- Integration of physical planning and infrastructure investment.
- Strengthening the local government revenue base through improving the efficiency of tax collection and broadening of the tax base, the cost recovery of urban public utilities, more appropriate cost-sharing between various levels of government and state enterprise, and private sector participation in urban services delivery.
- Strengthening self-reliance and community participation in infrastructure delivery to the urban poor.
- Establishing improved inter-agency co-ordination mechanisms in

urban services delivery and increasing local government capability through manpower development and training.[69]

In Indonesia, a nationwide approach towards the delivery of urban services has been initiated. It is known as the Integrated Urban Infrastructure Development Programme (IUIDP). This programme has the following features:

- It places *de facto* responsibility for planning, programming and implementation of urban services delivery at local level.
- In so doing, the programme endeavours to integrate the various components of infrastructure provision, both in a physical sense as well as in terms of the various sources of finance.
- The programme stimulates the mobilisation of increased local government resources through a process of analytical review of resource requirements and availability during the above medium-term period and the adoption of supporting financial/institutional development action plans.
- The approach embodies the preparation of multi-year infrastructure investment plans and their financing plans at local government level as well as annual budget proposals based on them.[70]

The comparison between the three approaches is revealing. 'While all programmes have as their objective the strengthening of municipal management and financial capabilities, the interpretation of this differs. A major difference in emphasis exists between programmes which focus on increasing the effectiveness of planning and programming of urban services (Indonesia, Philippines) and other programmes in which the emphasis is more on improving management structures and procedures, and the ways and means of increasing local government revenues (Thailand).'[71]

A summary of the (then) current experience is cited in Courtney and Lea (1985). It seems no less relevant now.

The metropolitan Manila CIF is now considered as a model for developing the budgets of other regions in the Philippines and for modifying the review of national infrastructure investment. It is important that both the metropolitan government and the national budget or finance ministry be involved in the capital budgeting exercises for large urban centres, since substantial central government funds are usually involved. Central ministries, key parastatals, and metropolitan and local governments should also be involved in planning the major sectoral investments.[72]

Again the importance of inter-agency planning mechanisms presents itself. This analysis compares unfavourably with another view. 'Thus metropolitan Manila does not have an effective form of government to direct planning and development ... This situation leaves the administrative system without co-ordination and, at times, in chaos.' Later, it is suggested that in Manila 'there is a conflict between the investment priorities of government and the basic needs of most of the population. Most of the investment is in primary infrastructure works ... In contrast, the population urgently needs different kinds of improvements such as adequate shelter ...'[73]

This is a real dilemma. The macro view is that network infrastructure will create the conditions for economic development. The micro view is that local improvements will improve the general well-being and absorptive potential of the mass of population. Inevitably, a balance between the two is required.

More recently, an article in *The Economist* cited Asia as the leader in attracting private capital to provide and (initially) operate major infrastructure, in the power and road sectors.[74] The distinction here perhaps is the potential major financial returns of rapidly developing Asia compared with the stagnant economies of Sub-Saharan Africa.

In summary, it is evident that innovative practice in Asia seeks to integrate planning, programming and budgeting in order to achieve sustained infrastructure provision.

As a general summary of this section it can be suggested that the provision of infrastructure is a key to urban economic development and helps to influence spatial determination. The fundamental need for clean water is too often overlooked, when evidenced by its associated diseases. The financing of infrastructure remains a perennial concern. The ability to organise for the planning and provision of infrastructure sees strong examples in Asia. Innovative practice in Asia seeks to integrate planning, programming and budgeting in order to achieve sustained infrastructure provision. The next section looks at more indications of the urban management process, through current strengthening work in the field.

INSTITUTIONAL STRENGTHENING

Under the heading of institutional strengthening, two ideas are considered: for urban management; the general challenge.

For urban management

There are two multilateral institutional development programmes running at present, which focus on the city. One is the Urban Management Programme (UMP), through the World Bank and UNCHS (Habitat). The other is UN–Habitat's Sustainable Cities Programme (SCP), which has since been incorporated in UMP.

The World Bank/UNCHS presents a standard justification for its urban management programme (UMP). 'Inside the cities, urban managers find it increasingly difficult to handle sewerage and refuse that pose serious threats to the health of the poor living in dilapidated squatter settlements. Only a shift from ad-hoc interventions towards integrated, multi-year planning and consistent, coherent policy frameworks can put environmental issues on the agenda of urban development.' A little later in the same report: 'the ability of cities to continue to perform their economic functions and to improve standards of living will rely heavily on the availability of infrastructure and municipal services. Efficient delivery of infrastructure and services, in turn, depends on the strength of local governments and the effectiveness of urban management'.[75] In its original guise, the programme had three subjects of concern: land management;[76] infrastructure;[77] and municipal finance.[78] A key objective was to develop operational models for urban management: 'to develop guidelines for the integration of spatial, sectoral, economic, financial and institutional planning so as to better achieve urban development goals'.[79]

The next programme document takes the programme a stage further by outlining its capacity building strategy, principally through a series of regional seminars. It also notes an additional subject for inclusion; that of the environment.[80] The notable absence from this document is any mention of developing operational models for urban management. It is not clear whether this is merely a lapse or a deliberate policy shift. Such a shift can only be interpreted, generously, as building the capacities of specific national and local governments to develop their own operational models.

Such a conclusion seems to be borne out by the third programme document. 'The primary aim of this expanded phase is to work with

countries to build their capacity to address urban issues . . . The overall goal is to improve developing countries' capacity to manage their
urban areas on a sustained basis.'[81] Again, there is no mention of developing operational models for urban management. At this stage, one
would think that was a primary focus for the urban management programme. An outsider simply notes that UMP's revised prospectus 'does
not define urban management although it details its project elements'.[82]
This seems a serious omission.

UNCHS presents another standard justification, this time for its sustainable cities programme.

> Addressing the critical issues produced by rapid urban growth in
> the developing countries requires new approaches to urban planning
> and management in general, as well as a new emphasis on environ-
> mental planning in particular, since many of the most pressing ur-
> ban management requirements, such as waste management and water
> supply, are also core environmental issues.

It goes on:

> it is therefore fundamental to achieving environmentally sustainable
> urban development that environmental management be incorporated
> at the formative stages of city-wide planning and investment strat-
> egies, and that it becomes a continuous routine. Integrating procedures
> are required so that environmental planning and management are
> incorporated into information collection and use; policy formulation
> across space, between sectors and over time; in municipal programming
> and budgeting; in project implementation; as well as in monitoring
> and evaluation.[83]

The next available document presents a number of objectives for
sustainable city demonstrations. The two most important are as follows. First, 'to prepare a strategic development plan for the city, including key components of environmental management strategies, sector
investment strategies, spatial planning, financial planning and admin-
istrative/legal requirements'.[84] Second, 'to strengthen local capacity to
plan, co-ordinate and manage urban development growth, with emphasis on improved multi-sectoral co-ordination and community based
participation'.[85] This programme started its work with client cities, the
first being Dar es Salaam in 1992.

The point about both the urban management programme and the

sustainable cities project is that both (whether implied in the first case or expressed in the second) are attempting to construct operational models for the urban management process, and to strengthen the relevant institutions to perform accordingly. In order to strengthen the institutions, their human resources must be decently equipped and utilised.

Observations on the human resource dimension can be made. Amos (1989) comments that: 'No matter how well designed systems may be, they will be of little value unless human resources are matched to the system ... Skills development falls into basic skills and systems and management.' Later, he continues. 'Institutional development differs from many other development projects in that it can never be finite ... If urban management is to be able to cope with the challenges it will face in the next two decades, then it is the development of the principal institutions which must be given priority over the better management of individual functions and projects.'[86]

In summary, it is suggested that the two programmes see planning as a holistic and integrated process. One expresses and the other implies the need to develop a resilient model of the urban management process.

The general challenge

The Asian Development Bank (1987b) summarises the challenge: 'Greater attention should be focused on building institutional capacity at national and municipal levels for formulating and implementing development programmes and managing urban areas. Toward this end, as well as for general policy improvement, a greater use of technical assistance, not necessarily tied to specific investment, is called for.'[87] The role of technical assistance as a mechanism for skills transfer has been discussed in Chapter 2.

The general views expressed above on the nature of institutional development for urban management in developing countries are reaffirmed. In the context of Asia, it is suggested by Rondinelli (1987) that:

... the ability of governments to respond to changing conditions in the future will depend to a large degree on the planning, management and financial capacity of local and municipal authorities. Much more attention needs to be given over the next decade to increasing the managerial and financial capacities of local governments. This will require national governments to support or conduct municipal management assessments to determine the level of capability within local governments and to increase planning and management capacity, where serious deficiencies are found.

He presents five areas for action. These include

upgrading the planning capability of local governments, developing the financial management functions and improving personnel management capabilities.[88]

UNDP records the experience of local government strengthening.

The big national programmes of the 1960s and 1970s undercut the authority and capability of local government . . . Almost everywhere in the developing world, local government remains unsurprisingly weak. That is why much international assistance in the past few years has begun to focus on upgrading the management of urban institutions and increasing the mobilisation of local resources for urban development.[89]

It also sets out an agenda for the 1990s. 'If cities are to contribute to human development, we need institutional mechanisms that promote equitable growth, encourage gender-sensitive, participatory development and improve the financial and managerial capacity of cities and towns'.[90]

UNDP goes on to highlight some key features of the urban management challenge and its associated institutional development needs.

Efforts to strengthen local government and administration should focus on decentralising power and resources to municipalities . . .[91]

The two faces of cities in developing countries – cities as engines of economic growth and as centres of increasing poverty constitute neither a crisis nor a tragedy. Rapid urbanisation presents opportunities for initiating innovative programmes for socio-economic transformation.[92]

Investment in urban infrastructure and services will become more important in developing countries not only to meet the basic needs for water, sanitation, education and health, but also to raise the efficiency of the private sector and to reduce production costs.[93]

Embracing the private sector is of fundamental importance.

The nature of such a challenge is highlighted in the work of Caputo (1989):

When drawing up a strategy for strengthening the capacity of a local government to undertake the task of resource mobilisation, the first question that should be asked is how can the productivity and the production capacities of these internal resources be increased and thereby promote the improvement of economic environments in the cities? The main strategic effects that can be obtained as a result of implementing a management approach based on the active participation and promotion of many small local businesses can be summarised as first, taxation systems and fiscal flows will be improved and second, the bottlenecks that slow down the development of small businesses will be reduced. The traditional approach (to urban management) has always ignored the importance of building upon the local economic aptitudes and strengths.[94]

Therefore, not only are the development of planning systems important to urban management but so also is the release of latent financial resources.

According to Hart and Rogerson (1989), the experience of Kenya is offering lessons for urban management in the new South Africa.

National urban policy should be embedded in (and not isolated from) national development planning. The policy neglect towards satisfying the needs of the poor should be rectified. Finally, all effort should go into avoiding the dangers that corrupt practices in urban management pose to the hijacking of the benefits of projects and policies supposedly targeted to the urban poor.[95]

Institutional strengthening is therefore concerned not only with building the positive aspects but also with avoiding the negative aspects of urban management in developing countries.

An agenda is offered by Bertone (1992) in relation to improving local government performance in Sri Lanka. The objectives are:

- To emphasise operation and maintenance of existing facilities over new municipal capital investments.
- To improve performance in revenue collection.
- To attain sound financial management and budgeting.
- To achieve affordability of municipal services.[96]

This looks like a very traditional notion of institution building. There seems to be no regard for the need to have a positive impact on local government's development environment – its towns and cities.

To conclude, it can be suggested that 'in reality, metropolitan management is an unglamorous inter-agency process; its accent is on consensus rather than command; its quality is a product of perseverance and team effort; its success in the long run is directly dependent on the degree to which that effort can continue to be maintained in the rapidly changing kaleidoscope of metropolitan life.'[97]

Shabbir Cheema (1993) reinforces the kaleidoscopic nature of the urban management challenge, justifying his book because of 'the scarcity of studies that provide a holistic perspective on urban management issues'.[98] This may have been written in ignorance of another book, which contains a strong advocacy for the holistic approach to urban development.[99] Yet, the general point about the kaleidoscopic nature of urban management remains central to the debate on urban management.

A summary of the deliberations of a senior policy workshop on cities and their challenge for developing countries makes the key point that the major multilateral agencies in the urban development field (World Bank, UNDP and UNCHS) 'have signalled a change in their ways of working, away from the traditional project approach to one that emphasises processes, that seizes opportunities as they arise, that stresses continuity, and, recognising the multi-sectoral nature of urban activities, also stresses the need to look at cities in a holistic way'.[100] This is certainly the inference from the multisectoral institutional strengthening work cited in this section.

In summary, it is imperative to address the human resource dimension and the strengthening needs of the local government planning systems.

As a general summary to this section; two multilateral agencies concur in their general approach to institutional strengthening for urban management. They see it as a holistic, integrated process. One strengthening programme implies and the other expresses the need to develop a resilient model of the urban management process. To achieve this, it is imperative to address the human resource dimension in strengthening institutions for urban management. It is also necessary to address the concept of power through the decentralisation of urban development finances. The central role for local government in urban management is the main justification for its strengthening needs.

Thus, at the end of this chapter, three key characteristics can be discerned from the scope of intervention.

4. Urban management should be seen as an external economy to the city.
5. Infrastructure is the key to economic development and helps to influence spatial determination.
6. Institutional strengthening must focus on the holistic concept or urban management.

The next section summarises the arguments from Part II.

Summary to Part II

Two authors encapsulate the nature of the urban management challenge. Linn (1983) suggests that 'the quality of urban management by the urban authorities may have an important effect on whether and how a city grows (the provision of adequate public utilities and so on)'.[1] This argues the function of urban management as an external economy to the city.

Davidson (1991) states that 'physical development objectives must be integrated with institutional development objectives, if there is to be a sustainable impact on urban management capacity'.[2] This identifies the central concerns of urban management; city and institutional development.

Part II has analysed the process (or function) of third world city management. Chapter 3 looked at various planning perspectives. Chapter 4 considered the scope of urban management interventions. The underlying issues from each of the six individual sections are summarised as follows.

PLANNING PERSPECTIVES

Cities and economic growth

Third world cities are growing and should be seen as a force for economic and social development. They already contribute disproportionately to gross domestic production. The idea of the city as an economic production unit is introduced. The downside is insanitary conditions, congestion, environmental degradation, poverty and disintegrating (or non-existent) infrastructure and services. Any approach to confronting this urban dilemma should seek to learn from third world practice and eschew the wholesale acceptance of Western perceptions. In essence, cities are seen as the powerhouse for economic development.

Required planning responses

Master planning is a long-term activity, divorced from the financing of its proposals. Planning interventions should be shorter term and tied

to a management perspective. This urban management should be dominated by a concern for processes. The process should centre on the
political economy of the city (e.g. poverty and wealth). The instrument of this intervention is an urban management process that incorporates planning, programming and budgeting. The suggestion of
integrating all the players and sectors in the process is introduced. In
summary, the planning response should focus on the political economy of the city.

From planning to integrated management

The shift from planning to urban management suggests a number of
general principles. There is a need for a holistic perspective to urban
intervention. The instrument of that intervention should embrace institutional arrangements and community involvement in order to develop
practical projects. The informal sector's major contribution to city building
must be harnessed. The danger is that the informal sector is (perhaps
unwittingly) being excluded because of the notion of 'bankable' projects.
The concept of bankable projects also fails to embrace the question of
environmental capacity. In summary, the informal sector's contribution to the city-building process must be harnessed.

SCOPE OF INTERVENTION

Operational parameters

Urban management must have a central concern for resource allocation across the spectrum of interventions in urban development. The
interventions should support economic development through the provision of infrastructure and services. The role of municipal government
is seen as crucial to this function. The output of urban management is
seen as an external economy, to support the development of the city.
The process of urban management encompasses both strategic and
operational thinking. The process should embrace all the players in
the city-building process. It should be seen as a holistic concept. The
key point is that urban management should be seen as an external
economy to the city.

Infrastructure

The provision of infrastructure is a key to urban economic development and helps to influence spatial patterns. The fundamental need for clean water is too often overlooked, when evidenced by its associated diseases. The financing of infrastructure remains a perennial concern. The ability to organise for the planning and provision of infrastructure sees strong examples in Asia. Innovative practice in Asia seeks to integrate planning, programming and budgeting in order to achieve sustained infrastructure provision. Essentially, infrastructure is the key to economic development and influences spatial determination.

Institutional strengthening

Two multilateral agencies concur in their general approach to institutional strengthening for urban management. They see it as a holistic, integrated process. One strengthening programme implies and the other expresses the need to develop a resilient model of the urban management process. To achieve this, it is imperative to address the human resource dimension in strengthening institutions for urban management. It is also necessary to address the concept of power through the decentralisation of urban development finances. The central role for local government in urban management is the main justification for its strengthening needs. In essence, institutional strengthening must focus on the holistic concept of urban management.

The conclusions to Part II are therefore as follows:

1. Cities are the powerhouse of economic development.
2. The planning response should focus on the political economy of the city.
3. The informal sector's contribution to the city-building process must be harnessed.
4. Urban management should be seen as an external economy to the city.
5. Infrastructure is the key to economic development and influences spatial determination.
6. Institutional strengthening must focus on the holistic concept of urban management.

These features of third world city management represent a set of general characteristics for the function. They will be returned to in Chapter 12.

Table 2.1   Variables for city management function

SCOPE OF THE FUNCTION	Frequency
Integrating all the players in the process	17
Holistic concept	13
Embracing the informal sector in city building	12
Tackling poverty	10
Institutional strengthening/decentralisation	9
Planning, programming and budgeting	8
Citizen involvement	7
Provide infrastructure and services	6
Integrating investment decisions	6
Infrastructure to support economic development	6
Prepare strategies	5
Protecting/improving the environment	5
An iterative or learning process	4
Planning as management	3
Planning in the political economy of the city	3
Operations and maintenance	3
Infrastructure for spatial determination	3
Spatial planning	2
MODES OF INTERVENTION	
Water supply	13
Sewerage systems	11
Solid waste management	11
Power	11
Roads	11
Drainage and flood control	6
Education	5
Health	5
Housing	2
Environmental protection and improvement	2

Note: The frequency denotes the number of times each variable is cited in Part II.

In conclusion, the importance of this analysis is to identify guides to thinking about the urban management process, without prescribing outcomes.

What remains is the need to introduce an initial conceptual framework for the function of third world city management. The suggested framework is in two parts:

- SCOPE OF THE FUNCTION
- MODES OF INTERVENTION.

Under each, a number of variables are identified. They are ordered according to the frequency of the citations in Part II. The conceptual framework is presented in Table 2.1. This will be returned to in Chapter 12.

Part III now analyses the form of third world city management.

Part III

City Management Form

Part III explores the characteristics of the form of city management. It does so in the knowledge of the literature's suggestion that there is no standard organisational arrangement for third world city management. Chapter 5 identifies some organisational dilemmas. Chapter 6 assesses the structuring criteria for organising city management. The Summary to Part III identifies the key characteristics of the city management form in the third world. An initial conceptual framework is introduced.

5 Organisational Dilemmas

The World Bank has established the connection between poor infrastructure and weak institutions. 'The poor state of physical infrastructure and the inadequacies of the services provided reflect the lack of coherence in sectoral policies and programmes ... the fragmentation of institutional responsibilities (and so on).'[1]

It is argued by Shabbir Cheema (1993) that 'the effectiveness of urban policies and programmes depends largely on the quality of institutions responsible for planning and implementing them'.[2] This involves (among other things) 'decentralisation of planning and management authority to urban local governments'.

Rondinelli (1988b) furthermore suggests that 'while the capacity of municipal governments to improve service delivery must be greatly expanded, that alone is unlikely to be adequate. In the long run, a variety of policy alternatives and organisational arrangements must be considered to cope with such a complex and pervasive problem' as third world urban growth and its attendant demands.[3]

The question is: what are the various organisational arrangements that can be brought to bear to give an appropriate setting to the process of city management? This chapter therefore seeks to identify the salient themes in the question of organisational structures. It considers three topics:

- ORGANISATIONAL MODELS
- THE DECENTRALISING PANACEA
- DECENTRALISATION FOR URBAN MANAGEMENT.

ORGANISATIONAL MODELS

Under the heading of organisational models, three ideas are considered: no formula; function to form; local government.

No formula

A decade ago, UNCHS was lamenting that 'not only is there no universal model of institutional arrangements for human settlement policies, but the arrangements adopted in any one country will change over time'.[4] The same point is made by Mawhood (1987). 'No single formula for administering local communities and promoting their development will be valid everywhere.'[5] More recently, Richardson (1993) has commented that 'the most difficult question to resolve concerns the appropriate institutional framework for metropolitan management in large cities in developing countries.'[6] Other authors make attempts to identify the ingredients to make decentralisation work.[7] There appears to be no common reference point for addressing the question of organisational arrangements for urban management.

There is a suggestion by Rakodi (1987) that 'the allocation of institutional responsibility for urban management varies from country to country, involving some combination of local and central government, and often, in addition, one or more statutory bodies.'[8] Invariably, these organisations are sectorally dominated.

The sectorally dominated organisational problem is defined by Baker (1989). 'The administrative structures of developing countries were generally inherited intact from the former colonial powers, and are typically organised vertically into sectoral, or functional ministries and departments (agriculture, health, education, etc.). This works reasonably well until the system encounters a problem of a very broad and highly integrated nature.' One example is obviously the urban question. Then, the sectoral structure 'tackles only the parts which are identifiable to each ministry and then each ministry tackles the symptom as a problem in, and of, itself.'[9] Arguments occur between a ministry of works and a ministry of local government, in the absence of a clear definition of which institution arbitrates on urban development issues as a whole. Is it:

- the ministry that prepares the land use plan, under town planning legislation,
- the local authority that prepares the development and funding strategy, under local government legislation,
- the ministry that executes and pays for the construction of the infrastructure (invariably through donor funds), under central government legislation, or
- a triumvirate of all three, sitting in regular co-ordination and, where required, arbitration?

The basic organisational dilemma facing third world local government is captured in an editorial to a theme issue of *Environment and Urbanisation*.[10] It states the dilemma as the failure of municipal governments in most Third World nations to fulfil their responsibilities in the management of urban growth (including the provision of infrastructure and services)... It is rare for local government to have any significant capacity for investment in expanding or extending infrastructure and services ... There is almost universal agreement that local government has important roles in stimulating and supporting development.

It goes on to note that

only relatively recently have donor agencies allocated much funding to institution building, training in urban management, local government finance and urban planning, and most of the planning for this has come from the World Bank – much of it in the last few years of the 1980s.[11]

Given the comparatively recent attention to third world urban management, it is interesting to note that 'there is a considerable network of third world researchers and research institutions who have long criticised the application of standard procedures and formulas to improve the efficiency of local government'.[12] So far, two weaknesses have been revealed in the current organisation for urban management. First is the sectorally organised central government. Second is the financially weak local government.

In summary, many authors admit that there is no single organisational model to deal with the urban management challenge in developing countries.

Function to form

In this context, it must be a requirement to define the appropriate role of urban government. According to Lee (1987), this will require 'striking the balance between central planning and direction on the one hand, and decentralisation of authority on the other ... Unfortunately, there is no clear-cut rule regarding the appropriate allocation of responsibility to urban governments'.[13] The Jakarta experience suggests a 'more comprehensive and less fragmented urban government' as a possible way forward. The Asian experience has already been noted for some innovative work in city management (Chapter 4). However, the functions of urban management have to be related to the alternative organisational forms available.

There is a view, put forward by Montgomery (1988) among others, that 'it would be convenient if the functions and levels of government could be designed afresh according to a few rational principles or by applying modern organisation theory based on experience . . .'[14] This is simply not possible. It was tried with the establishment of special urban development authorities. These have largely failed. Furthermore, Devas (1989) argues that, 'it was considered to be easier to invent new agencies rather than to reform and abolish existing ones. As a result, the proliferation of institutions has often become a major obstacle to effective urban management'.[15]

The debate as outlined by Rakodi (1990) runs that

> the initial reaction of many governments to the inability of existing city organisations to provide and maintain the infrastructure in conditions of rapid urban growth was to adopt a project oriented, sectoral approach (special works authorities), then a multi-sectoral approach – by way of establishing development authorities or special metropolitan governments . . . However, most have failed to adopt a truly multi-sectoral, metropolis wide approach or to solve the problem of the gap between installation and operation of urban services while the centralisation of power and the undermining of local government has further reduced the possibility of participation in city level decision making.[16]

The latest response is that of decentralisation. That is analysed more closely in the next two sections of this chapter.

The structural weakness of government organisations in the African context has been noted by Stren and White (1989)

> For African governments – both central and urban – the favoured organisational form is sectoral. The department of finance is staffed by economists, the ministry of works by engineers . . . Departments compete for scarce resources; they co-operate only when forced to do so by a higher authority . . . The African urban management crisis has highlighted the inefficiencies of the sectoral approach . . . Nothing short of a new approach to urban management can meet the scale of the present problems.[17]

In a later paper, Stren (1991) noted that, at the time, there was still no textbook on urban management – in Africa.[18]

UNCHS suggests that settlement management is undertaken at different administrative levels.

In most countries there will be some strategic development sectors that require central planning and management, while other sectors may only require extra guidance and technical support but can otherwise be approached at the local level. Most of the sectors related to the improvement of living conditions and to the management of the environment, even though they may follow national guidelines, are best managed at the local level.[19]

This is a first attempt at determining organisational form by urban management function.

UNCHS continues the argument.

The diversity in responses and experience [of institutional structures] makes it difficult to isolate and generalise characteristics, and suggest blueprints for institutional design [for urban management] ... Institutional arrangements for settlement planning, whether comprehensive or sectoral, can only be effective when they provide access to financial resources. Relationships between central government and local authorities in many countries are often far from harmonious, with central governments reluctant to relinquish control of allocation procedures and often critical of financial and administrative machinery at the local level, and local authorities resentful of their dependent position and often taking the view that they are unable to improve financial and administrative management without the support from central government.[20]

Whereas the functional determination of organisational arrangements is paramount, the question of financing the process will have a major bearing. This is looked at in Chapter 6.

UNCHS repeats the problem of contending with diversity.

No neat model exists, interrelating a range of institutional options in which finance, participation, administration and technical implementation work together as an analogue of the national socioeconomic goals which, in turn, are the explicit aspirations of the concerned popular constituents ...[21]

Yet, whatever difficulties exist in conception, there is a general acceptance that a new dynamic role is needed for local government (in urban management).

In summary, it is suggested that there is an acknowledged weakness in the sectorally organised central government in dealing with urban management.

Local government

In 1985, a report from the round table meeting in Stockholm recorded that its analysis points 'to a new, more dynamic role for local government in helping in the improvement of housing and living conditions (in cities)'. The text goes on to suggest that

> local governments generally have enormous legal and institutional responsibilities in the planning and management of urban areas. But they fulfil only a tiny portion of this responsibility, for they lack the power, resources and skilled personnel. Municipal governments have not grown in power, competence and revenue base, in line with the growth in area and in the population under their jurisdiction.[22]

The dilemma is that the post-colonial centralisation of power has dominated the thinking of governments. In consequence, central governments are now very reluctant to divest the power for managing the urban development process to local government.

Yet, it has been suggested by Ramachandran (1985) that 'the great strength of local government is its ability to come face to face with the people. As a vehicle of individual and community learning and as a means of establishing public participation as an integral part of the government process, it is probably unsurpassed'.[23] The argument is reinforced and extended by Harris (1990):

> The emphasis on government as facilitator makes urgent the need for effective local government. Yet in many countries, this is one of the most notorious areas of government incompetence. Often, local authorities are burdened with large financial deficits ... but are unable to expand their revenue sources because of the pre-emptive claims of central government ... Often they have been given new responsibilities without changes in finance or staff.[24]

The potential and desirable role for local government in running the city management process is apparent.

In the context of Malaysia, Hai (1988) has suggested that

the central challenge in the management of urban services is the fashioning of appropriate structures and providing them with the necessary authority and resources to carry out their tasks. It seems that appropriate structures are those that direct attention to the problems to be solved and that foster perceptions or understandings of these problems that are holistic or at least strategic enough to make possible the design of effective action measures. Appropriate structures therefore require prior identification of problems and some knowledge of their aetiology [their causation]. A structure that is appropriate for one problem or purpose may not be appropriate for another.[25]

Key words to stress are structures, authority and resources. The structures should be determined by a holistic perception of the problem.

In simpler terms, it is suggested by Bubba and Lamba (1991) that

several issues within the urban management system require prompt action. There is an urgent need to improve the local government system so it can react rapidly and flexibly to growing urban problems. Central government controls have been too stringent especially where finances are concerned. Local authorities need to improve their financial management . . . [they] need to make linkages with other institutions that are delivering urban services.[26]

This idea of linkages, in terms of inter-organisational arrangements, is important. It is returned to later in the text.

As a concluding overview, a current case of institutional strengthening outlines the scope of urban management from an institutional perspective. It seeks to analyse the organisational structure, activities and relationships in the urban management process. It seeks to understand the impact of financial management on urban management. It seeks to analyse the relationships between urban spatial planning and financial budgeting processes. Finally, it looks at manpower and training in relation to urban management issues.[27]

This is laudable but some would argue for an even simpler analysis. For example, Olowu and Smoke (1992) suggested that 'inadequate revenue generation – and a consequent inability to provide services effectively – is the most obvious local government weakness . . . At the core of revenue generation inadequacies and other major local government problems are central–local fiscal relations'.[28] The simple response to this is to be reminded that funds are a means to an end and not an end in themselves. Therefore, the need to take the whole (or holistic) picture into account, of local government and its impact on its development environment, is paramount.

In summary, all authors support the idea of a strengthened local government to deal with urban management.

As a general summary to this section, it is suggested that many authors admit that there is no single organisational model to deal with the urban management challenge in developing countries. There is an acknowledged weakness in the sectorally organised central government in dealing with urban development. All support the idea of a strengthened local government system to deal with the issue. In so doing, they show how the decentralisation panacea is pervading every corner of development administration. This is discussed below.   .

THE DECENTRALISING PANACEA

In considering the decentralising panacea, two ideas are considered: failures; reforming for decentralisation.

Failures

Decentralisation is pervading every corner of development administration. In essence, it is a response to the (perhaps inevitable) concentration of power in central government which took place after countries gained their independence from colonial powers. This is particularly so in Africa. However, whether in Africa or Asia, decentralisation is now advocated as a legitimate response to first, this initial centralisation and secondly, to the demands of a more complex urban management challenge.

According to Wunsch (1990a):

Decentralisation to a large variety of governments regulated by law makes possible the existence of a large number of flexible and diverse organisations. In turn, these can allow persons, groups and communities to act collectively to pursue their various conceptions of the good. This provides several possible advantages, including (1) the enhanced capacity to avoid and correct error associated with organisational redundancy, (2) the potential to reduce the intensity of political conflicts, (3) the capacity to articulate more closely to community values, and (4) the potential to neutralise tendencies to concentrate and abuse power at all levels of government . . .

With viable, functioning local organisations addressing the many social issues and needs, national leaders will be more able to focus
on the commanding heights of the economy; on national economic
policy, debt management, natural resource development, higher
and technical education, negotiation with foreign states and corporations, and evaluating the impact of national revenue, personnel and
so on.[29]

This lengthy quotation not only advocates decentralisation, it also attempts to specify the general functions that are legitimately a central
concern and those that would be more suited to local government.

The argument is continued by Werlin (1992), who states that

in most developing countries, there continues to be hostility to all
forms of decentralisation, including the delegation of authority to
local and regional governments, financial institutions, public utilities cooperatives, state owned enterprises, NGOs and so on.[30]

This is inevitably the case. Those who have power (in central government) are loath to see it wrested from their grasp (and transferred to
local government). This is especially so given the general circumstances
behind the centralised power. 'Once the assumption was made in the
post-independence era that development and unity required a highly
centralised, strong state, the role of local governing institutions became problematic'.[31] The feeling persists that local government is not
really up to the task.

In relation to the specifics of development, the policy of centralisation (still the current state in most of the developing world) has, according to Wunsch and Olowu (1990),

established institutions which have worked in three specific ways to
hinder, stifle, or even at times to erode broadly based human development in Africa. First . . . it facilitates exploitation and abuse of
the powerless by the powerful . . . Second, an erosive effect on a
broadly based development process has grown from human (and organisational) cognitive limitations: it stimulates a propensity to error . . .
Third . . . it has attempted to pre-empt and at times erode the local
social tools or technologies of human action; it has thus weakened
the diverse small-scale organisations needed for development. As
centralisation progressed in the post independence era, many African
states moved to restrict the ability of non-central state actors to

authoritatively allocate values, to engage in extra-state social organisations and to engage in private economic pursuits.³²

Centralisation therefore continues to pervert the potential for local development; an essential when, for example, attempting to harness the informal sector's contribution to the city-building process (stressed in Chapter 4).

Olowu and Wunsch (1990) summarise the consequences of such a perspective. 'By repressing the growth of autonomous organisations, the African state denied itself of two crucial elements of institutional development; criticism and legitimacy. Dissent was driven underground and voluntary or forced exile was the fate of those who could not conform to the mediocrity and sycophancy that resulted . . .'³³ An editorial to *Environment and Urbanisation* highlights the flaw of decentralisation in practice, in relation to such a disheartening perspective. ' . . . many national governments . . . have decentralisation programmes to deflect criticism of their failings. This can be characterised as decentralisation of responsibilities but not the powers and resources to meet them'.³⁴ In short, it is suggested by Oluwa (1987) that 'most of these [decentralisation] efforts have fallen short of expectations'.³⁵ Time and again, the literature attests to governments' failure to grasp the nettle of giving power (and resources) to local government to deal with matters that are genuinely local in nature.

It has subsequently argued that multilateral agencies 'blame failures (of decentralisation) on poor implementation . . . by the central government and its agencies. To them, implementation problems have included lack of clear objectives, ambiguous legislation, poor planning of the decentralisation process, inadequate resources, shortage of skilled personnel to service the reform as well as poor overall management'. The argument continues: 'the prescription for this is better planning for the decentralisation process, the commitment of more resources to decentralisation and the improvement of personnel skills'. Then the domination of the technocratic perspective in the arguments deployed is noted. '[There] is a clear tendency to overlook or underplay the political aspects of decentralisation and to emphasise the administrative/technical aspects.'³⁶ The political nature of decentralisation is the starting point. If it is not addressed squarely, no amount of technical excellence will compensate for the failure to address the political question.

Ake (1990) concurs with this view. 'Decentralisation is necessary. This will entail not only political and administrative decentralisation, but also the decentralisation of the planning process and the implementation of national development strategies. This will bring some power, resources and freedom to the level of the community where the strong sense of collective identity holds much greater prospects of grassroots contribution to development.'[37]

Furthermore, Olowu adds that 'the issue of all political organisation including decentralisation becomes clearly a fundamental economic and political rather than administrative problem. It is an economic problem in that it deals with enabling people to join with one another to solve common problems related to the production of goods and services. It is political in that it involves sharing power between the citizen and the official in such a way as to ensure order and facilitate collective action, while simultaneously protecting the citizens' predation by their rulers. The issue of local government is thus fundamentally, a constitutional issue ... In this regard, local self-governing units constitute one of the fundamental components of the polity.'[38] This argument responds to the immediate post-colonial legacy, especially in Africa.

In summary, it is clear that the decentralising panacea has, in practice, been dominated by a set of failures based on a technocratic view of the challenge.

Reforming for decentralisation

Other authors have identified four factors in considering the reform of local government. The three most significant are as follows. First, effective local government must be 'perceived as providing opportunities to involve long-neglected citizens in the decision-making process ... Secondly, mobilisation of local governments may be particularly important in African countries because many of them have been so severely affected by structural adjustment cutbacks in central government budgets.' Third is the question of urbanisation. 'Some analysts believe that local government initiative must be required to tackle the challenges of Africa's twin pressures, rapid population increase and urban growth ... Unfortunately, the literature on African local government is replete with failure.'[39]

The point is echoed in a World Bank paper from Israel (1992). 'Decentralisation is one of the institutional reforms that may have the highest potential for failure and distortion – for example through conflicts between levels of responsibility and authority, or responsibility and control.'[40] That may be so but the greater failure would be to continue with a centralised system of government control of urban management, which struggles to provide and maintain the infrastructure and services of towns and cities.

Uribe-Echevarria (1985) contributes a South American view to the discussion.

> The debate about decentralisation cannot be restricted to the realm of the organisation of the public sector. It involves nothing more and nothing less than a determination to seek a more egalitarian society, including a better access to the rewards of economic development and a stronger degree of participation in social decision making power.[41]

Decentralisation can be seen as the deconcentration of administrative authority or the relinquishing of real power. Deconcentration tends to be the common feature at present.

Blas (1985) also looks at South American experience to present an indicator for future success.

> It has been established that popular participation in development planning (policy formulation, decision making and implementation) is, at the same time, the aim, condition and the necessary means of achieving progress in development. And it has also been established that, for this and other reasons, genuine development presupposes the existence of some decentralised or deconcentrated instruments of planning and management of public activities. From these two premises, it follows that regional and local government are bound to play a very important role in this process and that it is a logical conclusion that the citizens have to be organised to participate within this same process.[42]

The article continues: 'all public decisions and actions affecting the population of a given territory should be directly controlled by its local administration. [Also] whatever can be carried out at a lower administrative level should not be carried out at the central level'.[43] This seems a credible starting point when considering decentralisation and urban management.

A simpler analysis is offered by Prud'homme (1989).

> It is the question of how to decentralise, in order to maximise the potential benefits of decentralisation, while at the same time, minimising the possible costs of decentralisation ... The real issues are

what specific expenditures and taxes can be decentralised, what subsidy system can be developed, and what kinds of co-ordinating mechanisms can be utilised.[44]

In this case, the key components are funding and inter-organisational arrangements.

A similar question is put by Kolo (1987):

Appropriate and feasible institutional frameworks are a necessary condition for implementing participation and decentralisation on an effective and sustainable basis . . . The need for such frameworks is increasing in terms of the misfit between institutional frameworks adopted from the developed world and local conditions and realities in the developing world.[45]

The question remains: what are the frameworks and how are they to be determined?

Of course, neither Kolo nor Prud'homme look to the decentralisation of power. The closest idea of power, in the technocratic sense, is that of finances. 'The decentralisation of power is more often declared in official documents than put into practice by governments. The transfer of power from the central government to local authorities is the prerequisite for any effective decentralisation.'[46]

This point is reinforced by Olowu (1990).

The issue of all political organisation, including decentralisation, becomes clearly a fundamental economic and political rather than administrative problem. It is an economic problem in that it deals with enabling people to join with one another to solve common problems related to the production of goods and services. It is political in that it involves sharing power between the citizen and the official in such a way as to ensure order and facilitate collective action, rather than imposing policy or solutions from the centre, to solve technical problems of administration.[47]

Again, funding and power are central ingredients to the decentralising challenge.

It is also suggested in Werlin (1992) that

the development process requires strong bureaucracies. The centrally directed, hierarchical bureaucracy has been ineffective in undertaking the complex, uncertain and resource-strapped task of third world . . . development. While I also criticise the rigid apolitical Weberian concept of hierarchy, rules, procedures, rights contractual duties and specialised positions or roles, I consider them essential for the successful functioning of organisations. What is necessary . . . is a high quality of political software for these bureaucratic requisites to be effective.[48]

Furthermore, 'supporters of the new development administration would insist that the merits of decentralisation be taken for granted.'[49] Yet as Wunsch (1991a) points out, 'decentralisation has not been a widely successful solution'.[50] The argument is taken up again by Werlin (1992).

Thus, while the political structures of such governments as Switzerland and Japan appear to be very different, both operate politically elastic forms of government, within which decentralisation and community development are meaningful. Until less developed countries move in this direction, I fail to see much hope for them.[51]

This seems a devastating indictment. However if the analysis is sound, then it compels urbanists to look less at the organisations themselves and more at the nature and quality of the relations between them; a matter explored in the next section.

In summary, it is evident that if decentralisation is to be successful, real power and resources must be devolved to the lowest level of government possible.

As a general summary to this section, it is suggested that the decentralisation panacea has, in practice, been dominated by a set of failures based on a technocratic view of the challenge. In consequence, the continued domination of central government has perverted the potential for local development, particularly in Africa. In turn, central government is loath to relinquish real power and resources to local government. If decentralisation is to be successful, real power and resources must be devolved to the lowest level of government possible. The test now is to relate decentralisation to urban management.

DECENTRALISATION FOR URBAN MANAGEMENT

Under decentralisation and urban management, two ideas are considered: tackling urban management; defining decentralisation.

Tackling urban management

UNCHS suggests that 'a clear trend to emerge from its review of the institutional imperatives of human settlement management and one seemingly common to a wide range of political systems and planning arrangements, is the tendency towards decentralisation'.[52]

UNCHS also suggests that

> the fundamental role of governments is to identify, within acceptable political parameters, where the management of human settlements will be enhanced by decentralising, devolving or sub-contracting any particular component of their current responsibility to any particular level. Clearly, for example, there would be a diseconomy in devolving responsibility for a central–local service to local government if local authorities did not have the skills and resources adequate to manage it. However, it should not be forgotten that the [dynamic] process of development is not always compatible with the most efficient [static] procedures for the administration of settlements. Long-term and short-term trade-offs between these incompatibilities involve complex political decisions.[53]

If the question of the availability of skills and resources is a precondition for decentralisation, no progress will be made because there will be no incentive to devolve resources and strengthen institutions to manage cities. First must come the commitment and practical steps to decentralise. Then can come the panoply of institutional development.

Malo and Nas (1991) pose a central question to the debate.

> The system of federal government [in Indonesia] which had been constituted at independence proved ineffective in coping with the complex problems confronting the newly independent country and the post-independence government came to assume the form of a unitary state government. Where city government was concerned, the course of decentralisation continued to dominate until 1965. However, the need to promote development after independence, while having to rely on relatively few skilled administrators, led to a fairly centralised approach to decision-making. As a result of these two trends, a central issue has been the struggle to arrive at an optimal configuration of central government intervention and local government autonomy.[54]

If the first challenge is to establish a commitment to decentralisation, the second is to identify the functionally based components of what is legitimately first, a central and secondly, a local government concern for urban management.

The need to address urban management is made clear by Shabbir Cheema (1993).

> Rapid urbanisation has substantially increased the demand for urban services throughout the developing world and, in most countries, the supply of services has not kept pace with increasing demand: transport, low income housing, piped water, public education, and public health services are in particularly short supply.[55]

There is an obvious need for an innovative approach that can offer developing countries a method for analysing and solving their urban development problems. The same author has warned of what has happened in the past.

> As the problem of urban management became more complex, some activities were taken over by other organisations because local governments lacked adequate administrative and technical capacity and had inadequate resources to deal with them. The central governments empowered urban local governments to perform many development functions but did not take the necessary steps to improve their financial position.[56]

This is obviously not the way forward.

UNCHS (1990b) offers an alternative prescription:

> It would be mistaken to believe that the re-arrangement by the public sector of any of its current commitments to the management of settlements necessarily means a decrease in its involvement. In fact, this is rarely the case: in devolving or sharing responsibility with another sector or a lower level of administration, it is the role of government to ensure that the partners are adequately equipped and supported to discharge their new roles. The objective is not decentralisation or partnership in itself but efficient settlement management.[57]

However, such a view must be in the light of an awareness that the organisation of urban management must be collegiate.

Sivaramakrishnan and Green (1986) again emphasise this point.

> Development administration requires a non-hierarchical and often collegial structure, which . . . is often informal, non-legalistic, relatively flexible and impermanent. The personnel are usually highly professional individuals who take on an intersectoral approach to urban issues. The organisation emphasises mobility (as opposed to security of tenure), merit (as opposed to seniority) and the recognition of authority and responsibility as functions of individual expertise and performance.[58]

Such a general view must be reduced to specifics if it is to have any practical meaning.

UNCHS attempts to give practical meaning to the general challenge of governing human settlements.

> In most developing countries, there are no holistic and integrated urbanisation policies. Investments are made by sectoral agencies and there have been few evaluations of the costs and benefits of alternative urbanisation strategies. However, there are important lessons to be learnt from case studies drawn from different national contexts from which a set of general issues and problems can be extracted.[59]

It goes on to identify some of the common deficiencies in current organisational arrangements that should be avoided in future structures. These include deficiencies in (a) structures and organisation, (b) processes of planning and (c) skills shortages.[60]

The clear challenge is outlined by Rondinelli (1986). 'Innovative combinations of policy alternatives and organisational arrangements will be needed to reduce urban service deficiencies in the face of rapidly growing urban populations and the increasing concentration of the poor in cities.'[61] The quest is to agree on the general approach to policy development and organisational arrangements.

Development planners are showing an increasing interest in metropolitan planning and management. Shabbir Cheema (1993) comments that 'this has been attributed to the need for (a) dealing with urban problems which extend beyond an individual local government jurisdiction; (b) improving urban infrastructure; and (c) increasing the efficiency of some services through economies of scale'.[62]

In this context, a fundamental analysis of the decentralisation issue has been prepared.

> In many developing countries ... urban services and infrastructure
> are either provided by central governments ineffectively and ineffi-
> ciently or by community organisations and private businesses only
> sporadically. The problems of providing and maintaining urban
> services and infrastructure have brought increasing calls for decen-
> tralisation and privatisation. Many governments are now decentral-
> ising responsibility for financing and managing urban development
> activities.[63]

The urban development activities centre on the provision and maintenance of infrastructure and services.

In summary, it is clear that urban management is seen as a legitimate concern of a decentralised system of government.

Defining decentralisation

In order to establish a suitable organisational pattern for the provision
and maintenance of infrastructure and services, decentralisation has been
held up as the organisational panacea. A clear definition of the concept has been offered by Rondinelli (1990a):

> Administrative decentralisation can be defined as the transfer of re-
> sponsibility for planning, management, and the raising and alloca-
> tion of resources from the central government and its agencies to
> field units of government agencies, subordinate units or levels of
> government, semi-autonomous public authorities or corporations, area-
> wide, regional or functional authorities, or non-governmental pri-
> vate or voluntary organisations.[64]

Within this general definition lie three specific characteristics.

> Deconcentration – the weakest form of decentralisation – is the re-
> distribution of decision-making authority and financial management
> responsibility for providing urban services and infrastructure among
> different levels within the central government.[65]

> Delegation is a more extensive form of decentralisation. Through
> delegation, central ministries transfer responsibility for decision mak-
> ing and administration to semi-autonomous organisations not wholly
> controlled by the central government but ultimately accountable
> to it.[66]

Devolution is a third type of administrative decentralisation. When governments devolve functions, they transfer authority for decision making to autonomous units of local government with corporate status. Devolution transfers responsibility for services to municipalities that elect their own mayors and councils, raise their own revenue, and have independent authority to make investment decisions. These characteristics distinguish local government from local administration.[67]

Though this is a standard definition, it does not appear to present a distinct classification to the decentralisation spectrum. From practice, the alternative view suggests decentralisation to be:

- deconcentration, within central government;
- devolution, to local government; and
- delegation, to the trading sector, whether private, NGO or government owned.

This argument is distilled by Mabogunje (1991). 'The first and most critical of the issues naturally revolves around the issue of local government autonomy, especially fiscal autonomy. The pertinent question here is: how is power to be devolved or decentralised to municipal authorities or local governments?'[68] This question is basic but obvious. How are cities to acquire 'the capacity and power to invest in, maintain and extend the water supply, sanitation, drainage, garbage collection, health care and other essential services . . . Powerful and well organised vested interests will oppose such changes.'[69]

In viewing the decentralisation issue and its provision of infrastructure and services in this way, one is conditioning the thinking towards a policy analysis perspective.

Policy analysts using public administration and finance theories usually take a different perspective on decentralisation than economists using public choice theories. The neoclassical economic approach is concerned with macroeconomic issues, while the policy analysis approach is concerned with specific decisions about political processes, organisational structures and financial resources.[70]

What is needed now is to take the general issues raised above and to turn them into practical organisational alternatives.

Ljung and Zhang (1989) help to summarise the issue.

A centralised approach to complex problems of metropolitan development could be viewed as inefficient and may not be politically desirable . . . Excessively centralised metropolitan planning systems, whatever their merits, often take away necessary unique elements, leading to the local community becoming less responsive to local requirements, and therefore, they are not up to a sustainable improvement in public services.[71]

The idea of responsive local government is explained by Meshram and Bansal (1989):

Another major issue with regard to the structure of municipal bodies [in India] relates to the accessibility and responsiveness of the municipal government. It is an accepted fact that common citizens in a city or town do not have ready access to their elected councillor or even to the municipal administration.[72]

Bearing in mind the fundamental importance of the informal sector to the city-building process, such a situation must be overcome.

In summary, it is suggested that the scope of decentralisation for city management must encompass the devolution of responsibility for planning and service delivery.

As a general summary to this section, it can be emphasised that city management is seen as a legitimate concern of a decentralised system of government. This perception demands that decentralisation passes real power and decision making from the centre to local government levels. A commitment to decentralisation must not be conditional upon prior local government strengthening; the transfer of authority must come first, giving substance to institutional strengthening measures. The scope of decentralisation for city management must encompass the devolution of responsibility for planning and service delivery. It is now necessary to look more closely at the alternative organisational arrangements for city management.

Thus, at the end of this chapter, three key characteristics can be discerned from the organisational dilemmas.

1. There is no single organisational model for successful urban management.
2. Central government retains the power of urban management, despite the efforts of decentralisation.

3. Decentralisation, to be meaningful, must include not only real power (to plan development) but also real resources (to implement development).

The next chapter looks at the question of structuring criteria for organisations in urban management.

6 Structuring Criteria

The challenge of city management is encapsulated by Sivaramakrishnan and Green (1986). 'In style and character, metropolitan management must be an active learning process in which the authorities continuously identify the critical metropolitan issues being thrown up by the forces of urbanisation and try to reduce the penumbra of uncertainty.'[1] In order to achieve such an outcome, it is necessary to consider the organisational alternatives. This chapter therefore seeks to identify the salient structuring criteria for urban management. It considers three topics:

- FUNCTIONAL DETERMINANTS
- ORGANISATIONAL ALTERNATIVES
- ORGANISATIONAL RESOURCES.

FUNCTIONAL DETERMINANTS

In discussing functional determinants, two ideas are considered: functions; organising from funding.

Functions

The functions of urban local government in Bangladesh can be listed in trying to understand the criteria for development. These range from liquid and solid based sanitation systems, water and drainage provision, road and street light provision and maintenance, to various regulatory activities (such as the licensing of vehicles).[2] There is no mention of planning for development. In this context, local government seems consigned to traditional infrastructure provision and maintenance. The observation on the functions seems to bear this out. 'The management of urban services by municipal bodies is handicapped by many constraints, the most outstanding of which is the resource constraint. On the other hand, overcoming the resource constraint is contingent upon effective urban management, particularly tax raising and the provision of municipal services. The potentialities in this regard have not been fully explored'.[3] This is a very traditional and limited concept of urban management.

The list of urban management functions, their executing and supervising agency, for Dakar, Senegal can also be presented. Land use
planning is a direct central government function. Transport, electricity,
water supply, drainage and sewerage are provided through private organisations though supervised by various ministries. Telephones are a
state function. Roads are a state function. Street cleaning and solid
waste are privately run but supervised by the metropolitan authority.[4]
Ngom (1989) observes that

> in spite of the effort that has been made to distribute power amongst
> the state, the CUD [The Urban Community of Dakar] and the com-
> munes, a great deal of confusion remains because of a lack of clear
> identification of the existing division of power and responsibilities
> amongst the various structures . . . Almost all urban services are con-
> tracted out by local authorities with very little follow up on deliv-
> ery. The role of local authorities in the provision of services under
> their jurisdiction remains highly theoretical.[5]

So far, a traditional approach to service provision has been contrasted
by a radical (extensively privatised) alternative. What this second view
does is signal the dangers of a plethora of organisations performing in
the urban management field without a central integrating function.

A survey of the nine SADCC countries in 1988 established what
services are provided in their countries. They ranged across the normal
activities:

> parks, street cleaning, sanitation and refuse collection, water and
> sewerage, road construction and maintenance, housing, primary edu-
> cation, [primary health] clinics, estate management, planning and
> zoning, fire and ambulance services, camping sites and recreational
> facilities.[6]

What is very important is that it goes to the heart of the matter confronting
those concerned with building organisations for urban management.

> The big question that is still haunting governments and local coun-
> cils are the division of responsibilities for the delivery of urban services
> between central government and its agencies and the local author-
> ities. The question is a policy issue [and] a political issue. [It is
> also] at the heart of the deteriorating state of affairs of urban ser-
> vices in our towns and cities.[7]

A more strategic view of the challenge is taken by Shabbir Cheema (1987). It relates specific functions to their executing and, where relevant, their supporting agencies. National urban policy is a national concern, supported by local government. Preparing urban development projects is a local government function, supported by sectoral agencies. The consistency and integration of programmes and projects by sector and metropolitan region is a central and local government function. The mobilisation of financial, political and administrative support is, again, both a central and local government function. The allocation and budgeting of resources for implementation is also a central and local government function. Project implementation is a local government and sectoral agency responsibility. Project co-ordination is a central and local government function. Monitoring, control and information systems is a client agency role, generally local government. Project evaluation is considered a specialist activity, supported by central and local government.[8] Again, while the functions are clear and follow the traditional planning and project development cycle, there is no sense of a central driving force that pulls the entire process together.

Batley and Devas (1988) also contribute to the debate.

> The concept of integrated development has been less prominent in the urban sector than in the rural sector, but the need for integration, particularly of infrastructure provision, has been increasingly recognised. This has called into question the approach, widely adopted by all aid agencies in the 1970s, of establishing specialist institutions for particular functions, unrelated to the overall urban development context. There has also been disillusionment with the so-called 'integrated' urban development authorities which, although intended to integrate urban infrastructure provision, have been divorced from traditional responsibilities for regular service provision and for operation and maintenance of the infrastructure provided by the development authorities.[9]

In recent years, there appears to be a recognition of the need to strengthen existing, multi-purpose institutions (local government) rather than creating new, specialist institutions.

To highlight the point, it is suggested by Brennan and Richardson (1989) that

> in many cities [in Asia], the specialist metropolitan authorities are either weak or non existent (e.g. Seoul and Jakarta). In some cases

there are conflicts between a metropolitan planning authority and the municipality, with the latter often turning out to be stronger (e.g. Bombay and Karachi). In other cases, key urban services and/ or major metropolitan investments are the responsibility of the central or provisional governments instead of a metropolitan authority (e.g. Seoul, Manila, Bangkok and Jakarta). Complexity of organisational responsibilities, especially for the already complex business of urban management, is a recipe for confusion, frustration and ultimately, dreadful services to the community, particularly the urban poor.[10]

Some principles are still required to establish organisational patterns for city management.

In summary, it is clear that the functions of urban management are wide-ranging. They straddle central and local government.

Organising from funding

What is recognised is the propensity of different urban services to be financed from various funding mechanisms.[11] This presents an interesting focus for analysing both the scope, funding and organisational structure for urban infrastructure and service delivery. In simple terms and taking such an analysis to its logical conclusion; a utility that is susceptible to direct user charges, such as water and sewerage systems, could be suitable as a self-financing organisation. A rates-borne function such as solid waste disposal could be a traditional local authority responsibility. By viewing the problem in this way, each component service can be analysed. The resulting organisational and financing matrix could determine both the functional and organisational pattern for future infrastructure and services provision in any given location.

It is possible to outline some urban services that are susceptible to private provision. These include public transport, waste removal and water supply.[12] Blore *et al.* (1992) make similar proposals for sanitation,[13] water supply[14] and solid waste management.[15] They suggest, in the context of Jaipur, that 'contracting out components of services, such as solid waste, transport, and the local distribution of water, should be explored'.[16] Roth (1987) also analyses the subject in great detail. The analysis explores the private provision of education, electricity, health, telecommunications, urban transport, water and sewerage. Each is susceptible to the option of private provision.[17]

Two tables have been presented in Moyo (1989) to illustrate the general argument. The first relates a service to a tier of government, whether central or local. The second relates a service to a source of finance. By way of example on the first; housing and water supply are local. Electricity is central. Sewerage, refuse collection and waste management are local. Secondary schools are central; primary schools are local. Examples from the second table are as follows. Bulk supply of water and the bulk supply of electricity are funded from tariff and user charges. Sewerage is funded from tariff charges. Land and transport planning is funded from rates and supplementary charges (a fixed rate on unrated properties).[18] This list illustrates the fundamental importance of first, establishing the function and its funding. Its organisational setting can follow from this. Put at its simplest, form follows function.

The argument is carried forward by Stren (1989c):

> Most functions that are considered genuinely local (refuse collection, the regulation of trade and building, transportation, preventative public health, the building and maintenance of roads, sewerage, and elementary education) are administered by departments of the council through the agency of the chief executive officer. Budgetary controls and administrative support are the responsibility of the central government ... Supplementing this structure in the provision of urban services are state or central government agencies such as housing corporations, water and electricity boards and town planning agencies.[19]

It is clear from this review that not only is the function of urban management wide-ranging but that the concomitant organisational arrangements are also going to be extensive. This takes us to the organisational alternatives in the management of cities. In essence, therefore, one is seeking to understand the settings for a wide-ranging process, whose functions straddle both planning and administration.

The contextual argument is reinforced by Sivaramakrishnan and Green (1986):

> The impact of politics on the process of administration – the influence of public interest groups, political parties, constituency interests, public opinion and internal pressures and conflicts within and between administrative departments – is increasingly being viewed as a critical factor in effective urban management.[20]

Later in the same volume, they comment,

appropriate networks need to be created between and within exist-ing organisations. The task force provides a clear alternative to the hierarchical command principle of the metropolitan development auth-ority and points to the direction in which improvements in manage-ment and organisation can be sought through appropriate elements of networking. Such networking must attend to the contrasting needs and operating styles of traditional urban bureaucracies and develop-ment administrations. Both types of organisation are fundamental to metropolitan management, and their differing processes can be inte-grated through conscious networking . . .[21]

What is therefore required is a clear exposition of the organisational alternatives for urban management.

In summary, it is suggested that a way of designing organisations for urban management could be established. The design could be by the location of function according to funding source.

As a general summary to this section, it can be declared that the functions of urban management are wide-ranging. They straddle cen-tral and local government. The greater the number of organisations involved in urban management, the greater the need for an overall support mechanism to assist the component parts. Specialist institutions (such as urban development authorities) have largely failed. Multi-purpose organisations are seen as a democratic way forward – the ideal pre-scription for local government. From this, a framework for determin-ing the organisational form to deliver the urban function can be established. The determination can be for each function according to funding source. The specifics of the organisational alternatives must now be explored.

ORGANISATIONAL ALTERNATIVES

Under organisational alternatives, three ideas are considered: options; inter-agency arrangements; economies of scale.

Options

UNCHS suggests that the following points have emerged (from its comparative research) which call for special attention in the area of institutional arrangements for human settlements:

- the need for integrating the budgeting and resource allocation functions with human settlement programmes;
- the need for effective co-ordinating mechanisms at all appropriate levels;
- decentralisation of human settlements functions and responsibilities to lower levels of government or specialised (sectoral) agencies; and
- the potential for involving non-governmental institutions.

In the context of this text, it is surprising to see that UNCHS also advocates the establishment 'of new institutions for human settlements development and financing'.[22] This runs contrary to the organisational themes discerned so far.

UNCHS presents an urban management matrix. It outlines a national planning process and applies its component activities to various levels of government and specialist institutions.[23] The thinking was correct (organisational form follows planning function). The outcome was a very traditional, central government dominated, urban management process.

Egunjobi and Oladoja (1987) suggest that

> a plethora of urban agencies and institutions have emerged in response to increasing complexity of urban growth and structure. Problems of housing, sanitation, health, traffic, employment and population have all called for the formation of one statutory body or another . . . In other words, the urban management function has not been seen in its true holistic perspective.[24]

At some point, there has to be a binding address; a clearly defined process to which the component parts of urban management can clearly relate.

A senior policy seminar echoed the point about the need for a binding strategy to overcome the sectoral domination of national governments. Recent urban programmes have 'mainly been concerned with infrastructure development, a set of projects with little relationship to any overall strategy of urban development. This was a common and recurrent problem deriving from institutional deficiencies'.[25] Two conclusions are drawn from this. First, organisational arrangements must be investigated. Secondly, intersectoral arrangements must be addressed.

Bahl and Linn (1992) go into some detail on three organisational alternatives for urban management. They suggest that the most common form of local government in developing countries is area-wide general purpose local government; that is, centralised metropolitan government. Under this form, most of the basic services provided in the metropolitan area are the responsibility of the city government, and no other general purpose local government (municipality) operates within the urban area. But the service area is usually overlapped by one or more special purpose districts, for example, a water supply authority or a bus company.[26]

They go on to suggest that

in functionally fragmented metropolises, the municipal government's responsibilities for services are limited, and basic functions are delegated to autonomous local bodies. The difference between centralised metropolitan governance and functional fragmentation is largely a matter of degree, because all urban areas are overlaid by some special districts; for example, water supply and sewerage are commonly provided by separate companies. In some metropolitan areas, however, this functional fragmentation has gone so far that local public enterprises have been created to finance and deliver even some of the traditional services of municipal government.[27]

Finally, they comment that 'jurisdictional fragmentation allows many general purpose local governments to exist within the same urban area. This structure of local government is most often associated with the USA, where single metropolitan areas may house dozens or even several hundred local governments with taxing power.'[28]

UNCHS offers a similar choice in the context of developing criteria for allocating the general planning function of the urban management process. First are centralised systems, 'where some or even considerable responsibility to prepare plans, programmes or projects may be assigned to lower regional levels of government'. Secondly are decentralised organisations, 'where all responsibility and all the corresponding power of decision are assigned to the lowest regional level'. Finally are mixed systems, 'where specific responsibility and power (are assigned) according to practical and political consideration . . . Only the third approach needs to be considered since it is the most relevant for practical solutions.'[29] From this, there is little functional determination for the form of urban management.

The challenge from the analysis above is to develop some criteria to assess the standard models against the needs of specific locations.

However, the urban management process does not fit easily into a pre-ordained local government structure.

This problem of 'fit' is placed into a practical context by Clarke (1992):

> While local government is the logical level for co-ordinated spatial/ sectoral investment planning, there may be situations where, because of the skewedness of city size, substantial financial dependence of local government on central government or for other reasons, it is appropriate to create institutional arrangements for co-ordination at the central government level. To oversee strategies for the development of the Bangkok metropolitan region (BMR), it has been recommended that a national urbanisation development board (NUDB) be created with the responsibility for integrated spatial development planning and programming.[30]

That is one solution. There are others.

In summary, it is clear that there are various organisational arrangements to govern the functions of urban management.

Inter-agency arrangements

The challenge of co-ordination in the urban management process is a central question, addressed by Shabbir Cheema (1987).

> Two types of co-ordination problems are discernable; horizontal, among the central, regional and municipal level agencies, respectively, in the city; and vertical, among related activities of several levels of government and administration concerned with urban development.[31]

The concern is to identify the best methods of co-ordinating the various components of the urban management process.

> There are several methods, techniques and mechanisms which have been utilised to ensure co-ordination in urban development planning and implementation. These include (a) exchange of information, (b) negotiation to resolve differences, (c) coercion if the negotiations fail, (d) specification of each agency's functional areas, (e) institutionalisation of procedures to ensure that views of all relevant agencies are incorporated in decision making and (f) delineation of guidelines by the supreme co-ordinating body.[32]

As every author seems to suggest, 'experience shows that there are no universally applicable institutional arrangements or structures for co-ordinating urban development activities . . .'[33] In the final analysis, however, one is seeking a mechanism for co-ordinating the complex inter-relationships in the urban management process. The suggestion is that

three types of co-ordination instruments or arrangements are needed:

- Metropolitan-wide horizontal and vertical co-ordination through the metropolitan local government.
- Municipality-wide co-ordination through the municipal government.
- Project-based co-ordination through a network of concerned implementing agencies headed by the local government or special authority, depending on the nature of the project.[34]

Sharma (1989) emphasises the importance of co-ordination.

Unless agencies have a common set of goals and targets, time-based and project-based action does not always work to the best advantage of city development. Municipalities have to perform their management tasks in isolation of the development inputs of various agencies. The process also takes on a random form because of the lack of (co-ordinated) programmes. Cities are replete with examples of unco-ordinated development even at project level because the priorities of different agencies often do not match and, at times, are even divergent.[35]

For example, in Calcutta, 'intersectoral horizontal communications are wanting. The planning sector is ignored by the operational sectors; its programme development is, more often than not, side stepped by project implementing departments'.[36] In Bangkok, 'co-ordination in planning and implementation is ineffective'.[37] . . . 'Co-ordination in the execution of projects . . . has always posed a problem'.[38]

The reason for such an inter-organisational impasse seems to centre on notions of power and influence. According to Franz (1986),

The example of the German inter-organisational network demonstrates that the organisations are primarily interested in ensuring their domains. This pragmatic and self-interested orientation fosters the maintenance of a very low level of co-ordination and stability. But this stability of the highly organised process of policy making bears the permanent risk that policies are not responsive to the interests and needs of the people affected by them.[39]

This analysis is equally applicable to the developed and developing world.

One model does exist to show that an inter-organisational planning and implementation process can work. As such, it reflects the argument – immediately above – of agencies that must 'have a common set of goals and targets, time based and project based . . .'[40] The model in question is based on the pioneering work of the Tennessee Valley Authority (TVA). Pearsall (1984) outlines the conclusions drawn:

> Several of the agency directors and planners were initially sceptical that an overall planning process could be developed which would not infringe on agency jurisdictions, which would not supersede agency planning processes, and which would enhance the success of agency initiatives. The Tennessee Protection Planning Committee has developed such an overall process. The Committee's work is accomplished through discussion and consensus development at the meetings and through the actions of individual agencies working alone or cooperatively after the meetings. Agency personnel have developed commitment to the process since its inception, primarily because the process enhances the success of their individual agency natural area programmes. It is therefore possible to establish a multi-agency planning process which neither replaces nor supersedes the individual agency processes. Such an approach requires that the agencies themselves coordinate a conglomerate of processes. The resulting overall process will be cyclical, creative and fragmented . . .[41]

This is, indeed, an ideal outcome. For a start, it shifts the emphasis from organisational structures to organisational processes. It also concentrates the mind on the nature of the inter-organisational relationships.

Allport and Einsiedel (1986) seem to concur. A new (urban) planning could

> only be achieved, either by giving the city government power (over government ministers) to dictate what should happen within its area or devising some form of inter-agency body comprising the city government and the major resource allocation and spending agencies, reliant

for its effectiveness on persuasion. Accordingly, a senior level inter-agency technical working group was formed, comprising senior representatives of all the key resource allocation and spending agencies, and chaired by the commissioner for planning.[42]

This example comes from Manila. A model of that inter-agency process is worth developing.

In contrast, it is suggested by Ostrom (1983)

that the dominant way of thinking about inter-organisational arrangements in metropolitan areas is false and should not be used in efforts to guide, control and evaluate performance in local public economies. The dominant view has presumed that certain facts are self-evident and need no critical investigation. One of these facts is that having many government units serving local areas is a priori evidence of chaos and malperformance. A second self-evident fact from this view is that small government units do not have the capabilities to perform effectively or efficiently. A third fact is that overlapping jurisdictions are wasteful and inefficient. A fourth fact is that most urban problems involve large spillovers and need to be dealt with in a comprehensive fashion by single organisations.[43]

The argument is that these supposedly self-evident truths

are all suspect. When a different theoretical approach is used to collect and organise data about inter-organisational arrangements in metropolitan areas, phenomena that appear chaotic are characterised by regular patterns of relationships between and among producing agencies and collective consumption units.[44]

The alternative approach 'opens up the possibility of a broad array of organisational arrangements that can be utilised to solve the complex problems present in local public economies'.[45]

Others appear to contradict such a radical perception. Bahl and Linn (1992) comment that

A jurisdictionally fragmented structure of local government seems to be least suited to the cities of developing countries . . . This would seem to leave metropolitan-wide government and functional fragmentation as the best choices of local government in the cities of developing countries . . . [However, in the latter case], the independence of autonomous agencies is both a blessing and a curse. It may enhance professionalism but it becomes more difficult to co-ordinate the delivery and financing of services.[46]

This alludes to the need for a centrally co-ordinated urban management process, to which disparate organisational contributions can relate.

Yet others conclude by strongly suggesting that from the Asian experience,

> to meet minimum organisational needs, emphasis should be placed on the formation of networks of existing institutions, in both the private and public sectors, to channel information and policy proposals to a metropolitan management team for overall planning purposes and, subsequently, to recommend related development projects and programmes to it for metropolitan review, selection and financing.[47]

Even a metropolitan management team, while an improvement in itself, is not going to satisfy its envisaged role, without the binding force of a commonly agreed urban management strategy. Such a strategy will have to embrace the 'scope of the process' and cover all the 'modes of intervention' presented in Table 2.1 at the end of Part II.

In summary, it is evident that a greater emphasis will have to be placed on inter-organisational arrangements. However, these arrangements can only work with a clear urban management process to underpin them.

Economies of scale

The general theme of exploring criteria to help determine an acceptable organisational form is explored in Sivaramakrishnan and Green (1986):

> It is not feasible to develop a common organisational design with a jurisdiction and structure capable of encompassing this complex [urban management] plurality of functions and organisations. Where a command-type, multi-sectoral authority has sought to accomplish many different tasks within the four walls of a single institution, its attempts have been largely unsuccessful or have led to serious inter-agency conflicts. Proposals for metropolitan government, designed to integrate all sectors, levels and kinds of activity have encountered formidable practical, political and social obstacles. The

dangers in attempting a premature institutionalisation of the metro-politan management process in its entirety must therefore be fully recognised.[48]

The authors go on to suggest that

the focus should be on accomplishing an essential minimum ... involving two main clusters of activity: one concerned with overall decisions on metropolitan development plans and policies (strategic matters) and the other, with the overall choice of programmes and projects to be implemented, the allocation of executive roles and the appropriate budgeting of financial resources (operational concerns).[49]

The organisational alternatives are summarised by Bahl and Linn (1992).

Each primary form of metropolitan government has advantages and disadvantages. One could make the case for each being optimal, depending on the criteria for evaluation and on whether one viewed the situation from the vantage point of central or local government. The norms for a good structure typically considered in such an evalu-ation are economic efficiency, technical efficiency, equity cost con-tainment and the autonomy of local government.[50]

At this point, one is considered central to the argument.

The technical argument centres on the notion of economies of scale. The cost of rendering a service, per head of population, decreases as the population increases, on the assumption that there is no corresponding increase in staff numbers. However, there is a critical difference in the provision of technically advanced services and infrastructure (i.e. capital services) and labour intensive, less advanced services. Again, Bahl and Linn (1992) comment:

The literature seems clearly to show that there are economies of scale for such hardware services as public utilities and transporta-tion. These economies may be captured if the government is large enough to make the substantial capital investment required, for example, to build the proper-size sewage treatment plant ...[51]

There is an example of this debate in Ecuador.

It is suggested by Fuhr (1994) that, given the limited resources and institutional weaknesses in that country, there is no 'promotion scheme for inter-municipal cooperation in water supply, sewage, drainage, solid waste disposal, etc. (where economies of scale are sometimes of crucial importance and synergy could be cost saving)'.[52] In countries where capital resources are particularly limited, the role of economies of scale to help determine the organisational location for the provision of infrastructure and capital intensive services (such as refuse collection, with its fleet of trucks and tip site graders) would seem a legitimate way forward.

Furthermore, Bahl and Linn (1992) state 'there is much less evidence that economies of scale exist in the provision of other public services. This is because such services – primary education, clinics and street cleaning – are labour intensive and have little room for capital–labour substitution.'[53] This is an important distinction. It can be used in the development of a normative framework for considering organisational alternatives for the urban management process.

Although a variety of organisational alternatives have been considered, there is still no clear picture of a best organisational arrangement. However, three sets of criteria are offered to help influence the organisational arrangements for urban management. The first is the need to consider styles of funding the particular functions. Second is the need to distinguish between strategic and operational functions. Finally, the third is the need to distinguish between capital- and labour-intensive functions. Whatever the analytical outcome, in institutional development terms, there must be a sufficient resource base to allow the urban management system to perform.

In summary, it is suggested that economies of scale may be one way of organising service delivery for urban management.

As a general summary to this section, it can be suggested that there are various organisational arrangements to govern the functions of urban management. Three organisational types are presented. Two types of organisational co-ordination are offered. In both cases, the problem is to fit the function of urban management into the forms presented. Great emphasis is therefore placed on inter-organisational arrangements. These arrangements can only work with a clear urban management process to underpin them. No general structure for such arrangements is agreed. It is therefore essential to consider the influence of resources in helping to assess the appropriate organisational alternatives for urban management.

ORGANISATIONAL RESOURCES

Under the heading of organisational resources, two ideas are considered: finances; personnel.

Finances

It is reported that the key recommendation on a workshop about strengthening institutions in Sub-Saharan Africa was 'the need to strengthen institutional capacity'. Adamolekun (1989) continues: 'the term "institutional capacity" was used to refer to the ability of an institution to make effective use of available human, financial and material resources for the achievement of the objectives set for it'.[54]

Cochrane (1983) asserts that 'no central governments have taken a comprehensive forward planning approach to strengthening local governments by attending to questions of personnel and finance'.[55] More recently, Stren (1993) has suggested that 'the degree to which urban management can be promoted, and find acceptance as a powerful approach to dealing with third world development needs, will depend on the elaboration of a coherent conceptual approach as much as it will depend on the presence of adequate financial and human resources'.[56] By way of example, Hart (1989) reflects on the comparison of financial and human resources available to the new South Africa compared with other major African countries. 'Large areas of South African cities are better endowed with the financial and human resources necessary for coping with urban growth.'[57] The point is, the role of financial and human resources to lubricate the urban management process, must not be overlooked.

The financing of urban development is a continuing difficulty for third world governments. Mathur (1987) suggests that:

What is crucial for developing countries is to take a view on the role of various agencies and institutions in the financing of urban development . . . For example, should urban development be financed by central government or should it eventually become a responsibility of local government? Should local governments raise resources on their own or rely on resources from above? Should the private sector be encouraged to invest or be kept away from this field?[58]

Prud'homme (1989) argues 'that some taxes can be more easily decentralised than others (but) by applying the principles of efficiency and fairness, it follows that expenditures and taxes should be decentralised differently . . .[59] Subsidies appear therefore to be an important corollary of decentralisation'.[60] Later, 'the real issues are what specific expenditures and taxes can be decentralised, what subsidy system can be developed, and what kinds of co-ordinating mechanisms can be utilised'.[61] Though stated before, it should be repeated; if decentralisation, as a means of strengthening local government, is to be relevant, funding arrangements must be an integral of that strengthening process.

Prakash (1988) has made an expansive contribution to the debate.

> City governments in the Asian developing countries provide a number of services on a self-financing basis. Water supply, sewerage and refuse collection are generally provided by most urban local governments . . . The recent efforts towards expanding the scope of self-financing activities and greater utilisation of user charges and pricing measures are important developments. They make the urban local bodies' revenue base more diversified. Generally speaking, local taxes have been found to be less income-elastic. Beneficiary charges, especially with rapid urbanisation, may be relatively more elastic.[62]

However, these points are qualified by identifying the crucial role of the private sector in urban development.

> Many development theorists and practitioners have argued that dynamic local government is crucial for development. It is pointed out that national economic development is a necessary composite of economic activities conducted at the local level. Local government is bound to be important either as an obstacle or an aid . . . While it is clear that governments will have to take a stronger role in providing urban services in the future, it should also be pointed out that the bulk of investments that affect urban development originate in the private sector. They represent the complex network of decisions by individuals, households and firms. Urban investment policies must thus be carefully designed to encourage maximum participation by the private sector.[63]

Bahl and Linn suggest a direction for the future in the private provision of infrastructure.

> It has long been a practice to create separate water and transportation authorities to make possible a more professional (and less

political) management, to avoid civil service regulations in employment practices and to create more autonomy in taxing, pricing and investment decisions.[64]

The dilemma is that the desire for increased professionalism tends to move away from the idea of democratic accountability. This may be an important factor, particularly in poorer countries.

Stren (1989a) expands on the role of external agencies.

Central government and parastatal agencies are responsible for a whole host of urban services and regulations. Among services typically performed by such agencies are water and electricity supply, refuse removal and public transport, public housing, land allocation and land-use planning.

The argument goes on to identify an inherent danger in wholesale privatisation.

The trade-off between the public and private sectors varies . . . but in Africa, where such a large proportion of the urban population is extremely poor, there is always a danger that the distributional consequences for the weakest groups will be, on balance, negative when a public service has been privatised.[65]

An interesting case study seems to be that of Calcutta, as detailed in Menezes (1985).

As part of a vigorous policy to strengthen local government, the state government and Calcutta Metropolitan Development Authority (CMDA) have adopted a two-tier (metropolitan and local) approach to developing the Calcutta metropolitan area. The CMDA's predominantly executive role will be restructured, while its coordinating, policy planning, monitoring and evaluation functions will be reinforced . . . The CMDA's role has been adjusted in several ways: it has been strengthened as a financial and policy intermediary by the addition of a strong appraisal, monitoring and evaluation unit; its metropolitan planning function has been reorganised and is being strengthened; certain responsibilities such as water supply and sewerage are being transferred to other agencies to gradually decrease CMDA's predominant role as an executive agency.[66] [In contrast] the municipalities have been given an expanded role in capital budgeting and in setting priorities within broad technical and financial guidelines set out by CMDA.[67]

The general argument is brought up-to-date by Bahl and Linn (1992).

Many countries have come to realise that strengthening local governments by granting them some fiscal autonomy is important to decentralisation. The evidence of this concern is a rash of government commissions on allocating fiscal responsibilities to local governments, restructuring intergovernmental grant systems, and solving specific fiscal problems of large cities. The role of local governments in development is in general, less often spelled out in national plans than included in administrative and legislative actions that become part of the planning process.[68]

In other words, local government decentralisation, to be both meaningful and practical, must be accompanied by greater fiscal autonomy and support. Rondinelli (1990b) is more cautious.

Decentralising responsibilities for the provision and maintenance of urban services and infrastructure, however, will require municipal governments to increase their revenues. World Bank officials urge governments in developing countries to use five major sources of revenue: self-financing and cost-recovery; co-financing and co-production; expansion of municipal general revenues; intergovernmental transfers; and expansion of municipal borrowing capacity. But the fiscal aspects of decentralisation are not the only, or even the most urgent, problems that municipal governments face in the future. A more immediate and crucial problem is improving the administrative capacity of municipal governments to manage revenue raising and expenditure operations more effectively.[69]

In summary, it is apparent that the nature of funding has an influence on the organisational arrangements for various components of urban management.

Personnel

Training is the key to strengthening administrative capacity in developing countries. Its bottom line is the transfer of skills from the expert to the recipient. This is outlined in Stren (1989a):

Failure of urban governments and other public agencies to provide adequate services is a function of both manpower inadequacy [including lack of experience] and the lack of financial means . . . [Institutional building] is a lengthy and complex process; only cautious and judicious programmes to improve revenue sources, to train the right people over a long period of time, and to develop local experience and competence in a number of different infrastructure and service areas can ultimately succeed.[70]

A similar view is offered in Sidabutar *et al.* (1991).

Present efforts to decentralise urban management (in Indonesia) can be seen in three broad and closely related areas.

- Innovative urban development projects, action oriented planning with a substantial degree of community participation and public/private partnership.
- Strengthening of institutional capacities and promotion of institutional modernisation: reform of the legal framework and administrative procedures; improving co-ordination between various central and local government agencies involved in urban infrastructure development.
- Supportive information and communication programmes.[71]

According to the authors,

none of these efforts can bear fruit without sufficient training, as it is always people and not plans that determine the course and speed of developments. Without appropriate human resource development, and innovative projects [urban] development policies as well as institutional changes, will remain meaningless, and unable to transform innovations into sustainable, regular activities.[72]

An operational example of the lack of training by Martin's (1989) case study of Kenya suggested that

it became apparent that, in addition to training concerning specific [urban management processes], there were major training needs within the local authorities. The rapid changes in personnel, the short history of many of the [Kenyan] local authorities and inadequate staffing levels had often created a serious management problem which the incumbents of the posts were ill-equipped to meet. Our diagnosis was that in-house workshops in which senior staff would participate for a few days, to be followed up on a regular basis, would tremendously strengthen management capacity.[73]

It is clear that manpower needs, as part of a total approach to human resource development, should be addressed in a rational manner.

> The point is that with the diagnostic [the rational] approach, the data themselves are used to help identify problem areas at an early stage, so that they can be understood and corrective actions considered that are relevant to the cause of the problem.[74]

From the total resource development perspective, this must involve the standard interventions such as 'recruitment planning, training strategies, industrial relations, pay and conditions, organisational changes, management attitudes and thinking'.[75]

The manpower need for urban management can be summarised in the following passage from Sivaramakrishnan and Green (1986).

> As the activities of government in [Asia's] great cities have become increasingly onerous and complex and the traditional urban administration model (typified by the local municipality) has been rapidly overtaken by events, the sectoral bodies set up to undertake urgent, large scale capital works have needed additional managerial talents for project identification, preparation and execution. The increasing size of the programmes has demanded ever greater attention to technical and operational efficiency. The introduction of multi-sectoral authorities has added yet another dimension of organisational complexity requiring emphasis on corporate planning and management. The tasks of metropolitan management in such an environment call for both experience and experiment so that conventional, day-to-day administration of services and upkeep of assets can be carried out at the same time that creative initiatives in urban development are actually pursued.[76]

The training for urban management is therefore going to have to span these two functional parameters. Part is concerned with routine tasks and part is concerned with the creative role of preparing and reviewing strategies.

To conclude, it is suggested

> That decentralising responsibilities for financing urban services and infrastructure in developing countries will be necessary to improve governments' capacity to meet rapidly expanding need ... A more important lesson of experience is that few central governments will

be able to decentralise financial responsibilities for urban services without first strengthening municipal administrative capacity ... Expanding their revenue raising authority alone will have little impact on improving the capacity of municipal governments to provide services if they continue to be plagued by inefficient organisational structures and operating procedures and lack clear legal authority to deal effectively with urban development problems.[77]

This is very important. While it has already been asserted that the devolved method of decentralisation must be accompanied by a strengthened fiscal resource base, the human resource base must also be seen as an essential ingredient for success. The difference is that the fiscal resources can have a direct bearing on the organisational arrangements for third world city management. The human resource base pervades all aspects of third world city management, irrespective of organisational arrangements.

Ultimately, one could argue that all local government in developing countries has, as its first object, a positive and supportive impact on its development environment. As such, one could therefore argue that an ultimate test for the institutional aspects of third world city management is incorporated in the International Union of Local Authorities (IULA) World-Wide Declaration on Local Self-Government. There are eleven articles. Extracts from two are offered below.

- Under Article 2: local self-government denotes the right and the duty of local authorities to regulate and manage public affairs under their own responsibility and in the interests of the local population;
- Under Article 8: the allocation of resources to local authorities shall be in reasonable proportion to the tasks assumed by them.[78]

In both extracts, a relevance to urban management can be discerned. In the first, a council is to serve the local population (provide infrastructure and services). In the second, government has to ensure a reasonable financial base for the council (to fund the infrastructure and services). In both, the strengthening of city governments is 'to ensure steady improvements in the provision of water, sanitation, storm drainage, garbage removal, health care services (and so on) ... This will usually demand changes in national governments' attitude to local government roles and responsibilities'.[79] It will also demand a change in the donor community where 'few aid agencies have a coherent policy for the support they provide to urban development [and where] it is rare for donor agencies to support projects and programmes to build urban governments' institutional capacity . . .' One donor agency did not even recognise the urban management issue under an urban classification: 'in ODA, "urban" has tended to be defined narrowly as old-style town and country or physical planning, which is not the appropriate focus'.[80] Fortunately, this situation has changed. 'ODA staff are now working on a more coherent urban policy for the agency'.[81]

In summary, it is evident that the quality of personnel has a direct impact on the productivity of the urban management process. The need to organise requisite training is clear.

As a general summary to this section, financial and human resources are the essential ingredients to make the urban management system work. The nature of funding has an influence on the organisational arrangements for various components of urban management. Decentralisation to local government is meaningless without fiscal autonomy. The quality of personnel has a direct impact on the productivity of the urban management process. The need for organising the requisite training is clear. While human resource capacity is a fundamental pre-determinant for successful urban management systems, of itself, it would not determine an organisational pattern for urban management.

Thus, at the end of this chapter, three key characteristics can be discerned from the structuring criteria.

1. The functions of urban management are wide ranging, straddling many authorities.
2. The idea of inter-organisational arrangements is being increasingly favoured.
3. The style of funding will help determine the organisational location for the various components of urban management.

The next section summarises the arguments for Part III.

Summary to Part III

Part III has analysed the settings (the form) for third world city management. Chapter 5 looked at various organisational dilemmas. Chapter 6 looked at the structuring criteria for organising urban management. The underlying issues from each of the six main sections are summarised as follows.

ORGANISATIONAL DILEMMAS

Organisational models

Many authors suggest that there is no single organisational model to deal with the urban management challenge in developing countries. There is an acknowledged weakness in the sectorally organised central government in dealing with urban development. All support the idea of a strengthened local government system to deal with the issue. In so doing, the decentralising panacea is pervading every corner of development administration. In essence, there is no single organisational model for successful urban management.

The decentralising panacea

The decentralisation panacea has, in practice, been dominated by a set of failures based on a technocratic view of the challenge. In consequence, the continued domination of central government has perverted the potential for local development, particularly in Africa. In turn, central government is loath to relinquish real power and resources to local government. If decentralisation is to be successful, real power and resources must be devolved to the lowest level of government possible. In summary, central government retains the power of urban management, despite the efforts of decentralisation.

Decentralisation and urban management

City management is seen as a legitimate concern of a decentralised system of government. This perception demands that decentralisation passes real power and decision making from the centre to local government levels. A commitment to decentralisation must not be conditional upon prior local government strengthening; the transfer of authority must come first, giving substance to institutional strengthening measures. The scope of decentralisation for city management must encompass the devolution of responsibility for planning and service delivery. In essence, decentralisation, to be meaningful, must include not only real power (to plan development) but also real resources (to implement development).

STRUCTURING CRITERIA

Functional determinants

The functions of urban management are wide-ranging. They straddle central and local government. The greater the number of organisations involved in urban management, the greater the need for an overall support mechanism to assist the component parts. Specialist institutions (such as urban development authorities) have largely failed. Multi-purpose organisations are seen as a democratic way forward – the ideal prescription for local government. From this, a framework for determining the organisational form to deliver the urban function can be established. The determination can be for each function according to funding source. Essentially, the functions of urban management are wide ranging, straddling many authorities.

Organisational alternatives

There are various organisational arrangements to govern the functions of urban management. Three organisational types are presented. Two types of organisational co-ordination are offered. In both cases, the problem is to fit the function of urban management into the forms presented. Great emphasis is therefore placed on inter-organisational arrangements. These arrangements can only work with a clear urban management process to underpin them. No general structure for such a process is agreed. In summary, the idea of inter-organisational arrangements is being increasingly favoured.

Organisational resources

Financial and human resources are the essential ingredients to make the urban management system work. The nature of funding has an influence on the organisational arrangements for various components of urban management. Decentralisation to local government is meaningless without fiscal autonomy. The quality of personnel has a direct impact on the productivity of the urban management process. While human resource capacity is a fundamental pre-determinant for successful urban management systems, of itself, it does not determine an organisational pattern for urban management. In essence, the style of funding will help determine the organisational location for the various components of urban management.

The conclusions to Part III are therefore as follows:

1. There is no single organisational model for successful urban management.
2. Central government retains the power of urban management, despite the efforts of decentralisation.
3. Decentralisation, to be meaningful, must include not only real power (to plan development) but also real resources (to implement development).
4. The functions of urban management are wide ranging, straddling many authorities.
5. The idea of inter-organisational arrangements is being increasingly favoured.
6. The style of funding will help determine the organisational location for the various components of urban management.

These features of third world city management represent a set of general characteristics of its form. They will be returned to in Chapter 12.

In conclusion, the importance of this analysis is to identify guides to thinking about urban management structures, without prescribing outcomes.

What remains is the need to introduce an initial conceptual framework for the form of third world city management. The suggested framework is in two parts:

- SCOPE OF THE FORM
- STRUCTURING CRITERIA.

Table 3.1   Variables for city management form

SCOPE OF THE FORM	*Frequency*
Decentralisation	12
Inter-organisational arrangements	10
Decentralisation of urban management (UM)	6
Importance of local government	5
Balance between central and local government	5
Decentralisation of resources	4
No clear rules to allocate UM functions	4
Failure of special development organisations	4
Holistic process	4
Functional determinant	3
Privatisation	2
Financing urban development	2
Failure of sectoral organisation of CG for UM	2
STRUCTURING CRITERIA	
Decentralisation	5
Sector	4
Sub-sector	3
Funding source	3
Economies of scale	3

Notes: The frequency is the number of times each variable is cited in Part III.

Under each, a number of variables are identified. They are ordered according to the frequency of the citations in Part III. The conceptual framework is presented in Table 3.1. This will be returned to in Chapter 12.

This concludes the theoretical analysis. Parts IV and V look at the practical aspects of institutional development in relation to third world city management.

Part IV

ID Practice: Organisational Strengthening

Part IV seeks to explore the first of two important aspects of the institutional development process. Ultimately, it focuses on the importance of the organisation–environment relationship. Chapter 7 looks at a case of project development in organisational restructuring and strengthening. Chapter 8 reviews the ID performance of the case. The Summary to Part IV identifies the key characteristics of this practice.

7 Project Development

This chapter seeks to analyse the process of organisational restructuring and strengthening. It will review the development and implementation of the project. The institutional focus is Lilongwe City Council, in the capital of Malawi. This chapter considers three topics:

- PROJECT FORMULATION
- OUTPUTS REQUIRED
- IMPLEMENTATION.

PROJECT FORMULATION

The British Overseas Development Administration (ODA) agreed to supplement the appointment of a town clerk and chief executive to Lilongwe City Council, in Malawi's capital city. The agreement was in response to a request from the Government of Malawi (GOM). GOM was deeply concerned with the deteriorating standards of financial management and general administration in the council. In particular, external audit reports in 1987 had identified a number of financial management weaknesses. These included delays in producing accounts, budgetary control difficulties, poor management of commercial enterprises (such as local produce markets) and inaction in tackling the mounting debtor list. The reports also identified the need to expand the council's income base, to cope with its rapidly growing city.

The overall objective of the project was stated to be 'institutional development'. It sought to strengthen the various capabilities of the city council to perform its services and achieve its ambitions on behalf of and for the citizens of Lilongwe. In particular, the project sought to improve the efficiency of the city council, improve standards of administration and financial management and train staff in the operation of the new systems, that would bring about the improvements.

While the symptoms of institutional malaise were evident, in terms of deteriorating finances, morale, services (like refuse collection) and the complete absence of any capital works, there were still some staff capable of contributing to an analysis of the problem. In the event, the 'town clerk's project' was negotiated between GOM and the British

High Commission and its development division (the ODA outpost, conveniently in Lilongwe). There was no consultation with the city council; whether through its councillors or its handful of remaining senior officers.

In summary, the project formulation was a discrete and closed process. The British government responded to a direct request from the Government of Malawi. The project was drafted by the British and Malawi government representatives in Lilongwe. There was no consultation with the client city council.

OUTPUTS REQUIRED

The project contained a number of specific targets. These ranged over both strategic and operational issues. On closer analysis, it was considered that certain improvements could be made:

- to reflect the immediate problems facing the council, and
- to highlight more clearly the strategic issues concerning its institutional development.

The adjustments to the project were intended first, to separate (i) the short-term urgent items from (ii) the medium-term strategic matters and secondly, to highlight the important stage of (iii) implementation. The project data sheet (the terms of reference) had mixed the three. The outcome, after submission to the city council, was sent to the Secretary for Local Government in February 1989. The result was a clearly structured four-stage project, as follows.

Stage 1 (February to April 1989).
SHORT-TERM URGENT TARGETS

1. Staff review.
2. Review of transport/equipment/construction.
3. Budget for 1989–90.
4. Action on auditors' reports.
5. Action on outstanding debtor accounts.
6. Plan for internal audit section.
7. Senior staff appraisal.

Stage 2 (May to November 1989).
MEDIUM-TERM STRATEGIC TARGETS

8. Review of services and performance targets.
9. Review of organisation and manpower.
10. Review of long-term training.
11. Budget for 1990–91.
12. Measures for increasing the revenue base.
13. Appointment of a counterpart town clerk.

Stage 3 (February to December 1990).
IMPLEMENTATION AND REVIEW

14. Implementation of institutional development.
15. Operational targets (further to 8).
16. General management manual.
17. End of tour report.

Stage 4 (January to August 1991).
CONSOLIDATION AND HANDOVER

18. On-the-job counterpart training.
19. Consolidating the new systems and procedures.

In summary, the project had specific outputs to be fulfilled over its duration. They were reorganised, in consultation with the client council. This was in order to match their short and medium term, operational and strategic nature.

IMPLEMENTATION

Stage 1

Target 1. The staff review identified a number of fundamental weaknesses in the council. Only 50 per cent of the established first- to third-tier posts (chief, deputy and assistant chief officer) were filled. This was despite the existence of a budget for the remaining 50 per cent. Consequently, there was a desperate shortage of good calibre managers in post. No organisation could work effectively with this staffing position. Only 44 per cent of the established supervisory posts were filled. This was, again, despite the existence of a budget for the remaining 56 per cent. Consequently, there was a desperate shortage of close supervision on particular council activities. No service could be efficiently delivered with this staffing position. The staff morale for each department was then judged, subjectively, as follows:

- Town Clerk's   Average
- Treasury   Average
- Landscape   Poor
- Health   Very Poor
- Engineering   Very Poor

The staff review concluded with a number of recommendations. First, that two chief officer and three deputy chief officer posts be reviewed as part of the second stage (concerning the organisation and manpower review). Secondly, eighteen vacant (or vacated) posts be filled by internal promotion. All these recommendations reflected the fact that the personnel involved were already satisfactorily performing the functions of the vacant posts and had been doing so (in each case) for at least a year.

Thirdly, thirty-five vacant (or vacated) posts were recommended to be filled by external advertisement. This was to allow some fresh talent to enter the system. Fourthly, three posts were recommended for immediate creation; a computer manager (to introduce a computerised financial administration system into the council); a town planner (to start work on government policy concerning the council's future take-over of traditional housing areas and the town planning function from, respectively, Malawi Housing Corporation and central government); and a personnel manager (to introduce a personnel management system – there was none). Finally, a number of short-term training proposals were presented. These included a supervisors' training programme in the engineer's department, a health assistants' course on child spacing (birth control) and a secretarial upgrading course. Each was no longer than two weeks. These recommendations were sent to the Secretary for Local Government in March, 1989. The internal promotions were rejected. The reasoning was that the existing staff had helped contribute to the decline of the city council.

Target 2. A situation was found where the transport fleet had been run down from over eighty vehicles to between twenty-five and thirty, depending on the state of repair of the increasingly ageing fleet. Basic items of equipment were simply not available such as for road maintenance. There was no capital programme. The council, as a deliverer of services, had been reduced to virtually two activities; pot-hole filling the roads and struggling to maintain the semblance of a public health and cleansing service. Essential items of transport were identified (cleansing vehicles, pick-ups and a car). A commercial loan was negotiated. Essential equipment was included; for road maintenance and computerisation (the council's financial management being entirely manual). A small capital programme was prepared. This reflected the government's development policy statement[1] and its outline zoning scheme (or structure plan) for Lilongwe.[2]

Target 3. At the start of the project in January 1989, no action was being taken to prepare a budget for year 1989–90. This was despite the fact that the statutory deadline for its submission to the Ministry of Local Government was one day later. It was finally submitted on 9 June that year; slightly over four months after the statutory deadline. A number of reasons explained this parlous condition. The city treasurer was a seconded civil servant. He had extensive accounting experience but this was from a civil (public) servant's rule-adhering perspective. He was not a budget man in the sense of thinking managerially about how to get the system to work. He was also incredibly badly supported by an overworked and largely junior staff. A new deputy had just been appointed. Within a year he was dismissed by government; his alleged American MA and PhD degrees turning out to be bogus. Equally, and as already noted, the other departments' senior management was in an equally parlous state. Consequently, there was no attempt from any of the other departments to help initiate the budget preparation process. Indeed, there were no regular chief officer meetings. The annual budget is the foundation of a local government's activity. Failure to produce it is to fail the most fundamental strategic management task for the organisation. This was evidence that the council was simply imploding. It was literally moving from day-to-day.

Target 4. Two external audit reports were prepared in financial year 1986–7. The auditor general, acting on instructions from the Ministry of Local Government, carried a special investigative audit of selected areas of the council's operations. A routine external audit by the council's private auditors, presented a number of operational irregularities and inefficiencies. These reports gave credence to the general evidence of how badly the council was being financially administered. Bearing in mind the date of the two reports, the required action from both was not formally instigated and reported to the council until April 1989.

Target 5. Of the cumulative rates debt of K13.4 million (one year's total council expenditure), K12 million came from the country's international airport, which was located in the northern (and essentially rural) sector of the city. Although action was already initiated, it amounted to little more than threatening noises to the operators of the airport; a parastatal organisation, supervised by government's Department of Statutory Bodies. The legal procedures for rates debt recovery were cumbersome. Properties upon which a rates debt was outstanding for at least three years could be sold by public auction. During that period, the council was statutorily restricted to charging a fixed interest penalty of 7.5 per cent per half year on the outstanding debt. With inflation never less than 17 per cent, property owners with particular financial acumen withheld their payments until the last possible moment; deposit interest rates were higher than the fixed penalty. No significant progress would be made until the law was changed: a first indication of the importance of the regulatory environment in which local government operated.

Target 6. No plan was prepared for the internal audit service. There were no professional audit staff to prepare such a document. In financial year 1988–9, the local government service commission (the central recruitment agency for all Malawi local government professional, technical, administrative and clerical staff) tried three times to recruit a professional internal auditor. It failed.

Target 7. The senior staff appraisal involved all first- to third-tier post holders; departmental chief, deputy and assistant chiefs. In a council of five departments, there were only seven people to interview. The review highlighted the following. Five out of seven staff had postgraduate or post-experience training from Britain. All were soundly trained in their technical disciplines. All were under considerable stress because of the lack of managerial and supervisory support staff. Most worked at some point most weekends. They were all constantly frustrated by the lack of transport and equipment. None had postgraduate management training. None displayed strong strategic management capabilities suitable for the post of chief executive officer.

This concluded the first stage of the project. The reports arising from Targets 2 to 7 were sent to the Secretary for Local Government in April 1989. Also sent was a detailed timetable for Stage 2. A report on the appointment of a counterpart town clerk and his subsequent training, was also presented.

This first stage of the project had taken care of the short-term urgent items. This stage had also offered an important opportunity to learn about and understand the detailed nature of the organisation. Implementation of Stage 1 could proceed without hindrance to the strategic concerns that were central to Stage 2; the cornerstone of the project.

Stage 2

The second stage required:

8. A review of services and performance targets.
9. A review of organisation and manpower, in relation to the targets.
10. A review of long-term training, in relation to the targets.
11. A budget for 1990–91, in relation to the targets.
12. Measures for widening the council's income base.
13. Appointment of a counterpart town clerk.

Target 8. The review of services and performance targets was a three-part exercise. The first had already been dealt with in Stage 1; all its targets contributed to a fairly intimate knowledge of the strengths and weaknesses (the dominant condition) of the council. The second part was to review the policy and government environment within which the council operated. This was to establish policy indicators for the review. The third concerned the need to establish an understanding of the concept of performance in local government.

On the review of services, government required (as of February 1989, through a presidential directive), the creation of a new cleansing department. This was in response to the weak cleansing service, (then) part of the health department. Government required, through its development policy statement, that the city councils should take over responsibility for the traditional housing areas from the Malawi Housing Corporation.[3] Also, it required the city councils to take over responsibilities for town planning from central government's physical planning department.[4] The Minister of Local Government reported, in an address to the city council on 14 June 1989, that the environmental health service 'must be strengthened, must have more equipment, must have more qualified staff and must have a better budget'. The World Bank's urban sector review identified, among other things, the need to strengthen the councils' personnel functions.

Concerning performance, there were both implicit and explicit references to financial performance in the original terms of reference. 'The revenue base of urban councils must at least keep pace with the increase in population if the standards of service provided are not to suffer . . . The decline in standards of financial management in urban councils has led to both a loss of revenue and to fiscal deficits even when a budget surplus had been forecast.' The financial issue was seen as the central concern; services and infrastructure clearly had to be paid for. The danger in the financial domination of performance assessment was to see the council as a trading entity; its acid test being the bottom line of its annual balance sheet. In a theoretical argument on the comparison of performance between business administration and public administration, an argument was presented for a three-level concept of assessing organisational performance, as follows:

Assessing organisational performance

LEVEL	BUSINESS ADMIN	PUBLIC ADMIN
1: 3–5 years +	Overall profitability and capital growth	Overall programme performance in relation to general socio-economic conditions (e.g. poverty)
2: 1–3 years	Specific market success and consequent profitability	Specific project success and citizen satisfaction (e.g. housing renovation)
3: 1/4–1 year	Operational efficiency, budget control, personnel morale and production management	Operational efficiency, budget control, personnel morale and project management

Source: McGill, 'Evaluating organisational performance in public administration', *Public Administration Bulletin*, No. 43, pp. 27–41.

The general thesis was that both business administration and public administration had a common discourse at the operational level of testing the efficiency of an organisation. Thus the three 'E' studies of the 1980s were dominated by a concern for public sector efficiency. This was not surprising. It was the only common language between the two traditions. Business and public administration diverged at the second and first levels.

> Whereas the business community has its automatic feedback mechanism of profit, public administration had no such mechanism. It must therefore construct its own [p. 32] . . . in the final analysis, one is arguing for an output and impact orientation to the [public administrative] performance evaluation [p. 33].

The argument was distilled and accepted by the council. It noted that performance could be assessed from the annual balance (whether the council was in financial surplus or deficit). It noted the efficiency and effectiveness of its services (just because a council may be in financial surplus is no guarantee that it is performing the services that people need – people pay their rates irrespective). It noted the implementation and effectiveness of the capital programme (there is no point in building things poorly and that nobody wants). It noted its potential impact on the overall social economy of the city (a very difficult matter to assess). The council accepted that in terms of performance:

- the annual balance sheet was a self-explanatory but limited test of performance for a non-trading organisation;
- the contribution of the council to the social economy of the city was difficult to assess (and therefore a long term policy target);
- the implementation and effectiveness of the capital programme concerned both concepts of efficiency (level 3 analysis) and the usefulness of particular projects; it was therefore immediately relevant;
- the central focus for council performance assessment would therefore be the efficiency and effectiveness of its services and capital programme.

The council then proposed that a specific set of operational performance criteria be established. This would be incorporated, eventually, into a council annual report – a long-term target.

Target 9. Having gained a thorough understanding of the internal operations of the council, scanned the policy environment in which the council operated and established the basis for assessing the council's performance, the project was ready to conduct the review of organisation and manpower in relation to the services and performance targets. The review presented the following proposals, additional to incorporating the creation of a new cleansing department. A new housing function would be created in response to government's development policy statement, for councils to take over traditional housing (around 80 per cent of the housing stock – including squatter residences). A new town planning function would be created, again, in response to government's development policy statement, for councils to take over town planning from central government. A new computer service would be created. To that date, the council had no computer system; all accounting and financial management, as well as personnel and general administration, was entirely manual.

The proposed new functions therefore responded explicitly to the three government requirements concerning housing, town planning, financial and general administration (computers). Additionally, it was proposed to transfer design and building control from the engineering (the council's biggest and weakest run) department to the new housing and planning functions; thereby creating a new housing and planning department. It would administer existing THAs (housing), develop new THAs (design) and integrate building control with the (transferred) development control function (of town planning). Finally, proposals were submitted for the strengthening of the environmental health service. In particular, preventative health care programmes were seen as central to that department's future activities. A public health education unit and a primary health education unit were the central features of the strengthening.

The fundamental principle underlying the proposed structure was to have each specific programme within a service (a department) led by a fully qualified officer at the third-tier (assistant chief officer) level. Thus in health, the primary (or personal) health care programme would be led by a fully qualified nurse. In housing and planning, the town planning programme would be led by a fully qualified town planner. This organisational structure of service, programme and (where applicable) task had far reaching (and intentional) consequences for the council's fledgling management information system; a system that was being constructed around its budget, staffing and operational performance criteria. This is dealt with later.

Target 10. The review of long-term training requirements concentrated on strengthening third-tier (programme leader) posts, particularly in and related to health and cleansing. It sought to ensure basic supervisory and technical skills at fourth-tier level (task leader), particularly in health, cleansing, engineering and treasury. Special attention was proposed for financial management and the fire brigade. These three areas of concentration reflected the priorities for the manpower and organisational review. In turn, they were the practical consequences of the review of services and performance targets. This is considered further under implementation; Target 14.

Target 11. Though plans were in hand to prepare the next financial year's budget, from October 1989, in time for the statutory deadline of 31 January of the following year, it was not submitted until 12 April; a two month improvement on the previous year but still a long way behind the statutory deadline. The reason was virtually the same as before. There were still no new staff. The manpower proposals for Stage 2 of the project were being submitted as the next year's budget process was starting. It would take another year before significant improvements in staffing and output would materialise.

Target 12. Six measures were outlined for increasing the council's revenue base. A strategy was being developed to encourage physical development. Every new building would be liable to a rate (a property tax). The more development, the more property taxes. There were many properties that were simply not rated because of the very slow progress made by central government's valuation service. The simple administrative task of getting these properties on to the valuation roll would yield additional income. Government conveniently exempted itself from paying a realistic grant in lieu of rates. Its actual annual payment to the city council was around 0.5 per cent of its total rates bill. The total bill represented (in 1989) over 45 per cent of the property tax bill for the city. The consequences for infrastructure provision were not hard to imagine. The rate itself had not been adjusted in the previous two years. Certain efficiencies remained to be squeezed out of the council's two enterprises; its resthouse and its produce markets. Finally, the council was keen to embark upon asset-creating ventures. This was in the context of not only the need to increase the income base of the council, but also the fact that the council was operating in a city where development land was held by government; the chances of acquiring freehold properties to encourage development, asset creation and income were very limited. Proposals for a 'housing for rent' scheme were approved; in the long term, to off-set the major annual rental bill for staff housing (one of the few benefits in working for local government). Redevelopment of a dilapidated (and condemned) resthouse into shops and offices, was approved. Phase 2 of a business centre was approved in a location where the council was able to buy a major piece of (very rare) freehold property. All three projects were being approached as property development initiatives; trading accounts would be opened. There would be no charge on the general rate fund. The long-term goal was asset creation. Any shorter term cash surpluses would be put back into subsequent phases or improvements.

Target 13. Notification of the vacant post of deputy town clerk and counterpart to the new town clerk was sent to the Local Government

Service Commission on 2 May 1989. This was immediately after the first stage progress review meeting with the ministry. The commission conducted interviews on 21 November that year. The interview took seven months to materialise. The impact of this and other delays in making key appointments is outlined in the section, constraints to progress.

In terms of Stage 2 of the project, the medium-term strategic concerns of institution building, the three key proposal reports were submitted to the Secretary for Local Government in September 1989. The submission covered the review of:

- services and performance targets,
- manpower and organisation in relation to the targets, and
- of long-term training requirements in relation to these targets.

The second progress meeting was held with the Secretary for Local Government in October 1989. At this meeting, the proposals for widening the council's income base and progress on the counterpart's recruitment were also reported. This second stage represented the fulcrum of the project. From this point on, the emphasis shifted from organisational restructuring and strengthening proposals to implementation, refinement and consolidation.

Stage 3

Stage 3 of the project was designed for the whole of 1990. In particular, it required:

14. Implementation of the institutional development plans.
15. Operational performance targets (to supplement the original services and performance targets review – as requested by the council).
16. A management manual; and
17. An end of tour report.

Target 14. The implementation of the institution-building plans were almost entirely dependent on the Ministry's response to the original three policy submissions for institutional development, submitted in September 1989. In particular, no organisational restructuring could actually be implemented until the organisational and manpower proposals were approved. Despite voiced approval in October, the Ministry refused to allow action to be taken until written consent for the creation of the posts (thus accepting the new housing and planning department for example) was issued. This was received by the council in August 1990; ten months after the original submission or 67 per cent into the 1990 year of implementation. In anticipation of this, the precaution had been taken to get approval to the key new third-tier programme leader appointments as part of the 1989–90 budget submission. These were the posts of town planner (to start on the housing and planning issue), the computer manager (to start computerising the council's financial and general administration) and a personnel manager (to start on the council's deplorable personnel management systems). They were approved, as part of the budget approval, in July 1989.

Despite this foresight, it still took the commission and the ministry ten months before a town planner was in post (May, 1990) and seven months for the computer manager to join. The personnel manager turned out to be an internal promotion, after interview. The implementation year of 1990 was therefore severely hampered. In terms of institution building, only a start could be made on town planning (from a standing start), computerisation (from a standing start) and personnel management (from an unsatisfactory state). The consequence was that, by the end of 1990, the reorganised structure was being presented in the council's new policy document (dealt with later) but that no new appointments, arising from the major review, had been made. However, some progress was made with the filling of existing posts. This was particularly so at the supervisory levels; that crucial operational tier of council activity. Despite the lack of progress on organisational and manpower restructuring, the development of systems and procedures were progressing. This would ensure, as the project data sheet correctly stated, that the new manpower would actually have something tangible to work to.

In the second half of 1990, financial reporting systems improved dramatically. By the end of that year, the council's budget and its concomitant monitoring systems were in place. Balances could be reported on a daily basis; it used to take weeks to extract the information from treasury. Income management improved, principally because of strengthened debt collection. Expenditure controls were tightened significantly. For the first time, service heads had to know and report the balance in the budget code as part of a submission to the purchasing sub-committee. Secondly, and perhaps more important, a double check was made that there were actually funds in the bank to cover the order(s). There was a slow but successful education process to get people to understand the difference between a budget (as a spending intention) and money (in the bank).

The council's management information system was lamentable. It took the whole of the first two stages of the project (in 1989) to get accurate base information on who was employed where and how these staff and overhead costs were budgeted and apportioned. This was particularly so in the central administrative functions of town clerk (general administration) and treasury (finance). In both cases, the establishment file listed personnel without reference to the functions they were performing. In the junior ranks of the professional and technical grades, staff were simply not able to explain under who they worked and what their precise responsibilities were. The starting point for constructing a management information system was the organisational structure. Within that structure (and additional to the project), salaries were completely revised, to relate accurately to tiers of management. The new salary structure then supported the restructured organisation, as a cascading system of services, programmes and (where relevant), separate tasks. During the second half of 1990, the existing budget document for that year was analysed into its component organisational units. Thus, each service had its central support of chief officer, secretary and so on. Each substantive operational programme then became the budget entity. For instance, in the town clerk's department, the budget and its base unit expenditure codes reflected the organisational structure exactly, namely:

Budget code	Programme
1.0	Central support
1.1	Administration
1.2	Legal
1.3	Computer system
1.4	Personnel
1.5	Internal audit.

Where operational codes contained specific tasks, the code was split again. For example, under 1.1 Administration, there were two tasks; 1.1.1 Committees, and 1.1.2 General duties. The budget therefore ceased to be a line item document; it became a programme budget.[5]

The council's management information was now centred on the programme. The programme was the council's unit of:

- organisation, as a management entity,
- budget, as a cost centre, and
- staffing, as an establishment centre.

Any programme could now be assigned to any service (any department) without loss to the programme's professional or technical integrity. Every programme could now be specifically monitored as to what it spent and what it earned, if anything. Every programme's staffing position was now explicit (previously, much was simply assumed). Finally, every programme was (or would be) led by a third-tier official. He or she would then be responsible for professional/technical outputs, personnel management concerning productivity and the programme's budget. What remained was performance criteria for each programme. This is dealt with under Project Target 15.

The impact of staff training was wide ranging. The object of the senior management training was to introduce all first- to third-tier staff members (who had sound technical skills but no management training) to the basic concepts and principles of general management. A total of four weeks training was completed by March 1991. The response was very good. First, people actually turned up. Secondly, the participants participated. This was particularly so in the sessions when operational performance targets were being conceived. Personal involvement and peer pressure ensured lively debate. The object of the supervisory management training was to introduce all fourth-tier staff (who, in the main, had reasonable technical training but no management training) to the basic concepts and principles of supervisory management. Four weeks of training were completed by the end of March 1991. At this level, it was decided to get written responses to a questionnaire on the perceived impact of the training being offered. The general tenor of comments was that too much ground was being covered in the week-long session. There was a demand for more in-depth consideration, particularly of supervisory skills. In general, the training was considered to be worthwhile.

Twenty-one individuals were identified for specific technical training. Funding was secured for only four. This individual technical training, being entirely dependent on external funding, was the weakest and most disappointing aspect of the training component of the institution building for the council. In contrast, over thirty junior staff took the opportunity to upgrade (or simply formalise) their secretarial and accounts clerk skills at local part-time courses. The council gave people the time off (day release) and funded tuition and examination fees (failure would mean repayment). Again, some staff had never had the opportunity to benefit from any kind of training, since school. The fact that the employer was now granting time off, and financial support for fee payment, was a major fillip to morale. There was no success in getting

a partner council in South Africa to host an in-house training programme for the fire brigade. The new treasurer started organising internal training courses for treasury staff. The low key, part-time technical
training was a success. The higher profile, externally funded technical
training proved to be a major failure, simply because funding was not
forthcoming, whether from government or donors.

The bottom line of the staff training and the second of two principal
components of the project was the development of key counterpart
staff. The programme for a counterpart town clerk had already been
submitted. By the time of the interviews, it was clear that action had
also to be taken to get a career appointed city treasurer. The counterpart town clerk took up his appointment on 6 March 1990. On 16
February 1990 (one day after receiving notification of his appointment), a training programme was submitted to the secretary for Local
Government, with a copy to the British Council (the funders). The
programme was in three parts. First would be the period March till
June. He would become familiar with the workings of the council and
the specific duties of town clerk. From June to December, he would
be in Britain. First, he would spend three months in a local authority,
gaining senior practical experience. He would then spend three months
at a university, studying financial and general management. The final
stage would be January to July 1991. At this time, he would receive
intensive on-the-job training and gradually take over from the ODA-
funded chief executive. He returned to his duties on the first week of
January 1991; the start of the last stage of the institution-building project,
concerning consolidation and handover. A similar programme was conceived for the future city treasurer.

A wide range of institution building clearly took place during the
implementation year of 1990 (to satisfy Target 14 of the project). Despite the lack of decisions on the organisational and manpower proposals, good progress was made concerning systems and procedures,
management information and training. What remained to be produced
for Stage 3 was operational performance criteria (Target 15), a management manual covering general and financial management (Target
16) and an end of tour report (Target 17).

Target 15. The operational performance criteria were developed, at
the request of the city council, to supplement the general institutional
building targets, presented under Target 8. They were also constructed
as a key technical component in the council's longer term ambitions
to prepare and distribute an annual report. The criteria were very hard

to develop. Two day-long internal seminars were held with all chief, deputy and assistant chief officers. The target was to establish a framework for determining how to present the operational criteria and then to generate the criteria itself. The resulting framework was in three parts, for each programme. The financial (input) criteria was simple enough. Every programme's budget was recorded. The end of year actual would be entered. The percentage variance from the programme's total budget would also be recorded. The input criteria was therefore entirely quantified. The efficiency (output) and effectiveness (impact) criteria were much harder to articulate. It was achieved. The majority of performance indicators were quantified. So, for example, under programme 1.5, internal audit:

- *Finance*: the budget for 1990–91 was K19,000; the actual was K18,000, a percentage variance of 5 per cent. This scored 4 out of a possible 5; the scoring being on target, 5; within 10 per cent either way, 4; within 20 per cent, 3; within 30 per cent, 2 and within 40 per cent, 1.
- *Efficiency*: audits had to be performed in accordance with the annual audit plan, within 5 working days of the original programme. The output was the specific audit investigation.
- *Effectiveness*: financial irregularities had to be kept to within 1 per cent of total expenditure. The impact was on the reduction of financial irregularities (whether through stupidity or petty corruption) on the financial system.

Target 16. The management manual, on general and financial management systems, was to be a central underpinning of the institution-building process. The published document's preface made an important technical point (Lilongwe City Council, 1991c):

There are two conditions when analysing a system. These are its structure and its processes. This manual is dominated by a concern for processes (i.e. the dynamics of the system – the things that make it work).

Chapter 1 outlined the general framework for policy and budgetary planning. Chapter 2 concerned the detailed preparation and review of the annual budget. This included the preparation of the capital programme and the revenue estimates, the review of the establishment file and the review of the budget itself. Chapter 3 outlined the process of committee administration. It focused on the annual committee cycle, managing committees and running the chief officers' management team. Chapter 4 presented the principles governing the embryonic computer financial management system. It described the fundamentals of general, transaction and cycle processing. Chapter 5 went into details. It outlined the computerised system for accounts and rates billing operations. It explained the logic of the budget codes. It reviewed the payroll and personnel systems' operations. The last chapter incorporated the council's (recently) submitted (31–8–90) internal audit plan (delayed because of personnel recruitment difficulties). It outlined the different types of internal audit and its annual programme for regular investigations. Two technical appendices were included. The first was the council's chart of accounts. The second was a schedule of fixed assets and their maintenance budget requirements.

In terms of Stage 3 of the project, implementing the institution-building programme, the two project documents (of operational performance targets and a management manual on general and financial management) were submitted to the Secretary for Local Government on 12 December 1990. There was no resulting review meeting held by the Ministry. What remained was the project's end of tour report, to be submitted at least six months before the end of the project. Among other things, it would report on the details of implementing the project (Target 14).

Target 17. The end of tour report was submitted to the Secretary for Local Government in January 1991, eight months before the end of tour. This was done to give the Ministry and the British High Commission a chance to respond to and act on the recommendations for continuing assistance. It was also submitted at the beginning of Stage 4 of the project in order to allow for a total concentration on the consolidation and handover stage of the project. This was particularly pertinent because the counterpart town clerk and treasurer returned to duty, from UK training, that week. There were only eight months left to ensure a smooth transfer of additional expertise and authority to the two key staff members who were to become responsible for the core administrative activities of the council; the central focus of the project.

The end of tour report's executive summary made two telling points:

- All the targets specified in the original project documentation have been achieved in the sense of policy development and the introduction of new systems and procedures. However, the new systems and procedures are not yet 'bedded down'. More time is required to guarantee not only their consolidation but also their sustainability.

- The weakest link in the project is the lack of time left for on-the-job training for the counterpart staff.

Chapter 2 of the report outlined the achievements of the project in terms of all the project targets. It concluded that the achievements had been to tackle the policy issues arising from each project target, to prepare and secure council approval to all the policy documents arising from the issues and to start implementing the approved recommendations. The impact of staff training was analysed. It concluded that it was difficult to discern changes in terms of improved productivity, it seemed positive in the sense of improved morale for the staff involved but it (was) only the start of a necessarily long-term initiative in manpower development.

The outgoing town clerk considered another strategic issue to be of primary concern and therefore worthy of inclusion and debate in the report. This concerned the need to develop a total urban management framework for the institutional development project. The state of the council was reviewed and summarised. It claimed that the (current, at January 1991) state of the council 'is a great improvement on its dire condition in January, 1989'. However, it argued that three fundamental weaknesses remained:

- the institution building is not yet complete in terms of staffing, the development of new skills and the consolidation of procedures,
- the financial position remains tenuous, simply because the council's largest debtor remains reluctant to pay (rates) and government continues not to pay a realistic grant in lieu of rates, and
- the management information systems have improved from being virtually non-existent but, in relation to the size of the organisation, remain in their infancy.

The last chapter considered the need for future assistance. It reviewed the role of the town clerk. It compared the comparative immunity from political pressures of a foreign town clerk compared to a local appointee. It acknowledged the improvements in financial management but that the system depended on too few key personnel. The recommendations for future assistance were considered in the light of possible future technical assistance; first from the ODA, as a second phase of the town clerks' project for Malawi. Secondly, these was the prospect of a World Bank-funded Local Government Development Project for Malawi. The recommendations were therefore restricted to rounding off the project as a prelude to possible additional assistance, arising from macro-policy work in government.

In summary, implementation concerned organisational planning, establishing systems and procedures, recruitment and training. The recruitment and training included that of a counterpart town clerk. The main instrument of ID was executive authority; the expert holding the principal line management role of town clerk and chief executive. It was supplemented by various training initiatives. Chapter 8 reviews the ID performance of this organisational restructuring and strengthening case.

8 Institutional Development Performance

This chapter seeks to identify the influences that determined progress in this case of organisational restructuring and strengthening. It therefore considers three topics:

- CONSTRAINTS
- ADDITIONAL ID
- IMPACT, SUSTAINABILITY AND HANDOVER.

CONSTRAINTS

The institutional development project document referred to the appointed town clerk being 'expected to operate in an executive capacity'. The statement suggested a requirement to take decisions on strategic and operational matters. The experience belied this intention. Ministry of Local Government Circular 13 of 1984 stated that the:

Local government service commission is responsible for all recruitment and discipline matters including transfers and the promotion of staff. In turn, matters involving administration and the running of councils will be the responsibility of the ministry of local government. The administration of day to day matters will remain the responsibility of the local authority.

It was a very illuminating passage and highlighted the essence of the context within which the project had to operate.

The Local Government Service Commission was a major constraint on the effectiveness of the project. Recruitment started in May 1989. From then, the recruitment process worked, at best, slowly. To cite the three key appointments required and proposed in advance of the organisational and manpower review; it took ten months to get the counterpart town clerk and town planner into their posts. It took seven months to recruit the computer manager. Admittedly, all these candidates required explicit ministerial consent before appointment. Nevertheless, it was an inordinate amount of time to recruit key personnel in a project that only ran for thirty months. Consequently, at the time of the end of tour report's submission, no staff had been recruited arising from the organisation and manpower review.

The Ministry of Local Government was the other major constraint on the effectiveness of the project. Two cases are cited. Both concerned organisational and manpower review matters that were fundamental to government itself and to the project in Lilongwe.

First, the ministerial instruction to create a new cleansing department was received in March 1989. The council approved proposals for the new cleansing department in April that year. The proposals were submitted to the Secretary for Local Government in May. The budget implications were incorporated in the budget submission in June. Budget approval was received in July. Permission to create the new cleansing department (i.e. proceed to get posts filled) was sent from the Ministry in December 1989; precisely seven months after the submission to the Ministry, and after reminder letters in June, August and September of that year. Then came the lengthy process of recruitment. The key third-tier postholders (three assistant cleansing officers) were finally in post in October 1990. From government directive to fully operational department took sixteen months.

Secondly, the organisation and manpower review was submitted to the Ministry of Local Government in September 1989. It was discussed and approved in principle at a ministerial project monitoring meeting in October. Government approval to create the new posts arising from the review was received in August 1990; ten months after the original submission. This was an inordinate amount of time to receive explicit ministerial approval to a fundamental component of an institution-building project that was only running for thirty months.

The consequence of the lengthy decision time was obvious. Nobody had (as of the end of tour report date of January 1991) been interviewed, let alone recruited to posts arising from the organisation and manpower review. If the short-term urgent appointments had not been made (ahead of the review) no significant progress would have been made on either the housing and planning functions or the computerisation proposals, during the course of the project. That was an absurd state of affairs. As the report went on to say: 'it is now unlikely that all the posts arising from the organisation and manpower review will be filled and settled in before the project ends. Time is simply running out'.

The implication of these constraints is the fundamental importance of city government's supervising environment. It can make or break not only a reasonable city management system but also its concomitant ID processes. In terms of analysis, the internal city management process must be related to its supervising environment. It is a general principle that must not be lost sight of in the totality of the institutional development process.

In summary, there were two major constraints to effective city council performance. Both were in the supervising environment. Firstly, staff were recruited by an independent recruitment commission. Its performance was very poor. Secondly, the parent ministry took an inordinate amount of time to reach decisions, especially on matters of organisational restructuring and related staff issues.

ADDITIONAL ID

In April 1989 (four months into the project), the councillors were informed that because of the parlous state of the council, the situation would deteriorate further before the institution-building plans would have a chance to arrest the situation. By the end of the second year therefore, and in view of the terms of reference, the project was on course, save for the organisation and manpower decision delays. However, the second (or implementation) year of the project not only saw its implementation, but also the development of a parallel initiative. It was argued that there was no point in building the institution of the council without a parallel activity; scanning and responding to the development environment (the city) in which it operated.

The project's terms of reference were a framework for institution-building. It was considered both dangerous and technically unsound to remain within them. The project was therefore reinterpreted as the need to develop strong urban management leadership in the context of a dynamic development environment. The process of city building was therefore seen as being central to the council's policy and budgetary deliberations. Institution building therefore became the means and not the end in itself (i.e. simply ensuring financial viability). The end was reinterpreted as the requirement to develop a total (or holistic) urban management framework. This would be to satisfy not only the needs of the project (i.e. strengthening the central and financial administration of the council) but also the needs of the city within which it operated and which it served.

The need to address the environment was articulated at two levels.

First, there was the requirement to recognise and organise the process of city building. This was in order to ensure the availability of proper infrastructure and services so that, ultimately, the city would contribute to and not be a drain on the national economy. The cause of this need was the frequent inability of urban government to organise itself to anticipate its own urban growth. The consequence was the inevitable collapse of urban infrastructure and services provision in rapidly growing third world cities.

Secondly, at the time of the initial conceptual thinking (very early in the project), there was no city-building capability in the city council. The population projections, at 6 per cent a year, predicted a city of over half a million people by the turn of the century and (if the growth continued) another doubling within the following decade. The argument was put forward that the city council had an opportunity to avoid the potential collapse of infrastructure and services provision, in the light of the projected growth in population and its consequent demands on infrastructure and services. Till that point, the issue was not recognised by local government in Malawi. This was despite central government's requirement for city councils to take over the traditional housing and town planning services, when ready. The driving force had to come from local government itself. It was pointed out that collapsing services and infrastructure occurred where council expenditure outstripped its income, where strategic planning was non-existent and where there was no central urban management leadership. The urban management leadership and concomitant planning systems had to be installed.

The importance of city government in the city-building process was stressed. The ability of cities to continue to perform their economic functions and to improve standards of living would rely heavily on the availability of proper infrastructure and services. The efficient delivery of infrastructure and services, in turn, depended on the strength of local government and the effectiveness of urban management. In this sense, the need was seen to integrate the infrastructure, services, organisational and financial planning so as to better achieve urban development goals. This would be done more successfully if the process of city building was channelled through an integrated urban management system.

A first attempt to present a coherent urban and institutional development framework to the council, the Ministry of Local Government and the donor community, was the integrated development strategy of May 1990. At that time, the World Bank and the United Nations Development Programme (UNDP) were in the process of forming the draft of a local government development project for the country. The strategy was seen as a way of influencing matters. In particular, it was designed to place as great an emphasis on infrastructure provision as possible, so that the anticipated project would reflect that priority. The next edition of the strategy was available in November that year. It was published in tandem with the budget for the following year. It was technically strengthened, with the benefit of hindsight and responses to the first edition.

The integrated development strategy was a combination of infrastructure and services planning, and organisational and financial planning, within an annual policy and budgetary cycle. The respective concerns were therefore external to the council (city building), internal to the council (institution building) and the binding planning process (policy building).

At this point, the institution-building exercise in the first two stages of the project was combined with the wider notion of the council, in a symbiotic relationship with its development environment (its city). In turn, the infrastructure and services development had been integrated with the organisational and financial development. What remained was the integration of policy and budgetary development within an annual planning cycle. This would ensure a continuous review and preparation of the strategy and its budget. This was fundamental to the concept. It completed the circle of urban and institutional development planning. The key was the sequential integration of policy and budgetary planning. The annual policy and budgetary cycle was therefore the process that bound the integrated urban management system of infrastructure, services, organisational and financial planning together. In turn, the integrated development strategy was the heart of the integrated urban management process of strategy, manual and review.

The heart of the process was based on simultaneous thinking about infrastructure and services provision (to support the economic development of the city) and organisational and financial arrangements (to ensure the council's ability to do the providing). This wider concept of urban management, to which the city council was advised to aspire, was considerably in excess of the traditional (organisation centred) notion of institutional development contained in the project's terms of reference. By the beginning of Stage 4 of the project (consolidation and handover), the integrated development strategy was already an accepted body of knowledge and experience within the city council.

In summary, the major additional ID work focused on the justification to break out of the confines of a traditional, or organisation centred notion of institutional development, as a test of performance. Instead, the council's impact on its development environment (its city) and the mechanism to plan for that impact was conceived; an integrated development strategy.

IMPACT, SUSTAINABILITY AND HANDOVER

The sole concern for Stage 4 of the project was to get the returning counterpart staff (the future town clerk and treasurer) into a fit condition to take over the running of the council (Target 18) and to consolidate the systems and procedures (Target 19).

Target 18. The counterpart staff returned to duty the first working week in January 1991. No more project documents were required. However, the council was promised a revised strategy (to take account of World Bank project negotiations and indicative commitments for infrastructure provision), an updated management manual (simply to improve upon the first edition) and a full annual report (as an expansion of the operational performance targets). A departure report was also considered necessary.

The counterpart town clerk was given increasing responsibility for the running of the council. The handover was virtually imperceptible. By the Easter of 1991, the acid test was that the incumbent town clerk had ceased to accept incoming correspondence (of which there was an abundance every day). By then, he saw mail by exception only. He had turned his role into an adviser to the future town clerk. The future city treasurer was treated in the same way by the outgoing treasurer who departed in July 1991. The new treasurer was firmly in place by then.

Target 19. In July 1991, the outgoing town clerk submitted a departure report to the Secretary for Local Government. A comparison between the start of the project (January 1989) and the end of the project (as of July 1991) was offered. The report noted that it was 'ultimately a matter of debate whether the project has been a success'.

Two failures were recorded. First, the airport rates issue had still to be resolved. Secondly, the takeover of development control had not been implemented. Both were the result of a failure of government to make a decision: in the rates case, to agree a proposal that had been jointly presented by the council, central government's department of lands and valuation and the airport, in December 1990; in the development control case, there was simply no decision from the parent ministry on a report prepared jointly by the council and central government's Commissioner for Physical Planning.

The departure report concluded that 'in the final analysis, the test of success will be whether the institutional and city development proposals, brought about by the past two and a half years, can be consolidated, sustained and self-perpetuating'. Much would depend on the nature and quality of future assistance and the system's ability to retain good personnel.

In August 1991, the outgoing town clerk submitted to the Secretary for Local Government, a revised integrated development strategy and management manual. The original operational performance targets were also extended into a full annual report. Each document's introduction described its role in the total urban management process. The three documents were designed to govern the performance of the council.

> The first is the strategy the council is trying to implement. The second is the method by which the council performs in order, ultimately, to implement the strategy. The third is the framework for reviewing the council's performance. Although published as separate documents, they represent the three stages in the council's total urban management process, namely, policy development, implementation and review.[1]

The integrated development strategy incorporated and updated the project development work submitted to the World Bank in May 1991. The management manual refined the policy and budgetary chapter on the preparation and review of the integrated development strategy. The annual report was a new document. Operational performance criteria had already been prepared and submitted (Target 15). Having constructed a major policy and urban development process through the integrated development strategy, it was clear that any operational performance criteria had to be part of a wider policy review exercise. It was therefore included in the council's first annual report.

The project was completed. The handover had taken place to competent local staff. The systems and procedures for general and financial management had been introduced and recorded. The management information system had been established. The basic implementation of the institution building had proceeded as far as it could in the time. The supervising environment had proved to be a major constraint to progress, particularly on the organisational and manpower proposals. Additional advisory support was to be forthcoming (see Part V).

In summary of this section, in terms of impact, there was a clear difference as a result of the ID; a planning process, the planning for infrastructure provision, organisational and financial development. With a measure of continued support for the local government system, the ID was seen to be sustainable. There was a smooth and successful handover to the counterpart chief executive.

Summary to Part IV

Part IV has analysed a case of organisational strengthening and restructuring in a third world city council. Chapter 6 reviewed the project. Chapter 7 looked at various aspects of its institutional development performance. The underlying issues from each of the six individual sections are summarised as follows.

PROJECT DEVELOPMENT

Project formulation

The project formulation was a discrete and closed process. The British government responded to a direct response from the government of Malawi. The project was drafted by the British and Malawi government representatives in Lilongwe. There was no consultation with the client city council. In essence, the project was imposed by the council's host ministry; there was no consultation on project formulation.

Outputs required

The project had specific outputs to be fulfilled, for its duration. They were reorganised, in consultation with the client council. This was in order to match, their short and medium term, operational and strategic nature. In essence, short- and medium-term outputs were identified.

Implementation

Implementation concerned organisational planning, establishing systems and procedures, recruitment and training. The recruitment and training included that of a counterpart chief executive. The main instrument of ID was executive authority; the expert holding the principal line management role of town clerk and chief executive. It was supplemented by various training initiatives. In essence, the main instrument of ID was executive authority.

INSTITUTIONAL DEVELOPMENT PERFORMANCE

Constraints

There were two major constraints to effective city council perform-ance. Both were in the supervising environment. Staff were recruited by an independent recruitment commission. Its performance was very poor. The parent ministry took an inordinate amount of time to reach decisions, especially on matters of organisational restructuring and re-lated staff issues. In essence, the supervising environment was a major constraint to progress.

Additional ID

Additional ID work centred on the justification to break out of the confines of a traditional or organisation centred notion of institutional development, as a test of performance. Instead, the council's impact on its environment (its city) and the mechanism to plan for that im-pact was conceived; an integrated development strategy. In essence, the traditional notion of institutional building had to be widened to take into account the organisation's relationship with its development environment.

Impact, sustainability and handover

In terms of impact, there was a clear difference as a result of the ID; a planning process, the planning for infrastructure provision, organis-ational and financial development. With a measure of continued sup-port for the local government system, the ID was seen to be sustainable. There was a smooth and successful handover to the counterpart chief executive. In essence, the impact and handover was achieved; sustainability would require further assistance.

The conclusions to Part IV are therefore as follows:

1. The project was imposed by the council's host ministry; there was no consultation on project formulation
2. Short- and medium-term outputs were identified.
3. The main instrument of ID was executive authority.
4. The supervising environment was a major constraint to progress.
5. The traditional notion of organisation centred institution building had to be widened to take into account the organisation's re-lationship with its development environment.

6. The impact and handover was achieved; sustainability would require further assistance.

At this stage, the executive role of implementation, the constraining
influence of the supervisory environment and the efforts to develop an
explicit organisation–environment relationship should be noted.

Part V

ID Practice: Planning Capability

Part V seeks to explore the second of two important aspects of the institutional development process. Ultimately, it focuses on the importance of testing sustainability. Chapter 9 looks at a case of project development for a policy and planning capability. Chapter 10 reviews the ID performance of the case. The Summary to Part V identifies the key characteristics of this practice.

9 Project Development

This chapter seeks to analyse the function of city management through a case of developing a policy and planning capability. It will review the development and implementation of the project. The institutional focus is the four major urban councils in Malawi. It therefore reviews:

- PROJECT FORMULATION
- OUTPUTS REQUIRED
- IMPLEMENTATION.

PROJECT FORMULATION

The British Overseas Development Administration (ODA) agreed to appoint an urban management adviser to the Ministry of Local Government. The agreement was in response to a request from the government of Malawi (GOM). It was keen to see an extension to the first town clerks' project. The idea was that the adviser would be a source of support and technical assistance to the newly trained town clerks as they wrestled with the practicalities and challenges of running their councils. In contrast to the first project (Part IV), where a crisis had arisen that required external assistance, this second project was to build on the achievements of the first. It was also to be a technical assistance component of the forthcoming World Bank-funded Local Government Development Project.

The overall objective of the project was stated as 'to consolidate the handover of authority to the newly trained Malawian town clerks and to develop their urban management capabilities'. In particular, the project sought to instil a policy planning capability in the four urban councils.

Specifically, the project was required to advise the selected urban councils on institutional and urban development initiatives arising from the original town clerks' project and the forthcoming World Bank's local government development project. It was required to give specific support to the new town clerks. It had to prepare a performance monitoring framework. It had to get the councils to prepare and update annually their (forthcoming) development strategies. It had to advise the Ministry on policy co-ordination in support of the councils.

In summary, the initial project formulation was a less discrete but still, essentially, a closed process. However, this applied only to the outputs for the first quarter (the first six months) of the project. The British government responded to a request from both the government of Malawi and the World Bank, to carry the policy and planning experience of Lilongwe to the other three major urban authorities. The project was drafted by the World Bank, with ODA and government of Malawi observations. Consultation with the identified adviser was undertaken.

OUTPUTS REQUIRED

Specific outputs were identified for the first six months of the two year assignment. In consultation with the Malawian town clerks, it had to:

1. Identify the specific institutional development and urban development initiatives to be pursued for each city/municipality arising from both the ODA assistance and the World Bank's proposals.
2. Highlight specific difficulties arising from their assumption of responsibilities from the departing town clerks.
3. Establish an annual planning and review cycle for the institutional and urban development issues identified in (1) above, as a framework for developing both an urban management capability and to follow progress on the reform and strengthening measures arising from the forthcoming World Bank project.
4. Prepare the first review of each council's development strategy or, if none exists, to ensure the preparation of each council's first strategy.

In consultation with the Ministry of Local Government, it had to:

5. Consider a framework for co-ordinating the ministry's policy development and monitoring activities in support of the four councils.

In summary, the project had specific outputs to be achieved for its first six months. During that time, the adviser, in consultation with the client councils, had to develop a programme for the remaining eighteen months of the assignment. This was done.

IMPLEMENTATION

Stage 1

The city councils had, up to the first week of January 1992, benefited from an institutional development project funded by ODA. Lilongwe and Blantyre had received thirty months of support; Mzuzu, thirty three months. The councils also participated in the formulation of the World Bank's Local Government Development Project. During this time, Zomba had no equivalent ODA institutional strengthening initiative.

In terms of policy and budgetary development, Lilongwe was the most advanced in its plans for infrastructure and services provision. It also had a clear organisational and financial development strategy to support these plans. Blantyre lacked an overall development framework within which it could plan its provision of infrastructure and services effectively. However, it did have a clear organisational and financial development strategy for its (then) perceived needs. Mzuzu had the rudiments of a strategy for its infrastructure, services, organisational and financial development. It needed to integrate the assorted thinking into a development strategy. Zomba had no foundation (in the form of recent technical assistance) for the publication of its thoughts on infrastructure, services, organisational and financial development.

Target 1. The infrastructure and services needs for each council were assessed in terms of a checklist of development requirements. Arterial infrastructure concerned the fundamental needs of public health and general movement. This included water supply, sewerage and sanitation, power and roads. Serviced land for general development focused on the provision of infrastructure to allow residential (except traditional), commercial and industrial development to take place. Serviced and upgraded land for traditional housing locations concerned the provision of infrastructure to allow new locations to be developed and existing ones to be improved. Urban development focused on particular building projects (as opposed to infrastructure provision, to allow others to build), such as offices and industrial space. The Lilongwe figures were taken straight from its integrated development strategy. No equivalent data existed in the other councils. Intensive work was therefore undertaken with the other councils' town clerks and their support staff in order to get a first indication of what confronted their councils and their cities, with the predicted population increases. The resulting analysis revealed, for the first time, Malawi's urban sector infrastructure needs.

The result of the services assessment was that all four councils still required a considerable amount of institution building. This was despite the efforts in the three cities, through the previous town clerks' project. Each council now had a local town clerk. That was an achievement in itself. Blantyre had to resort to recruiting an expatriate treasurer. The other councils had local treasurers. Zomba's treasurer was particularly weak. There was a general acceptance of the need to improve the existing cleansing service and to expand the solid and liquid waste management system into the traditional housing locations. These made up an average of 80 per cent of each city's housing stock. This would be a major institutional and equipment undertaking. The development functions were the weakest in the system. Each council needed to improve its construction and maintenance abilities. Each wanted to develop a full town planning capability.

In order to meet the challenge of providing infrastructure and services in the urban sector, the urban management adviser submitted the above analysis to satisfy Target 1 of the project, in January 1992. It set out to identify all the matters to be addressed, the issues arising, action required and a timetable for implementation. In so doing, it highlighted the building blocks for developing the urban management process, namely, policy and budgetary development, infrastructure and services development and organisational and financial development. From this analysis, Blantyre, Mzuzu and Zomba would be in a position to prepare their first strategies; Lilongwe would revise its strategy, already in its third edition. These strategies would present the councils' infrastructure and services proposals, and the organisational and financial plans to show that they were in a fit condition to provide, operate and maintain the infrastructure and services.

Target 2. This concerned the performance of the new town clerks. Within each council, there were key organisational outputs based on the annual policy, budgetary and committee cycle. They included a set of financial and administrative monitoring activities. Each town clerk could be judged initially on whether he had been able to ensure the production (or outputs) on the following; the council's development strategy, the budget and capital programme, the external audit, capital programme monitoring, revenue budget monitoring, financial balances and staffing levels.

The list was a simple but fundamental reflection of the process-dominated activities each town clerk had to ensure were performed by his council. This was basic local government activity. If the council failed to perform these tasks, its town clerk failed at the first hurdle. Additionally, it was necessary to reflect on the personal output of the town clerk. Was he performing? On the assumption that he was, was he performing because of or in spite of the system? Were supporting interventions required from the supervising environment – the Ministry of Local Government?

The new town clerk of Lilongwe assumed sole responsibility for the running of the council in August 1991. He had the advantage of inheriting an established policy and budgetary system. The council's development strategy was already in its third edition. By 30 March 1992, he had prepared the strategy's review report, on time. He prepared the budget and capital programme, submitting it to the Ministry only three weeks late. He was unable to fulfil the external audit; the new computer manager had been poached back to his former private sector employer, thus rendering the computerisation programme in a state of limbo (rates billing and salaries had been computerised; the accounting system was next on the agenda). He prepared quarterly capital programme and budget monitoring statements. He prepared regular financial balances statements. The staffing situation was reported quarterly. The town clerk admitted that the council was slow to respond to his first budget's preparation. Otherwise, he was satisfied with his own outputs. He regarded the system as working reasonably well.

The new town clerk of Blantyre assumed sole responsibility for the running of his council in January 1992. He had the advantage of inheriting an already submitted budget and capital programme for 1992–3. In turn, he prepared the council's first development strategy, with technical assistance. He ensured the conditions for fulfilling the external audit for 1991–2. He held his first quarterly capital programme and budget monitoring meetings. He produced financial balances for the committee cycle. He reviewed his staffing levels. In terms of basic organisational outputs and given the time he had been in post, his biggest challenge was the preparation of the council's development strategy. He did well to respond quickly to the technical assistance on the subject. The result was the council's first strategy, on time and to a required standard.

The new town clerk of Mzuzu assumed sole responsibility for the running of his council in December 1991. He inherited no advantages. Consequently, he prepared the council's budget and capital programme, submitting it to the Ministry on time. He prepared the council's first development strategy, with technical assistance. He was unable to fulfil the external audit requirements because of problems in the treasury service. He held his first quarterly capital programme and budget monitoring meetings. He produced financial balances for the committee cycle. He reviewed the staffing levels. In terms of basic organisational outputs and given the time he had been in post, his biggest challenges were to prepare the budget and the council's first development strategy. He did very well to produce both documents on time (by 31 January and 30 April respectively). He responded well to the technical assistance on preparing the strategy. He had the advantage of being a qualified town planner.

The town clerk of Zomba was transferred from his newly promoted third-tier post in Lilongwe, in February 1991. Zomba was in a dire condition. It needed someone in post to hold the system together, while the previous incumbent went to Britain on training for a year. The new postholder had no advantages of direct technical assistance under the ODA-funded town clerks' project. The consequence was plain to see to the point that the urban management adviser was asked to give early emphasis to Zomba, ahead of his formal programme of work. The first result was an organisational and financial analysis of the council, submitted to the ministry in December 1991. It made a number of recommendations about staffing and a financial strategy. The second result was a restructured budget, capital programme and financial strategy for the council. This was submitted to the Ministry by the council within the statutory deadline of 31 January 1992. Finally, the town clerk was assisted in getting his council's first development strategy prepared. In this regard, he was blessed with the support of a particularly dedicated US Peace Corps volunteer architect. He absorbed the technical assistance, which resulted in Zomba's first development strategy, on time. Despite a serious absence of support staff, the town clerk's work was commendable under very trying circumstances. The final accolade was that on the previous post holder's return from Britain, the council requested that they retain their temporary town clerk, permanently. The ministry had the good sense to agree.

Target 3. This concerned the preparation of an urban management performance framework. It was argued that this would combine two specific objectives:

Target 5.	To advise the Ministry on policy and co-ordination of its activities in support of the four councils, and
Target 3.	To establish an annual planning and review cycle as part of an urban management performance framework.

When the system was viewed in its entirety, it was seen that the two requirements blended into a total urban management performance framework.

This framework had four parts. First was the council's annual planning and review cycle. That was the necessary foundation of the urban management system. Secondly was the need to establish a framework for co-ordinating the Ministry's activities in support of the councils. Thirdly there was the obvious requirement to simply track all the urban and institutional development proposals; were they progressing to a point when they became absorbed into the mainline system? Fourthly was the need to assess each council's performance against explicit criteria. Finally, it was necessary to establish comparative performance criteria between the councils.

By April 1992, each of the four urban councils had an explicit annual policy and budgetary cycle. It was contained in each council's development strategy. The essence of the cycle was two-fold. The first half of the financial year was concerned with reviewing and reporting on development (strategy) and financial (budgetary) performance. It included the need to articulate issues for the following year's strategy and budget. The second half of the year was then dominated by preparing and submitting the following year's strategy and budget. It was logical therefore that any framework for the Ministry's support and co-ordination for the councils should relate to the councils' annual planning cycle. The Ministry agreed. It would host two development progress meetings a year. The first meeting (in early June) would review the previous year's performance of each council. It would also identify issues for the following year's strategy and budget. The second meeting (in early October) would see the development of the issues into clearly specified and costed urban projects or institutional proposals. These would be discussed as part of the following year's draft strategy and draft summary budget. The idea was that the meetings themselves would develop an agenda of specific matters that the ministry would be required to act upon in support of the councils. Furthermore, the councils and Ministry could share in the identification of issues and possible solutions. This represented the process framework which, for the Ministry, did not exist before. What remained was the product framework; the criteria for assessing council performance.

At the first level of product analysis, the demand was to see the various urban and institutional development proposals actually being implemented. Performance therefore concerned things like 'have the plans been prepared for tendering?' or 'has finance been secured for the technical assistance?'. It was fairly mundane. Yet it was a fundamental requirement in the too often ill-managed process of implementation. The result was the refinement of the original urban and institutional development checklist for each council, submitted as part of the urban sector's development issues report. Only after urban and institutional developments had been completed did they become part of the mainline operational system (and budget) of the council. The second level of analysis therefore concerned the performance of the capital developments and service delivery of each council. For example, is the capital project (say, a new market) or the service (say, primary health care) satisfying some explicit performance criteria? At this stage (April 1992) it was too early to advise on the development of operational performance criteria for each council. Lilongwe already had its criteria, as part of its draft annual report. The target for agreeing the other councils' criteria was therefore set at October 1992.

What remained, under the urban management performance framework, was to develop standard criteria for assessing the councils' comparative performance. The judgement criteria was conceived under seven topics. Development concerned the various aspects of funding each city's infrastructure requirements. Trading concerned the basic business efficiency and returns on revenue for council enterprises. Running costs was a comparison from differing perspectives. Staffing and vacancy levels were self-evident. General health centred on each council's underlying financial position. Logistical strength concerned the council's ability to be mobile (transport) and to manipulate information (computers). The performance indicators covered actual costs or numbers. The comparative components covered the costs or numbers as a proportion of a population unit; normally, per head. The comparative performance tables were submitted. They revealed some interesting analysis. Though Lilongwe had the largest infrastructure bill, Mzuzu's was greater in relation to its population. In contrast, Zomba's was the largest in relation to its annual income. The two smaller authorities of Mzuzu and Zomba had significantly higher staffing levels per head of population than the two larger councils. The analysis was revealing and original. Such comparative data had never been available to the ministry or the councils before.

Target 4. This concerned the preparation of the councils' development strategies, or a first review if they already existed. By 30 April, each council had its first strategy; Lilongwe had its first review of its strategy's third edition. The three new strategies flowed from the previously submitted urban and institutional development issues report (Target 1). The first development strategies were appearing at the time of the suggested annual reports. It was important to get the new councils on to the learning curve of preparing the documents. The next editions would appear, in accordance with each council's annual policy and budgetary cycle, and the Ministry's policy support system, by December of 1992. They would include an additional level of analysis. Each city's total infrastructure requirement was presented in each strategy, in project definition and cost terms. However, the total need (and therefore the total cost) of additional (particularly traditional) housing, being generated by the population growth, had still to be calculated.

At the time, thinking was limited to existing and potential plans. The wider shortfall had still to be articulated in order to close the circle of analysis. Also, each strategy went into some detail on the question of affordability. In essence, without full government contributions in lieu of rates, the councils would remain dependent on the largesse of central government. The details of this analysis also had to be expanded, in time for the next edition of each council's strategy.

With the substantive targets for Stage 1 satisfied, it remained to present the outcome of discussions with the four client town clerks; a work programme for the next eighteen months of the project. The conclusion to the submission made it clear that the assignment was dominated by the process of urban management. It sought to introduce and bed-down a system of organisational behaviour that would allow the councils to cope with their rapidly growing cities. The process domination was also an inevitable consequence of the need to make sure that the development proposals (concerning the councils and their cities) were actually progressed to the point of successful implementation. Without implementation (that is, the development actually taking place), the process would be meaningless. The project was therefore presented as follows.

Stage 1. (November 1991 to April 1992).

INITIAL DEVELOPMENT FRAMEWORK

- Zomba: initial assessment.
- Zomba: budget strategy.
1. LL, BL, MZ, ZM issues report.
2. Town clerks' progress.
3. Urban management framework.
4. Development strategies.

Stage 2. (May to October, 1992).

ADDITIONAL POLICY ANALYSIS

5. Development progress report.
6. Development strategies.
7. Town clerks' progress.
8. Operational performance criteria.
9. Housing needs assessment.
10. Infrastructure/financial shortfalls.
11. Ministry support to councils.

Stage 3. (November 1992 to April 1993).

REVIEW OF PERFORMANCE

12. Development performance.
13. Operational performance.
14. Supporting performance.

Stage 4. (May to October, 1993).

CONSOLIDATION AND HANDOVER

15. End of project report.

This programme of activities, along with the analysis for Targets 2 to 4, were submitted to the Ministry of Local Government, ODA and the World Bank in April 1992.

This submission, which concluded Stage 1 of the project, was summarised as follows. All three town clerks, recruited and trained under the original town clerks' project, not only remain in post, but also show clear signs of developing into good urban chief executives. Additionally, the town clerk for Zomba (now part of this project) had shown remarkable resilience and determination under very difficult circumstances. With the prospect of additional assistance, his situation can only improve. All four councils submitted and received ministerial approval to their budgets, before the beginning of the next financial year. This was a significant improvement on the beginning of the first project in 1989, when no council achieved this target. Each council now had a development strategy to govern their urban (infrastructure and services) and institutional (organisational and financial) development.

There was now an urban management performance framework as a common reference point for the councils and the Ministry to gauge their absolute and relative performance. This included a new system of ministerial support and co-ordination of policy meetings with the councils. Stage 1 of the project was completed and to a reasonable level of success, especially concerning policy development and strategic thinking.

Stage 2

Target 5. Development progress involved the conception and production of a development performance framework for each council. The framework would allow each council (and its parent ministry) to follow progress and to co-ordinate and monitor development. The framework centred on each council's development strategy (already prepared/revised under the first stage of the project). Each strategy focused on infrastructure, services, organisational and financial development. The output was a technical analysis and the production of the development performance framework for each council. The impact was the absorption of this analysis into the routine development progress assessment by each council's town clerk.

Target 6. The publication of each council's first development strategy (the first review for Lilongwe) was recorded in the first progress report. Since then, a review and updating process had taken place. This was incorporating additional technical analysis (see below). The review and preparation cycle saw the formal incorporation of the Ministry of Local Government into the process. It chaired its first review meeting in early June, and its first planning meeting in early October. The output was to assist each town clerk to absorb the technical analysis concerning the future urban development of their cities. It also involved the revision of each council's strategy. For the parent ministry, it was to steer it through its first review and planning meetings with the cities' town clerks. The impact was the revision of the strategies with a contribution from the Ministry of Local Government.

Target 7. The town clerks were guided on the various technical aspects of the urban management framework, including the development of operational performance criteria. The output was dominated by technical submissions for and explanations to the town clerks on four key items. These were the development performance framework, the operational performance framework, the housing needs assessment and the infrastructure and financial shortfalls for respectively, their cities and their councils. The immediate impact was the incorporation of this work into their revised development strategies. The longer term test would be to see if the town clerks could reproduce both the technical analysis and to incorporate it into subsequent editions of their strategies. At this time, they depended on the urban management adviser.

Target 8. The operational performance criteria was conceived and structured for all four councils. The model was taken from the previous work in Lilongwe. The output was to lead the technical debate on the performance criteria for each council. The impact was the acceptance of the criteria by all the town clerks. The operational performance criteria was similar for each council.

Target 9. The housing needs assessment involved the construction of a framework for assessing urban growth and the resultant need for serviced plots for housing. It was a technical contribution to each council's strategy. The output was the technical analysis and production of the assessment framework for each council. The impact was the incorporation of the analysis into each council's development strategy. This should not be underestimated. The original development strategies (including Lilongwe's) reflected feelings, as opposed to hard analysis, about what was needed. This was tempered by the existing institutional capacity of the councils to provide the infrastructure for the serviced plots for (particularly) traditional housing – which made up about 80 per cent of each city's stock. With the analysis in place, the emphasis could shift to strengthening the capacity, systems and procedures of the councils to satisfy the quantified need for serviced plots.

Target 10. The infrastructure needs of each city and the financial consequences for each council were contained in each council's development strategy. The need was to extract that information in summary form, to allow for local and comparative analysis. It was also a required follow-up to the outcome of the housing needs assessment. The output was a technical analysis of the infrastructure needs and financial shortfalls for each city and its council. The impact was the incorporation of this analysis into each council's development strategy. Again, this analysis should not be underestimated. It was alluded to in the original cities and councils development issues report (Target 1).

Target 11. The councils' urban management performance was conditioned by the support offered by their policy and supervising environment; in this case, the Ministry of Local Government (MLG). This ranged from the speed of decisions on specific recommendations (requiring MLG approval), the extent of progress on negotiating about development issues with other government departments (requiring MLG action on behalf of the councils) to the progress towards securing technical assistance (requiring MLG action on the World Bank's Local Government Development Project, for the councils). The specific technical output was to prepare a performance framework for the Ministry of Local Government. The immediate impact was to crystallise MLG's activities and specific actions required, in support of the council's urban and institutional development. Two major constraints were identified.

At the beginning of the assignment, the urban management adviser was asked by the Ministry to prepare a report on the institutional (organisational and financial) difficulties facing Zomba Council, as a matter of urgency. The report was first submitted in December 1991. In September 1992, a summary review was presented to the Ministry, arising from a regular field visit. Progress was scored at 40 per cent. Three key posts had still not been approved for creation. The general manpower proposals, as part of the organisational development component of the council's first development strategy, had still not been considered.

At the first ministry review meeting in support of the council's development initiatives, issues were raised concerning central government's responsibility for (a) funding the construction of new arterial roads and (b) funding the services for development land. The Ministry was unable to get the Ministry of Works to respond to an issues paper presented in March 1992. The Ministry had not even raised the issue of development funding with the government's Department of Lands and Valuation. The result was that progress towards releasing funds for badly needed infrastructure was thwarted.

The analysis for Stage 2, was submitted to the Ministry of Local Government, ODA and the World Bank on 30 October 1992. It was summarised as follows. All three town clerks, recruited and trained under the original town clerks' project, are still in post. Each month, they develop stronger technical skills and acclimatise themselves to the sometimes turbulent nature of urban management, both from a political (councillors) and technical (officers) point of view. The municipality of Zomba's town clerk is weaker, not having benefited from the original ODA-funded town clerks' project. Additional support is in the offing for him. All four councils now have an established annual planning and review cycle. This integrates their policy and budgetary planning systems. All four councils have development strategies. They integrate infrastructure and services planning with organisational and financial planning. They are currently being revised and updated, based on the additional analysis (noted above). The development of appropriate co-ordination and monitoring instruments for the urban management process for, (a) the development and (b) operational performance frameworks of the councils and (c) MLG's development performance in support of the councils, has been established. Finally, concern was expressed about the sustainability of the established urban management process, after the urban management adviser's departure. This last point is discussed in Chapter 10.

Stage 2 of the project was completed and to a reasonable level of success, especially concerning additional policy analysis, performance assessment criteria, and a system of policy support and co-ordination from MLG.

Stage 3

Stage 3 was dominated by an assessment of the established urban management system's performance. Arising from all the preceding analysis under Stages 1 and 2 of the project, the concept of the urban management performance was considered as three separate components; development, operational and supporting performance.

Target 12. In urban terms, development performance concerned all those matters that took a project from initial proposal to the start of construction. In institutional terms, it meant all those matters which turn a proposal into new organisational structures and/or processes. In both cases, only after the development had taken place, did the project or proposal become operational. There were three areas of development performance. They concerned policy, urban and institutional development. The aggregate percentage scores for each component of development performance were:

- Policy   100 per cent
- Urban   32 per cent
- Institutional   66 per cent

Policy development concerned the activities and processes involved in each council's development strategy and budget. The councils had all done uniformly well, at 100 per cent. They each prepared strategies in April (as an initial review). Their consolidated annual strategies appeared by Christmas. Their budgets were regularly monitored (at least quarterly). Their new budgets were submitted within the statutory deadline.

Urban development concerned all the infrastructure and services proposals to have a direct impact in each city. In particular, it concerned arterial infrastructure, serviced land for (non-traditional area) development, serviced and upgraded land for traditional housing areas (THAs), and specific urban projects. The councils' general performance was rated as a poor 32 per cent. The two bigger councils achieved an average (poor) 45 per cent; the two smaller, an average (very poor) 22 per cent. There were mitigating circumstances for this. First, the councils were only starting to build a meaningful urban development capability (including the administration of traditional housing areas (THAs) recently taken over from the Malawi Housing Corporation). Secondly, their collective engineering capacity remained desperately weak (despite efforts to arrest the situation). Finally, because the development strategies sought to integrate all agencies in the development process, they had to accept that over half the funding responsibilities were entirely outside their control. This simply illustrated the enormity of the task facing the city councils as they:

- fought for infrastructure funds to lever private sector investment in urban development generally, and
- sought to encourage parastatals and central government to fund their components of the infrastructure need.

Institutional development concerned those specific measures being introduced to strengthen existing or develop new services in the cities. The councils' general performance was rated as a modest 66 per cent. In the end, only two projects were accepted under the Local Government Development Project (LGDP) for direct benefit to the councils; a maintenance expert(s) to improve systems and procedures. The other was the establishment of a Town Planning and Housing Management Service (to take over town planning and traditional housing responsibilities from, respectively, central government and the housing corporation) all in accordance with the government's general development policy for the country.

In summary, each council's development planning systems and their documents were now in place. However, implementation of the various proposals was (inevitably) much slower. LGDP's emphasis on strengthening MLG's technical capacity, to allow it to support the councils, would go some way to strengthen the councils' development and implementation capacity. However, the councils themselves also needed to strengthen their own project development, implementation and financing capabilities. Arguably, this was the focus of LGDP; its first component for the city councils being the preparation and review of development strategies and the supporting processes and techniques.

Target 13. There were three areas of operational performance. They concerned finance (inputs), efficiency (outputs) and effectiveness (impacts). Their respective aggregate scores were:

- Finance   45 per cent
- Efficiency   69 per cent
- Effectiveness   63 per cent

The financial assessment concerned a basic variance analysis; comparing end-of-year (predicted) expenditure with the budget for that year. The councils' general performance was a poor 45 per cent. All scores hovered in the fifties, except for Blantyre; it scored a surprising 28 per cent, based on its estimates for 1993–4 (which included revised figures for 1992–3). A small improvement to Blantyre's returns would lift the general rating from poor to modest.

Efficiency was the test of a council's departmental programmes (or tasks) against explicit and quantifiable performance targets. The specific concern was for the output of the operations. The councils' general performance was a modest 69 per cent. This was, in fact, encouraging because it missed the good scoreline by only one per cent. Mzuzu scored a surprising 80 per cent under this category.

Effectiveness was the test of a council's departmental programmes (or tasks) against explicit and quantifiable performance targets. The specific concern was for the impact of the operations. The councils' general performance was a modest 63 per cent. The score was slightly depressed by Lilongwe's 58 per cent against an upper sixties in the other cities. This depressed score was a result of the council's inability to implement its ambitious capital programme. The simple reason was a lack of finance.

In summary, the system in general was operating modestly. The required improvements were all in the realms of traditional operational management practice. Despite the rating, this represented the best of the three performing components of the urban management process.

Target 14. Supporting performance concerned the environment in which the local government system operated. In this case it was the legal and policy environment of the government, implemented through the Ministry of Local Government. Three categories of performance were involved. These concerned general policy reviews and studies, general development issues (shared by all the city councils) and specific proposals (in this case, for Zomba). The summary percentage scores for each city were as follows:

- Policy   22 per cent
- Issues   34 per cent
- Zomba   63 per cent

Policy concerned all the matters arising from the World Bank's Local Government Development Project, that had a direct bearing on the city councils. These were essential policy reviews (like the review of legislation) that would improve the legal environment within which the individual local authorities operated. Progress was rated at a very poor 22 per cent. This was partly because there was a delay in achieving credit effectiveness (from October 1992 till January 1993). Consequent administrative activities, to get things moving, were delayed. ODA contributed to the low score by not having separate funding available for the second phase of the review of local government legislation.

Issues concerned all the matters that were of central concern to the councils, that were directly influenced by the government through the Ministry of Local Government. These were essential matters such as the need to clarify responsibility for funding arterial (or trunk) roads in the four cities. Progress was rated at a modest 33 per cent. The government was simply slow when dealing with its urban sector.

At the start of the project, and at the request of the ministry, a quick review of Zomba Council's situation was undertaken. This was in the context that no institutional development had been offered to the council under the previous first phase of ODA's city councils' (town clerks') project. The result was a set of organisational and related recommendations. Progress was a modest (but encouraging) 63 per cent. The principal reason for this score was the Ministry's approval to upgrade the council's salaries (this performance variable, or component, being given a high weighting, in the support performance schedule).

In summary, the nature of the development being considered was disparate and subject to various administrative delays. Progress was slow but in Zomba's case, it was in the right direction (such as on the Zomba salaries).

In this project, urban management as a process was seen as three inter-related activities. They concerned the development and operation of, and support for, the local government system. In this case, the focus was four urban councils. The aggregate scores for each component was:

- Development   41 per cent
- Operations   59 per cent
- Support   31 per cent

To summarise the general performance assessment, the urban management system just made the modest performance category. An ideal standard to aim for was a uniform good. This would mean aiming to improve the scores for each variable to something over 69 per cent. The system had some way to go. The strongest component was the councils' policy development. The weakest component was MLG's policy support. All these ratings and scores were taken from the individual council assessment sheets, averaged for the collective scores.

The system's ability to generate development was hampered by technical and financial weaknesses in the four councils. Also, many supporting agencies (such as central government's Department of Lands and Valuation – DLV) seemed frighteningly inactive (e.g. in the provision of serviced land for general (i.e. non-THA) development).

The system's financial operations remained weak and needed to be strengthened. The efficiency of the system received the highest overall rating. With the quantified performance targets, the scores helped to belie some ill-informed judgements about how the major councils were performing. The effectiveness score was a bit less but remained reasonable, given the current technical, logistical and financial constraints.

The system's support mechanism was the weakest link. It was hampered, in part, by the disparate nature of the help required. Policy decisions, in support of the urban sector, took time to emanate from government.

The two larger cities just made the modest category because of their relatively stronger development performance. The two smaller cities scored at the top end of the poor category. Despite relatively stronger scores in operational performance, the smaller councils were significantly weaker in development performance.

This was the first time the urban management system had been fully tested as a quantified process. The results confirmed impressions about weak development and supporting performance. The surprise was the reasonable showing on operations. However, the system needed to upgrade itself across the board before it could achieve a uniform target of good, or at least 70 per cent.

The analysis for Stage 3 was submitted to the Ministry of Local Government, ODA and the World Bank in April, 1993. Apart from the continuing progress on the four main elements of the project, particular mention was made of the town clerks' developing skills and maturity in having to contend with both the pressures of the (then) proposed referendum and secondly, a stringent financial environment. The summary noted:

> The town clerks have had to guide their councils to absorb the unprecedented (and not budgeted for) salary and wage increases . . . With no consequent rates increase in any city, to take account of the increased labour costs, the councils have had to fall back on their reserves and cut general expenditure, particularly on development. Without that shock to the local government financial system, each council would have been in a more robust position at the start of the financial year 1993–94.

Stage 4

Target 15. What remained was to prepare an end of tour report. It was submitted in August 1993. The report suggested that the real test was to compare the city councils and their development thinking at the start and the end of the project. The assertion was that progress had been significant.

In terms of developing and transferring a process of urban management and its supporting techniques, the required (development strategy) outputs had been achieved. As the report stated: 'They are now reviewed and updated annually.'

In terms of enhancing the capabilities of the town clerks, their policy and budgetary cycle, and the policy co-ordination function of their parent ministry, the output had been real; 'the impact was discernible'.

The urban management system's performance (that is, the product of the established urban management process) had an aggregate weighted score of 50 per cent and was (just) rated as modest. The main strength was in policy development (very good). The main weaknesses were in the technical and financial capacity to turn the development strategies into infrastructure provision (poor).

Many of the obstacles to individual council performance resided in the supervising environment. These were now to be addressed through a series of policy review studies and related technical assistance, under the World Bank's Local Government Development Project.

Part of Chapter 10 reviews the question of sustainability.

A short fourth progress report was submitted in November 1993, at the project's conclusion. It made observations on each of the four components of the terms of reference; the annual planning and review cycle, development strategies, co-ordinating and monitoring, and the town clerks. The observations on the first three components were that 'no further action is required'. On the fourth, it was recommended that ODA considers supporting 'a succession strategy for potential future town clerks'. After three years, the incumbent British-trained Malawian town clerks were beginning to show signs of a desire to face new challenges.

In conclusion, after a second year of labour unrest, and after the pressures that were brought to bear on the councils by the wage settlements of 1992, 'one can safely suggest that the Malawian town clerks have come of age'.

In summary, implementation focused on policy analysis, planning documentation and skills transfer. The main instrument for ID was an advisory role; the expert was located in the supervising ministry. He made frequent visits to each of the four urban local authorities. Chapter 10 reviews the ID performance of this policy and planning capability case.

10 Institutional Development Performance

This chapter seeks to identify the influences that determined progress in this case of developing a policy and planning capability. It therefore considers three topics:

- CONSTRAINTS
- ADDITIONAL ID
- IMPACT, SUSTAINABILITY AND CONSOLIDATION.

CONSTRAINTS

It was noted above that there were two major constraints to the progress on the project. One was the lack of progress in presenting issues to other ministries for resolution, on behalf of the councils. The second was the seemingly endless delays in making decisions on recommendations requested urgently by the same ministry almost one year previously, for the weakest of the major councils. By the end of the assignment report, significant progress had been made. On the first, the level of difficulty and frustration felt by the town clerks, over the lack of support from government in general, especially on the general issue of encouraging the city-building process, through the urban management system, was addressed at the policy and co-ordination (review) meeting of July, 1993. Immediately after, the Ministry of Local Government called meetings with the other offending ministries and government departments to address the following issues. First, was access to development land for traditional and general development. Secondly, was the provision of the arterial road network in the cities. Thirdly, was the formal transfer of (the already informally transferred) local planning and development control processes. Each item was an attempt to force the pace of central government policy on decentralisation (in this case, of the city-building process) to the major local authorities. In turn, each item illustrated the classic symptoms of (a) institutional resistance to change and (b) central government's reluctance to decentralise power and resources to local government.

209

On the second topic, decisions started emerging in favour of Zomba Municipal Council. The first included the upgrading of staff salaries (to allow it to compete in the labour market with its city council competitors). The second was to approve the creation of three key new posts (two of the four departments – engineering and health/cleansing – having no chief officer post; the third having ambitions to computerise from scratch, but with no computer operator post on the establishment).

In summary, there were two constraints. First was the supervising ministry's seeming inability to push for support for all aspects of urban and institutional development, through the other relevant government ministries and departments. Second, was the inability to reach decisions (again) on organisational and manpower issues.

ADDITIONAL ID

There were two additional outputs identified, in the course of the assignment. One concerned the production of an urban management manual. The second concerned the production of an urban infrastructure paper.

In the second progress report, it was noted that the town clerks 'are the established counterparts to this assignment'. Despite this, concern was expressed, both by the counterpart town clerks and ODA, at the lack of a counterpart in the supervising ministry. It was noted that the ideal scenario is that the town clerks will be able to produce their strategies and review reports regularly and in accordance with their annual planning and review cycle. The Ministry would merely have to respond with understanding and action where appropriate. However, the need for a back-up or contingency mechanism in MLG to support the councils was seen to be reasonable. The idea of an urban management manual was therefore agreed.

The urban management manual would concern itself with the processes required to satisfy the annual planning and review cycle. It would identify and describe the key activities, offer a timetable, and maximum and minimum times for their completion. The manual would be made available to the councils (to reinforce the existing systems of analysis and processes for production) and to the ministry. The ministry's supporting role, particularly in the processes, would be emphasised. This was seen as a reasonable way of reinforcing (a) the technical capability of the town clerks and (b) the supporting role of MLG. The first draft of the manual was included as an appendix to the assignment's third progress report.

The third progress report hoped that the end of assignment report would include a policy paper on the pressing issue of funding urban infrastructure provision. It was felt that this was an important additional component of analysis. It concerned the need (and mechanics) for, and the consequences of not providing, the infrastructure urgently required in Malawi's rapidly growing cities. If that paper could be achieved, it was felt that the circle of analysis, starting with the development strategies (outputs and bids) and finishing with implementation (impacts and consequences), would be completed. The paper was attached to the end of assignment report. It argued for the development of a strategy, programme, budget and consequence or SPBC analysis.

The strategy (**S**) was the base point for concerted action to provide the infrastructure to support the construction of buildings (houses, shops, offices, factories) or superstructure. The programme (**P**) turned the strategy into a set of timed investments. The budget (**B**) ensured the funding capacity to implement the strategy, through its programme. The consequences desired (**C1**) were the ideal outcome of the strategy's implementation; hence **SPBC1**.

Each council's likely programme was calculated (**SPBC2**). These programmes presented an increasing backlog in infrastructure provision (consequences or **C2**). In terms of serviced housing plots, the depressing picture was one of squatting increasing as a percentage of serviced housing stock. This was to the point where squatting overtook serviced housing as the main form of shelter provision. This would represent an abject failure of the urban management system.

Clearly both additional items of technical assistance were required. The first would ensure a practical and robust relationship between each council's strategy and budget. The second would highlight the consequences of that relationship in terms of the twin urban bottom lines of squatting and infrastructure shortfalls. What remained was to assess whether any of this work had a practical impact and was sustainable.

In summary, there were two additional major outputs. First was the need to prepare an urban management manual to strengthen: (a) the technical capacity of the chief executives; and (b) the supporting role of their ministry. Secondly was the need to prepare a policy paper to spell out not only the need for infrastructure provision in the urban sector, but also the consequences of it not being provided.

IMPACT, SUSTAINABILITY AND CONSOLIDATION

The project was dominated by the challenge of establishing an urban management system in the four largest urban councils. Quoting from the councils' new urban management manual:

> Urban management is the process of (a) planning for, providing and maintaining a city's infrastructure and services, and (b) making sure that the [city's] councils are in a fit state, organisationally and financially, to do so. The council is therefore concerned with both urban and institutional development.

The tangible documents were the councils' development strategies and their performance reviews (the latter subsequently incorporated in their first annual reports). The question was to gauge the impact of the new urban management system by testing its sustainability.

The four town clerks collectively addressed the question, 'is the urban management system sustainable?' The question was asked in relation to the four components of the project's terms of reference: the town clerks; the annual planning cycle; development strategies; and co-ordination and monitoring. For each component, a number of activities were considered.

The sustainability of the town clerks was assessed in relation to three management activities. First, was advising the councils (the need for intellect, tact and patience). Secondly, was working with councillors (the need for rapport, humour and guile). Finally was managing staff (the need for some human resource development skills). The 'bottom line' was that, all other things being equal, would the various management skills needed to give technical leadership to the councils, be sustained and be likely to self-development? The collective sustainability rating was very good, with a score of 95 per cent. All four town clerks felt equally confident with this component.

The sustainability of the annual planning and review cycle was assessed in relation to four management activities. First, was to ensure the process of a strategy and budget review. Secondly, was to ensure the preparation of an annual report. Thirdly, was to ensure the process of strategy and budget preparation. Finally, was to ensure the preparation of strategy and budget documents. The 'bottom line' was that, all other things being equal, would the various management skills needed to give the driving force to the urban management process, be sustained and be likely to self-development? The collective sustainability rating was very good, with a score of 91 per cent. There was a 10 per cent variation in individual scores. Two town clerks emerged as very good; the other two as good. The lowest score was 85 per cent.

The sustainability of preparing and reviewing the development strategy was assessed in relation to six technical activities. The first set of three concerned the strategy. These were population growth and housing need/supply analysis; strategy, programme, budget and consequence (SPBC) analysis (i.e. of planned and likely outcomes); and finally, financial analysis of the strategy in relation to council resources. The second set of three concerned the reviews of development performance, operating performance and comparative performance. The 'bottom line' was that, all other things being equal, would the various technical skills needed to prepare the development strategy and annual review report, be sustained and be likely to self-development? The collective sustainability rating was very good, with a score of 90 per cent. There was a 15 per cent variation in individual scores. Again, two town clerks emerged as very good; the other two as good. The lowest score was 82 per cent.

Whereas the first three items were a direct function of the councils, through or by their town clerks, this last item was a matter for the supporting ministry. The sustainability of the co-ordination and monitoring system was assessed in relation to two activities. First was the technical one of reviewing supporting performance. The second was a managerial one of holding review and planning meetings. The 'bottom line' was that, all other things being equal, would the technical skills and managerial effort to implement the policy and co-ordination process be sustained and be likely to self-development? The collective sustainability rating was modest, with a score of 30 per cent.

The ratings and scores were taken from the individual council assessment sheets, averaged for the collective scores. The town clerks were confident that if left to their own devices, they could sustain and develop their own capabilities. They felt equally confident about the annual planning and review cycle. There was slightly less confidence about the technical analysis required to prepare the development strategies; given time, that would take care of itself. The least confidence was felt about the likely support to come from the ministry. In all respects, the parting gift from the assignment was the urban management manual.

A collective sustainability rating of good and score of 87 per cent was encouraging under the circumstances. However, it had to be remembered that the new urban management process was dominated by operating and technical constraints. These existed within the local government system as a whole. No matter how well the town clerks and their urban management process could perform, its supervising environment and its component technical weaknesses remained. These weaknesses had to be addressed. What the urban management process offered was a dynamic and integrated policy framework for each city council, within which other support could be placed. The other support would concern the urban management system's supervising environment. It would therefore focus on regulatory and procedural reform.

In summary, the impact was determined, in consultation with the client chief executives, in terms of the four main components of the project. Sustainability was therefore quantitively assessed in terms of the probability of 'self-development'. If the chief executives were not interfered with, the sustainability analysis was rated as good with a score of 87 per cent.

Summary to Part V

Part V has analysed a case of developing a policy and planning capability in the urban sector of a third world country. Chapter 9 reviewed the project. Chapter 10 looked at various aspects of its institutional development performance. The underlying issues from each of the six individual sections are summarised as follows.

PROJECT DEVELOPMENT

Project formulation

The initial project formulation was a less discrete but still, essentially, a closed process. However, this applied only to the outputs for the first quarter (the first six months) of the project. The British government responded to a request, from both the government of Malawi and the World Bank, to carry the policy and planning experience of Lilongwe to the other three major urban authorities. The project was drafted by the World Bank, with ODA and government of Malawi observations. Consultation with the identified adviser was undertaken. In essence, the project was requested by the ministry, after discussions with client councils; the councils were not involved in project formulation.

Outputs required

The project had specific outputs to be achieved for its first six months. During that time, the adviser, in consultation with the client councils, had to develop a programme for the remainder of the assignment. This was done. In essence, three-quarters of the project's outputs were determined in direct consultation with the client councils.

Implementation

Implementation concerned policy analysis, planning documentation and skills transfer. The main instrument for ID was an advisory role; the expert was located in the supervising ministry. He made frequent visits to each of the four urban local authorities. In essence, the main instrument of ID was an advisory role.

215

INSTITUTIONAL DEVELOPMENT PERFORMANCE

Constraints

There were two constraints. First was the supervising ministry's seeming inability to push for support for all aspects of urban and institutional development, through the other relevant government ministries and departments. Secondly was the inability to reach decisions (again) on organisational and manpower issues. In essence, the supervising ministry was weak in its attempts to persuade government in general to support various development initiatives.

Additional ID

There were two additional major outputs. The first was the need to prepare an urban management manual to strengthen (a) the technical capacity of the chief executives and (b) the supporting role of their ministry. The second was to prepare a policy paper to spell out not only the need for infrastructure provision in the urban sector, but also the consequences of it not being provided. In essence, the additional ID was a natural consequence of the iterative and learning approach, concerning the need for a manual and an urban development policy paper.

Impact, sustainability and consolidation

The impact was determined, in consultation with the client chief executives, in terms of the four main components of the project. Sustainability was therefore quantitively assessed in terms of the probability of 'self-development'. If the chief executives were not interfered with, the sustainability analysis was rated as good with a score of 87 per cent. In essence, the impact, sustainability and consolidation were achieved.

The conclusions to this chapter are therefore as follows:

1. The project was requested by the ministry, after discussions with client councils; the councils were not involved in initial project formulation.
2. Three-quarters of the project's outputs were determined in direct consultation with the client councils.
3. The main instrument of ID was an advisory role.
4. The supervising ministry was weak in its attempts to persuade government in general to support various development initiatives.

5. The additional ID was a natural consequence of the iterative and learning approach, concerning the identified need for a manual and an urban development policy paper.
6. The impact, sustainability and consolidation were achieved.

At this stage, the advisory role of implementation, the exploratory nature of the project's development and efforts to measure the prospects for sustainability should be noted.

The tabulation of the urban management system's sustainability analysis is presented in Table 4.1.

Table 4.1   Is the urban management system sustainable?

TERMS OF REFERENCE	COMPONENTS (M = managerial; T = technical)		OBSERVATIONS	Probability % score	% weight	Weighted % score
1. TOWN CLERKS	1. advising the council	M	Full confidence expressed in these three components, and scored accordingly.	100	9	9
	2. working with councillors	M		90	8	7
'To support the cities town clerks in developing local urban management leadership'	3. managing staff	M	[Opinion shared by all town clerks.]	95	10	10
2. ANNUAL PLANNING & REVIEW CYCLE	1. plan & budget review	M	Full confidence expressed in the two process items. Slightly less	100	6	6
	2. review (annual) report	M	confidence, though still very well scored, on the production of the	79	4	3
'To establish an annual planning & review cycle on key institutional & urban development issues'	3. plan & budget preparation	M	reviews and strategies.	100	8	8
	4. plan (development strategy) & budget documents	M	[Slight variations agreed by all town clerks.]	83	6	5
3. DEVELOPMENT STRATEGY	**Strategy preparation:**					
	1. housing need / supply analysis	T	The one potential (relative) weaknesses is in the technical work	64	8	5
'To give particular attention to the four councils' preparation, implementation & review of development strategies, ensuring that both institutional	2. SPBC analysis	T	for the strategy.	74	10	7
	3. funding analysis	T	[Slight variations agreed by all the town clerks.]	100	8	8
	Performance review:					
	4. development performance analysis	T	Full confidence expressed on the	100	8	8

(organisational & financial) & urban (infrastructure & services) issues are addressed'					
5. operational performance analysis	T	technical aspects of the performance review.	100	8	8
6. comparative performance analysis	T	[Opinions shared by all town clerks.]	100	2	2
4. CO-ORDINATION & MONITORING					
'To advise MLG on policy & co-ordination of MLG activities in support of the four councils, including the creation of appropriate co-ordination & monitoring instruments'					
1. supporting performance analysis	T	Little confidence in MLG's ability to prepare supporting performance analysis.	10	4	0
2. review & planning meetings	M	Even chance of MLG calling the annual review and planning meetings. [Town clerks have agreed a contingency arrangement to help MLG ensure that these strategically important meetings take place.]	50	1	1
		Totals: n/a		100	87

Rating for sustainability scores. e.g. VG = very good chance of sustainability & self-development. Over 89% = VG; 70–89% = Good; 50–69% = Modest; 30–49% = Poor; Under 30% = VP.

SUSTAINABILITY RATING & SCORE   GOOD: 87%

Part VI

Institutional Development Synthesis

Part VI synthesises the lessons from the two institutional development projects in relation to the earlier theoretical text. Chapter 11 offers a structure to ID in relation to the conclusions in Part I. Chapter 12 identifies the key features of city management and the institutional development imperatives for third world city management, in relation to Parts II and III.

11 Structuring ID Practice

This chapter seeks to identify the basic operational characteristics of the institutional development process. It therefore considers two topics:

- SYNTHESIS OF THEORY AND PRACTICE
- STRUCTURING THE PRACTICE.

SYNTHESIS OF THEORY AND PRACTICE

An initial conceptual framework for the institutional development process was presented at the end of Part I. This was in terms of its scope, its modes of intervention and factors for success (see Table 1.1 at the end of Part I). This section now looks at these variables of institutional development in theory and practice. This is a precursor to settling on an operating structure of the process that draws on the strengths of both the theory and the practice.

Scope of the process

Authors presented the idea of sustainability to be the key to all institutional development. Without some prospect of sustainability, the ID would, at best, facilitate specific project implementation, dominated, as it usually is, by various forms of technical assistance. When this technical assistance was withdrawn, the strengthened institutional performance would lapse. In practice, the conclusion to the organisational restructuring and strengthening case offered a qualified prognosis on sustainability, subject to additional assistance. The conclusion to the policy and planning capability case presented a structured and quantified assessment of the sustainability of the established systems and procedures.

Authors suggested that the iterative, learning and experimental model of ID was to be favoured above the stricter project approach. The practice gave out mixed signals. The first case saw a project prepared by the host government in consultation with a bilateral donor; there was no consultation with the client city council. The learning and experimentation (concerning the conception of development strategies) was in spite of the terms of reference. The second case saw a project prepared by the host government, in consultation with a bilateral and multilateral agency and with the proposed technical adviser. The learning and experimentation was built into the terms of reference by only prescribing one quarter (the first half year) of the outputs required. The remainder unfolded in direct consultation with the client town clerks.

Authors offered the concept of the value of an organisation to be the binding component of an institution. Value, beyond the mere instrumentality of the organisation, turned it into an institution. The practice produced little evidence to suggest that value was the intrinsic quality of the local government system. Despite this, efforts were made to develop the local government system to the point where it would be recognised in the country at large, as a force for the good.

The theoretical view was that the nature of ID encompassed a political and not a technical rationality. The two related case studies would suggest a strong concern for technical outputs. However, it is contended that these outputs were seen as a means to an end and not an end in themselves. The end was the desire to intervene in the political economy of the city (supporting economic development and the informal sector). It was argued that this end was not expressed in the technical rationality of, say, land use patterns or council financial surpluses.

Authors suggested that institutions have a pivotal role in the development process. In essence, all development needs are filtered through institutions and carried out by institutions. From the two related case studies, the institution of local government (assuming value beyond instrumentality), was seen as the driving force to an embryonic urban management process. In turn that process sought to understand the needs of the city and to ensure each council's provision of infrastructure and services to satisfy those needs.

Authors suggested the need to release local potential for self-help. At every stage of the case studies, the desire was to establish structures, systems and procedures in consultation with the clients and to support the opportunities for self-development. In turn, the output of that ID (an urban management system) was designed to provide the infrastructure to allow enterprises and households to expand for themselves.

A concept of political software was introduced. This is an allusion to the quality of relations between people, departments and organisations. The first case study developed a corporate management system. The second case study saw an inter-organisational planning and monitoring process being established.

A concern for human and financial resources was seen as an important feature of ID. It is. These resources lubricate the whole system. A concern for these resources underpinned both case studies. The first was as part of a general strengthening of the organisation. The second was to develop expertise to prepare, and funds to pay for, the development strategies.

Structures, processes and outputs were the last general characteristics of the scope of ID. Organisational structures dominated the first case, and organisational processes dominated the second.

Modes of intervention

Assessing the environment was seen as the necessary precursor to strategic intervention in the organisation. The influence of the environment was forced into the first case and written into the second.

Structures and organisation were the second most commonly cited variables. They dominated the first case of organisational restructuring and strengthening.

Policy and management processes were the second equal most common variable. It dominated the second case of building a policy and planning capability.

Personnel and training was also signalled as a central feature. It pervaded both cases; the first in terms of a training strategy to tackle specific weaknesses, the second in terms of the building the specific skills to run an urban management process.

Finance was identified. It also pervaded both cases; the first in terms of strengthening the position; the second in terms of funding infrastructure and services.

The legal framework and government regulations was recognised by multilateral practitioners. It did not feature in either case. However, it was clear that the regulatory environment had to be tackled, in order to create a more supportive style of relationship between the parent ministry and the local authorities. The allusion here is to a decentralised local government where, for example, the parent ministry is not having to take decisions on appointments and organisational structures. Both were sources of frustration, particularly in the first case.

Inter-institutional arrangements were seen as an important shift of emphasis, from the preoccupation with individual organisations. This was an important concern of the second case study. In particular, the local authorities encouraged their parent ministry to take a more positive role in persuading other ministries and government departments, with responsibility for urban infrastructure provision, to perform.

Remuneration and incentives to performance became a de facto element of the first case, where a new salary structure was conceived. It reduced the salary range from thirty-four overlapping grades to a linear spine of ten grades. The grades were then set against the tiers of staff. Finally, the tiers of staff and therefore the salary grades became comparable in the local authorities; an important feature in trying to achieve government's desire for a unified local government system.

Factors for success

Project leadership and environmental support were seen as very important by certain authors. The project leadership in the first case was a donor-funded expert holding an executive position within the organisation to be strengthened. The project leadership in the second case was a donor-funded expert holding an advisory position in the ministry, supervising the client councils. The environmental support in both cases was from the parent ministry. In each case, the constraints section identified various aspects of poor support, in terms of slow or non-existent decision making from the supervising ministry.

Project clarity and clear goals were seen by authors as the second most important factors for success. In both cases, the project goals and specific outputs were clearly presented. This aided the success of the first and second cases. In particular, the first case highlighted the importance of tackling short-term urgent items before moving on to the medium-term strategic aspects of manpower reviews and organisational restructuring, in relation to future development priorities. The second case highlighted the importance of getting on to the learning curve of preparing a quick (and inevitably incomplete) development strategy. With the first attempt in place, it was easier to add additional analysis and build on the experience.

Beneficiary and counterpart involvement was seen by authors as important to ID success. It figured prominently in the first and second cases. However, training permeated all aspects of the local government system. The training proposals were drawn by the ministry; favouring itself in specific recommendations, despite the vast majority of employees being in the local government service. From that point, the client councils were not closely involved in preparing the training strategy.

Autonomy and accountability were acknowledged features of success. In both cases, there were regular (half-yearly) review meetings to account for progress. There was an almost excessive autonomy in the two cases.

Writers suggested that project scale (i.e. small and with few components) was a factor for success. The first case had 19 specific outputs to be fulfilled. The second case had 15 specific outputs. While project scale is important, in order to retain the clarity of outputs required, it is also necessary to keep (almost ruthlessly) to the agreed time-table. The amorphous nature of the ID process can lead practitioners to drift and let target dates slip. That should be avoided at all costs. An organisation can get a sense of forward momentum if the ID leader displays a driving force and enthusiasm for the task in hand.

Authors favoured the use of local resources where possible. Long-term expatriate resident advisers were to become the exception. Local experts should be recruited, where available. Local consultancies should be favoured if possible. In both cases, long-term resident expatriate advice was used to bolster local resources and expertise.

In summary, it is apparent that the practical material went some way to satisfy the conceptual framework outlined in the Summary to Part I. It is now necessary to take the preceding analysis and present a structure of the institutional development process.

STRUCTURING THE PRACTICE

It is suggested that from the practice, the stages of the ID process are as follows:

- project formulation
- outputs required
- implementation
- constraints to ID performance
- additional analysis
- impact and sustainability.

Each is reviewed from a theoretical and practical perspective.

The literature implied that project formulation should be a participative exercise; extensive consultation should be undertaken with the client. Project leadership should be defined from an early stage. Autonomy and accountability should be built into the process. The project scale should be manageable. The use of local resources should be a central feature. The scale of the project must be weighed against the chances of ID sustainability. Monitoring and reporting must be an implicit fea-ture of the project's formulation. Thus, any ID process should have as its first set of considerations:

Project formulation

- client involvement
- scale of the project
- leadership
- monitoring and review arrangements.

The literature was scant on the nature of the outputs required. Instead, apart from dwelling on the modes of intervention, it considered factors for success (project formulation) and the general scope of the process. It therefore remains for the practice to guide the nature of the outputs required. There were two sets of outputs. These were conditioned by the individual components of ID being addressed. In both, an iterative, learning and experimental character was, to varying degrees, built in to the ID. This was in the nature of the outputs required. While a regulatory reform case is not recorded, sufficient indications from the first two cases, concerning the constraining influence of the supervising environment, offer indications on an ID pattern in any regulatory reform practice. Thus a second set of considerations suggests:

Outputs (according to the component of the ID spectrum)

ORGANISATIONAL RESTRUCTURING AND STRENGTHENING

- short-term urgent targets
- medium-term strategic targets
- implementation and review
- consolidation and sustainabilty test.

POLICY AND PLANNING CAPABILITY

- initial development framework
- additional policy analysis
- review of performance
- consolidation and sustainability test.

REGULATORY AND PROCEDURAL REFORM

- consultation with client organisations
- ID proposals (including legal and regulatory reviews)
- resulting ID of supervising organisation (including law reform)
- consolidation and sustainability test.

The literature was not overly concerned with implementation. The closest it came was in identifying the specific modes of intervention (such as policy and management processes). For ID, it is the challenge of skills transfer, as part of the institution-building process, that is at the heart of the matter.

The first case was dominated by the executive role. The institutional development project was entirely dependent on the postholder as the chief executive officer of the city council. He executed the project as far as possible within the scope permitted by the supervising environment. In essence, two development roles were combined in one. The chief executive acted as both adviser and implementor. The executive role had the advantage of carrying some weight to implement. In the development business, such a role is, by far, the exception.

The second case was dominated by the advisory role. The city management project was entirely on advice and technical supplementation to the counterpart chief executives. It depended on a creative response and acceptability by the counterpart personnel. In this case, the advice can be accepted or rejected. If accepted, it has to be incorporated into practice by the recipients. All else being equal therefore, the role stands or falls on the strength of the advice. This is in contrast to the executive role where force of personality can overcome technical weaknesses. The advisory role, in the second case, worked. It is suited to development countries because the host accepts the responsibility for implementation.

Project development was in hand for regulatory reform in the supervising environment (through the World Bank's Local Government Development Project). This process was dominated by the consulting role. Here, experts would literally be flown in to the country. They would gather a wealth of information from existing publications and discussions with key personnel. They would produce a report. The report would be accepted in whole or in part. After the process was completed, a report would sit in someone's in-tray, waiting for its recommendations for implementation to be introduced. Implementation was normally divorced from its author. It highlights an essential frustration with the itinerant consultant's mode of operation. He or she is rarely involved in the implementation of his or her work. Too much depends on the quality of the report's advice on implementation. It is a one-way process. It is suggested that the consultant role, divorced from implementation, is a flawed concept given the long time spans involved in third world institutional development.

Any ID process should therefore have as its third set of considerations:

Implementation

- executive role
- advisory role
- consulting role.

The literature does not address the issue of constraints to performance. Instead it attempts to identify those factors of success, that should be incorporated in the project's preparation. The practice saw the constraints to performance emanating from the supervising environment (external). In essence, it concerned the difficulty of the supervising ministry to reach decisions within a reasonable time. It also concerned its inability to act within government itself, on behalf of the local authorities. A third case would seek to address the issue of the constraining effect of the supervising environment. Constraints could also exist within the organisation (internal). From the practice this was not so. Any ID process should therefore have as its fourth set of considerations:

Constraints

- external
- internal.

The literature advocates the concept of a learning process to ID. The first case saw short-term urgent matters as being both an immediate intervention but also a basis for learning and further development. Nevertheless, its major learning required the additional development of the institution, beyond its original terms of reference. The second case saw the initial development framework as being both a quick intervention but also a means of stepping on to the learning curve of preparing development strategies. Additional outputs were identified in the course of the project; preparing an urban management manual and preparing an analysis of the urban development challenge facing the urban management process. Any ID process should therefore have as its fifth set of considerations:

Additions

- structures
- processes
- supervisory environment.

The literature is replete with references to sustainability in the ID process. It is central to the activity. If the ID is not sustainable, it has failed. In the first case, sustainability was considered subjectively. The key staff had been recruited and trained (chief executive and treasurer). They had assumed responsibility for their functions and were performing well. The assessment of sustainability rested on assumptions about interference, a reasonable measure of co-operation and continued advice for at least two more years. The second case presented a quantified assessment of its sustainability. Each TOR objective was analysed into its component parts. Each part was given a probability percentage score and a weighting out of one hundred. The result was a sustainability score and rating (see Table 4.1). Any ID process should therefore have as its sixth set of considerations:

Sustainability

- component activities (from terms of reference)
- percentage probability of success
- weighting (out of 100)
- score and rating.

The one issue that has not been mentioned is that of training. Training should pervade all aspects of ID. The literature has many references to training as part of urban management. Looking closely at this literature, two styles of training are apparent. First is the general approach to strengthening the system. Secondly is the specific approach to imparting coherent skills and addressing practical problems. The first case was a mixture of both approaches. The training needs were identified as technical (a scattered approach) and managerial (more focused). The second case was specifically focused and practical problem solving. In both general and problem-specific approaches, the style of training can encompass on-the-job, in-house, local external and foreign external locations. Malawi's newly appointed chief executives received on-the-job, in-house and foreign external training. Training has to be an integral part of any ID process. Any ID process should therefore have as a seventh set of considerations, ideally to follow the identified outputs of the ID project:

Training

- general (qualification-seeking)
- problem-specific (e.g. establishing processes).

In summary, it is suggested that the structure of the institutional development process incorporates those features identified above. They are summarised in Table 5.1. The table suggests that:

1. Project formulation is an exploratory and, therefore, a non-mechanistic process (client involvement is essential).
2. Outputs should write in a basic morphology or stages of learning (short-term before medium-term strengthening; initial before full development strategy).
3. Training should seek to achieve practical outcomes and be clearly structured (following the functions being addressed through ID).
4. Implementation should be participatory (whether through execution, advice or consultants).
5. Constraints should be accepted as an inevitable outcome of the political nature of ID (whether internal or external to the organisation).
6. Additions (and even deletions) are the natural consequences of exploration in ID.
7. Sustainability must be tested; without the test, the cycle of the ID process is not complete.

From both theory and practice, it is apparent that ID is still a fledgling discipline. Yet, that discipline is beginning to generate some strategic and operational principles to guide the instrumentalities of the institutional development process.

The next chapter reviews the city management function and its institutional development imperatives.

Table 5.1   Structure of the institutional development process

---

Project formulation
- client involvement
- scale of the project
- leadership
- monitoring and review arrangements

Outputs
(according to the component of the ID spectrum)

ORGANISATIONAL RESTRUCTURING AND STRENGTHENING
- short-term urgent targets
- medium-term strategic targets
- implementation and review
- consolidation and sustainability test

POLICY AND PLANNING CAPABILITY
- initial development framework
- additional policy analysis
- review of performance ,
- consolidation and sustainability test

REGULATORY AND PROCEDURAL REFORM
- consultation with client organisations
- ID proposals (including legal and regulatory reviews)
- resulting ID of supervising organisation (including law reform)
- consolidation and sustainability test

Training
- general (qualification-seeking)
- problem-specific (e.g. establishing processes)

Implementation
- executive role
- advisory role
- consulting role

Constraints
- external
- internal

Additions
- structures
- processes
- supervisory environment

Sustainability test
- component activities (from TOR)
- percentage probability of success
- weighting (out of 100)
- resulting score and rating

---

12 City Management and its ID Imperatives

The immediate challenge in the development of institutions for third world city management is two-fold. First, is the need to organise urban management according to its functional determinants. This is the obvious argument that form follows function. Secondly, is the need to be guided by a set of institutional development imperatives, that are specific to the fledgling urban management discipline in developing countries. This chapter seeks to review the first in order to arrive at the second. It does so by considering the following:

- CITY MANAGEMENT FUNCTION
- CITY MANAGEMENT FORM
- INSTITUTIONAL DEVELOPMENT IMPERATIVES

CITY MANAGEMENT FUNCTION

Functional variables

The variables for the city management function have been analysed to a summary table (see Table 2.1 at the end of Part II). Each variable is briefly reviewed below.

Scope of the function

Integrating all the players in the process was frequently cited as a purpose of urban management. That is, the process itself and its resulting strategies were to be the vehicle for that integration. In practice, integrating all the players in the process was a specific objective. This was both in the preparation and review of the development strategy. It became an explicit component of the inter-organisational annual urban infrastructure meetings, as a precursor to the parent ministry's own annual review exercise with the city councils.

The holistic concept of urban management was advocated in recognition of the totality of the urban challenge. In practice, each strategy

234

contained statements confirming its view of the urban management challenge as being holistic. The nature of that holism embraced four sets of relationships:

- urban and institutional planning;
- infrastructure and services planning;
- policy and budgetary planning; and
- council and other agencies' planning.

Each of the four sets was seen as part of the integrated urban management process.

The theory saw the informal sector as being the key to a successful city-building process. This was because of its latent potential to help itself (given the right conditions) and because governments were becoming relatively poorer as the demand for infrastructure and services increased. In practice, embracing the informal sector in the city-building process was an explicit intention in each strategy. With between 40 and 60 per cent of each city's residents being squatters, the strategies planned for the infrastructure needs of the formal and informal sectors. In both, the primary consideration was the provision of serviced land, either for site and service schemes or for squatter upgrading. For the informal sector, the desire was to create the conditions to nurture self-help schemes.

Tackling poverty measures were seen as a central concern of the urban management process. In practice, anti-poverty measures were a desire. A major programme of supplying potable water to squatter areas was introduced. However, the infancy of each council's social welfare and community development programmes precluded any major service proposals to alleviate poverty.

The theory suggested that institutional strengthening and decentralisation were the fundamental precursor to any meaningful city management. City management was therefore the legitimate concern of the lowest competent level of government. In practice, institutional strengthening was a central purpose of each council's development strategy. The strategy itself was the mechanism to decentralise policy and planning for urban development from central to local government.

Planning, programming and budgeting were frequently cited as being central to the instrumentality of city management. In practice, planning, programming and budgeting were introduced as explicit components of both the planning (strategy) and review (annual report) process. This was particularly so in the strategy, programme, budget and consequence (**SPBC**) analysis, introduced as part of the planning process and described in the resulting urban management manual.

Citizen involvement was seen in the literature as a fundamental requirement for successful urban management. It was considered as helping to legitimise the urban management process. In practice, citizen involvement in the annual planning and review process was zero. At such a general level, community involvement was through the ward councillors, in council committees. In contrast, where a specific location was being proposed for site and service and squatter upgrading proposals, there was major involvement in the nature and details of the project. This extended to encouraging the local chiefs of the traditional administrations to persuade local squatters to be committed to upgrading their plots (after tenure was granted).

The theory had a central concern for the provision of infrastructure and services. This was seen as the essential ingredient to nurture economic development. The primary focus of each council's development strategy was the provision of infrastructure and services. This was the key mode of intervention; it is looked at more closely, under the modes of intervention (the next sub-section).

Theorists advocated the requirement to integrate investment decisions. Integrating investment decisions was a primary purpose of each councils' development strategy. Among other things, each strategy sought to 'integrate all the (funding) players in the city building process'. A table showing each proposal, its cost and its funding responsibility (whether council or others) was included in each strategy.

Infrastructure provision was seen as the vital external economy to support the economic growth of cities, enterprises and households. In practice, this was the justification for each strategy's dominant concern for the provision of infrastructure.

The theory frequently talked about the preparation of strategies but never articulated its form and contents. The medium of policy and planning in each council was the annual preparation and review of the strategy document. The strategy's form and contents is looked at more closely in the next section, concerning the structure of the urban management function – the functional checklist.

The environmental issue has gained prominence in the literature. Protecting and improving the environment was a desire. However, the infancy of each council's technical programmes precluded any environmental contribution to the planning process, beyond basic public health concerns, such as the provision of clean water.

The literature suggested that the idea of learning through planning and review was an important concept. It reinforced the demise of the master plan approach to urban planning. In practice, an iterative or learning process was part of the reason for building a constant plan and review system, into the annual policy and planning process.

Planning as management viewed the demise of master planning from a different perspective. Authors presented the notion (from practice) that local governments, in order to survive, must plan their urban interventions having a direct eye on the resources available. Traditional master planning precluded an explicit concern for resources. Planning as management was another central feature of the development strategies. The strategies were seen as part of, and a contribution to, the total urban management process of planning, implementation and review.

Authors viewed urban management intervention as a concern for human welfare and economic development. Planning in the political economy of the city was therefore a reference to viewing issues of human need (such as water and poverty) as opposed to spatial patterns and land use. In practice, the urban management process was concerned with the former.

Operations and maintenance was the logical conclusion to every additional item of infrastructure provided. Operations and maintenance was not an explicit component of the strategy. Each strategy's financing chapter included projections to illustrate the desired and likely levels of expenditure and income (SPBC analysis). This covered both capital and current expenditure. Within this framework, the councils were developing separate infrastructure maintenance programmes, quantified according to the anticipated need for repair.

The literature noted the role of infrastructure provision in helping to determine the spatial development of cities. Infrastructure for spatial determination was advocated, through threshold analysis (through a geographical information system – GIS), as the way to move the strategies beyond site-specific proposals to the wider perspective of urban structure and spatial pattern. No significant progress was made because of the infancy of the system and the inability to manipulate information on the spatial distribution of utilities.

Spatial planning was cited in the sense of its demise in relation to the new urban management process. It was positively cited on two occasions. Spatial planning did not figure in the Malawian practice as part of the urban management process. However, specific site-based infrastructure provision was always spatially located.

Modes of intervention

- Water supply was the most frequently cited item of infrastructure in the literature. Water supply was seen as fundamental to life and was always first in the Malawi city councils' urban development checklist.
- Sewerage systems was the second most frequently cited item of infrastructure in the literature. Sewerage systems always followed water supply in the Malawi city councils' urban development checklist.
- Solid waste management was a prominent item for the writers on urban management. Solid waste management always followed sewerage systems in the Malawi city councils' urban development checklist. In practice, all three were considered to be fundamental to life and public health.
- The authors made reference to power – the supply of electricity. Power was never raised as an issue in the Malawi practice. The strategies made reference to it and its supplier, a national parastatal organisation.
- Roads are fundamental to transportation and therefore economic performance. Roads were classified as arterial (or trunk) and site-specific. Both categories figured prominently in the strategies.
- Drainage and flood control was important to the authors. It was not expressed as a concern in the Malawi urban sector. However, it always figured in the site and service and squatter upgrade plans as an issue, when determining specific proposals for the informal sector.
- Education was the first service to be identified by the authors. Education was not a central issue in Malawi's urban local government sector. This was partly because its provision was a central government responsibility. It was also because the councils simply did not have the capacity to think about the service. Occasionally, opinions were expressed that primary education should become a local government function.
- Health was rated as important as education in the literature. In Malawi's urban sector, health ranged over clinical care (a central government function), primary health clinics, social welfare and public health (city council responsibilities). At this time, the city councils were only beginning to think about the nature of service provision plans; to become an explicit component in future development strategies.

- The literature identified the provision of housing as being an important concern of urban management. Housing was central to each of Malawi's integrated development strategies. This was in the sense that serviced land for housing had to be provided, for both the formal and informal (or traditional) sectors of the economy. The councils were not housing authorities, in the sense of the landlord of housing stock.
- Environmental protection and improvement was identified by some authors. Environmental protection did not figure in the Malawi city councils' integrated development strategies.

Functional checklist

Both the theory and practice identified the fundamental importance of water-based infrastructure: water supply and sewerage systems. They also identified solid waste management. The theory highlighted drainage and flood control. The theory highlighted power. The practice highlighted roads. The suggestion is that all these matters represent the infrastructure and service networks that bind the city together. Any integrated development strategy should therefore have as its first set of urban interventions:

Network infrastructure

- water supply
- sewerage systems
- solid waste management
- drainage and flood control
- power supply
- trunk roads
- road rehabilitation and reconstruction.

The theory identified housing and serviced land in general terms only. Other land uses, say for industry, were not mentioned. No distinction was presented between the formal and informal economic sectors. In contrast, the practice saw all non-network infrastructure as being site-specific (and therefore susceptible to plot beneficiary or user charges, to recover costs). Also, the practice presented a clear distinction between the formal and informal sectors. Thus, the modes of intervention follow primary land uses for site-specific infrastructure provision in both sectors. Any integrated development strategy should therefore have as its second set of urban interventions:

Serviced land (general formal sector infrastructure)

- housing (according to category)
- commerce
- industry
- others (such as institutions or government).

Any integrated development strategy should therefore have as its third set of urban interventions:

Serviced and upgraded land (traditional, including squatter area infrastructure)

- site and service schemes
- squatter upgrade schemes
- existing official area upgrading.

Having covered all aspects of infrastructure provision, the strategy should look at key superstructure requirements, such as business premises. The theory only identified markets. The Lilongwe practice outlined, among other things, business premises. Major building requirements that need public funding should be presented. Smaller scale projects, such as markets, can be included in the council's annual capital programme. Any integrated development strategy should therefore have as its fourth set of urban interventions:

Buildings

- major government proposals
- council property initiatives (business premises)
- smaller scale projects (markets).

What remains is specific services. The theory identified education and health. The practice was only starting to consider the details of its service provision to its cities. The importance of this topic, however, is to distinguish the capital component of service provision (equipment for refuse collection; buildings for schools) from its current costs. The capital element would be included under the appropriate infrastructure or building head. The concern here is for the nature of the service being provided. The service issue should be defined. The function and activities of the service to be provided should be articulated. Thus, the concern is for the nature of the service being provided and its current costs. This should feature in a service development section. Any integrated development strategy should therefore have as its fifth set of urban interventions:

Service development

- health
- education
- other services provided by the council that have a direct impact on the community, such as parks.

Once the services have been identified, the institutional changes to bring them about become internal concerns for the council and therefore become a council building (as opposed to a city building) concern. In order to differentiate the city building from the council building text, the latter is the focus of the appendices (on organisational, financial and policy strengthening).

This concludes the modes of intervention in the urban management process. What remains is the preceding discourse to set the scene for the intervention and the financial analysis for the strategy. Then comes the institutional strengthening measures to ensure that municipal government is in a fit state to plan, provide and maintain the infrastructure and services required of its growing city. Taking the strengthening measures first; the range of institutional development offered from the practice is in three parts. Any integrated development strategy should therefore have as its first set of institutional interventions:

Organisational development

- structures and personnel
- planning processes
- contextual reforms.

Any integrated development strategy should therefore have as its second set of institutional interventions:

Financial development

- cost-saving and efficiency measures
- revenue-increasing measures
- long-term asset creation and management policy.

Any integrated development strategy should therefore have as its third set of institutional interventions:

Policy development

- specifying the annual budget cycle
- specifying the policy budget cycle
- developing their explicit relationship.

The first institutional intervention is designed to establish the correct structures, processes and policy environment for the human resources to perform as efficiently as possible for the community. The second set of institutional interventions is designed to establish as strong a financial base as possible to allow the council to perform effectively in the community. The third set of institutional interventions is designed to ensure that it can plan on behalf of the community, as efficiently and effectively as possible.

What remains is the preceding discourse to set the scene for the intervention. This involves the scope of the city management function.

The case material presented one chapter (after a short introduction), to set the strategic and policy context for the specific interventions. The four councils' strategies presented a population projection, an outline of the formal and informal economic sectors, an outline of the land-use structure and, finally, housing projections (as a basis for subsequent proposals). In terms of the scope of the function (outlined above), three items were not included in the practice: infrastructure networks (for spatial determination), anti-poverty measures and protecting and improving the environment. It is arguable that all should be included to help determine the contextual framework for intervention. Thus, for example, the infrastructure networks would be highlighted to identify the most efficient locations for future urban development (or redevelopment). The environmental topic could follow network infrastructure. It would highlight any major issues that need to be addressed in the strategy and spell out any spatial determinants. The question of poverty is less clear. All interventions have a potential to alleviate poverty (providing clean water; building schools). It would be reasonable to introduce the issue of poverty, after the general housing projections. In order to ensure their inclusion in specific interventions, the infrastructure network, the environmental and anti-poverty consequences of each proposal should be stated. Additionally, the role of city government as the integrating force in the city-building process, should be stressed. Any integrated development strategy should therefore cover in its contextual chapter:

The general context for development

- population growth
- economic characteristics
- land-use pattern
- infrastructure networks
- environmental issues
- housing projections
- poverty issues
- city government's importance to city building.

Finally, comes the inevitable question of finances. The theory talked about planning, programming and budgeting but did not explain how to view the question from an urban management stance. The Malawian practice was more explicit. The purpose of **SPBC** analysis is to present the holistic urban and institutional development picture, as one financial entity. A decision on the scope of any compromise (say, not to develop housing land) and its justification should then be made. The consequences of not developing the housing (in terms of housing shortage and resulting squatting) would then see the organisational issue of saving money against the urban issue of increased housing problems, with public health consequences. Any integrated development strategy should therefore cover in its financial chapter:

Financing the strategy

- the strategy's total cost, by agency
- funding the council's shortfall
- strategy, programme, budget and consequences desired (**SPBC1**)
- strategy, programme, budget and consequences likely (**SPBC2**)
- the compromise and its justification.

In conclusion, it is suggested that the practising framework for the city management function, as expressed through an integrated development strategy, could be as presented as in Table 6.1.

Thus, it is suggested that the weaknesses to be addressed in practice are the need to:

Table 6.1   Structure of the integrated development strategy

CITY BUILDING

The general context for development
- population growth
- economic characteristics
- land-use pattern
- infrastructure networks
- environmental issues
- housing projections
- poverty issues
- city government's importance to city building

Network infrastructure
- water supply
- sewerage systems
- solid waste management
- drainage and flood control
- power supply
- trunk roads
- road rehabilitation and reconstruction

Serviced land (general formal sector infrastructure)
- housing (according to land-use densities)
- commerce
- industry
- others (such as institutions or government)

Serviced & upgraded land (traditional & squatter infrastructure)
- site and service schemes
- squatter upgrade schemes
- existing official area upgrading

Buildings
- major government proposals
- council initiatives such as business premises
- smaller scale council projects, from revenue

Service development
- health
- education
- other direct impact council services, such as parks and amenities

Financing the strategy
- the strategy's total cost, by agency
- funding the council's shortfall
- strategy, programme, budget and consequences desired (SPBC1)
- strategy, programme, budget and consequences likely (SPBC2)
- the compromise and its justification

COUNCIL BUILDING

Organisational development
- structures and personnel
- planning processes
- contextual reforms

Financial development
- cost-saving and efficiency measures
- revenue-increasing measures
- long-term asset creation and management policy

Policy development
- specifying the annual budget cycle
- specifying the annual policy cycle
- developing their explicit relationship

- Make explicit the decision-making relationship between infrastructure networks and development proposals.
- Make explicit the decision-making relationship between environmental constraints and development proposals.
- Make explicit the decision-making relationship between poverty alleviation and development proposals.
- Develop a more rigorous analysis of service needs, involving the delivering agencies as appropriate.

In conclusion, it is suggested that the scope and mode of the city management function, expressed in the structure and contents of an integrated development strategy, represents the outcome of the synthesis of theory and practice. It offers a functional checklist for the urban management process.

The functional checklist to govern the preparation of an integrated development strategy is presented in Table 6.1.

CITY MANAGEMENT FORM

Organisational variables

The variables for the city management form have been analysed to a summary table (see Table 3.1 at the end of Part III). Each variable is briefly reviewed below.

Scope of the form

- The theory suggested that decentralisation was seen as the central issue to be addressed. It had three manifestations: deconcentration to regional or local offices of central government; devolution of powers and resources to local government; delegation of functions to the private, including the non-government organisation (NGO) sector. In this context, decentralisation was conceived as the need to transfer powers and increase the autonomy of local authorities. In practice, decentralisation was hailed as the main reason for the Local Government Development Project in Malawi.

- Authors reported that inter-organisational arrangements were another major theme. Some argued that there was a clear shift in emphasis away from the traditional idea of setting up new organisations, such as development agencies, to manage urban growth to accepting the all-embracing or holistic nature of urban management. The consequence was that more attention should therefore be given to inter-organisational arrangements, to reflect the complexity of the urban challenge. In practice, the question of inter-organisational arrangements was only beginning to be addressed.

- Writers on urban management advocated the need to see the function placed firmly in the local government arena. In practice, decentralisation of urban management was expressed as an over-riding intention. The strengthening of local government's planning capability was viewed as a vital component in the decentralisation of urban management from central to local government.

- Authors stressed the importance of local government to the urban development process. In practice, the importance of local government was the reason for the Local Government Development Project; a comprehensive institutional strengthening package.

- Theorists on organisational arrangements were conscious of the need to strike a balance between central and local government. This was the attempt to address the political issue of power and resource deployment. The balance between central and local government pervaded key areas of the practice. It materialised in issues of financial support and authority to recruit senior personnel. Again, these were to be central features of, respectively, the financial management and legal reviews.

- Authors repeatedly linked decentralisation with the re-allocation of resources to lower levels of government. Decentralisation of resources was a concomitant of a general intention to decentralise. In practice, this was (to be) a central feature of the policy and regulatory reform. For example, the emphasis was to persuade government to pay rates on its considerable property holdings in the four Malawian cities.

- The theory presented no clear rules to determine the allocation of urban management functions. Patterns of organisational style were advocated. They revealed various levels of sectoral distribution of functions. In practice, everything was carried on the principle of decentralisation and general strengthening.

- Authors accepted the general failure and ultimate demise of special development organisations. This may have coincided with a re-awakening of a local democratic consciousness. These organisations were not a feature of the practice.

- Writers acknowledged the holistic nature of urban management and, therefore, the need for organisational arrangements to match that complexity. The practice made no acknowledgement of the holistic nature of urban management.

- Authors recognised the importance of function in determining organisational form. The practice made no acknowledgement of the fact.

- Writers saw privatisation as one major option in the delivery of some urban infrastructure and services. Privatisation was not a feature of the practice.

- Financing urban development was seen as an endless quest for alternative funding and cost recovery mechanisms. The practice went to considerable lengths to establish a funding vehicle for urban infrastructure provision.

- Authors saw the sectoral organisation of central government as being a structural weakness when dealing with the inter-sectoral nature of urban development. In practice, the failure of sectoral organisations (e.g. ministries) to contribute to the urban management process was only beginning to be addressed.

Structuring criteria

- Decentralisation was the most frequently cited organisational style. Of itself, it has little specific meaning. However, the literature suggests three distinct elements in an attempt to grade the extent of decentralisation. Deconcentration is the minimal approach. It concerns the dispersal of administrative responsibility from headquarters to regionally based arms of central government. Devolution is the middle approach. It involves the transfer of administrative and funding responsibilities from central to local government. Delegation is the maximum approach. It requires the transfer of funding responsibilities to the private sector, in the sense of a trading activity. While decentralisation was central to the practice, the concomitant organisational analysis was not.

- Sector is inextricably linked with the style of decentralisation. However, an important qualification must be made. The private sector embraces all agencies that trade for their existence and judge success according to profit (the excess of total income over total expenditure). Thus, a trading parastatal organisation that is supervised (or even owned) by central government is, in practice, a business operating in the private sector, whether or not as a monopoly. Hence business organisations include the parastatal sector. The sectoral organisation of urban management was not a feature of the practice.

- Sub-sector flows from the sector and the style of decentralisation. The deconcentrated, central government sector involves the headquarters and regional arms of central government. The devolved, local government sector concerns two tiers (metropolitan and municipal) or one tier (integrated) of local government. The delegated, private sector involves private business, government (trading) parastatals and non-government organisations. There was no sub-sectoral consideration in the practice.

- Funding sources are seen as a practical analytical tool in helping to determine the organisational responsibility for an' urban management function. Thus, for example, if the function (say, water supply) was susceptible to direct user charges, the logic would suggest the delegation of the activity to the private sector. Conversely, if a function was more suited to tax funding (say, preparing the development strategy, under political control), its location would be within government. Funding source analysis was not a determinant of organisational style, in the practice.

- Economies of scale; that is, reducing the overhead costs of capital-intensive functions, was seen as one way of determining the allocation of organisational responsibility for urban management. This would be particularly relevant when determining the allocation of a function in a two-tier local government system. Thus, for example, capital-dominated trunk road construction would be more likely to be a metropolitan tier responsibility. Road maintenance would more likely be a municipal-tier function. Economies of scale were not considered as a determinant of organisational arrangements, in the practice.

Organisational checklist

Both theory and practice is dominated by the principle of decentralisation. The practice in Malawi turned out to be more circumspect, with deconcentration to regional offices of the ministry being the only early proposal. Any organisational analysis for the urban management process should therefore have as its first set of considerations:

Decentralisation

- deconcentration
- devolution
- delegation.

Neither theory nor practice presented a structured argument about the benefits of one sector over another, in determining the location of urban management functions. As such, the item still needs to be addressed. In the first instance, therefore, it is necessary to identify the organisational classifications. These follow the decentralisation types, respectively, as central government, local government and the private sector. Any organisational analysis for the urban management process should therefore have as its second set of considerations:

Sector

- central government
- local government
- private sector.

Neither theory nor practice presented a structured argument about the benefits between sub-sectors, in determining the location of urban management functions. There was simply the general contention that it was more efficient and effective to have urban management decentralised from central to local government. The private provision of urban services should also be considered. As such, the item still needs to be addressed. In the first instance, therefore, it is necessary to identify the sub-sector classifications. These follow the sectors respectively, as central government, local government and the private sector. Any organisational analysis for the urban management process should therefore have as its third set of considerations:

Sub-sector

- headquarters or regional administration
- one or two tiers
- business, including parastatals and NGOs.

The theory presented no clear rules for allocating the functions of urban management, save the panacea of decentralisation. Individual authors attempted to offer structuring criteria. These were according to funding source and by economies of scale. The practice showed no signs of analysing the urban management function according to either criterion. Any organisational analysis for the urban management process should therefore have as its fourth set of considerations:

Financing

- funding source
- economies of scale.

Thus, it is suggested that when the form of urban management is being considered, the following matters should be addressed:

- The nature of the desired decentralisation should be specified and justified.
- The sectoral implications should be highlighted.
- The sub-sectoral consequences should be identified.
- The link between sub-sectoral location and funding source should be made explicit, in order to distinguish between a tax and a user-charge burden.
- The economies of scale should be quantified, when determining the allocation of a function between a tier of local government.

In conclusion, it is suggested that the structuring criteria for determining the organisation of urban management conforms with the original theoretical analysis. It offers an organisational checklist for the urban management process.

INSTITUTIONAL DEVELOPMENT IMPERATIVES

It is now necessary to combine the functional and organisational conclusions. This is in order to highlight the institutional development imperatives, arising from the combination. The suggestion is that there are three institutional development imperatives for third world city management.

Integration

In terms of the strategic aspects of institutional development, the first most salient point seems to be the fundamental importance of integrating all the players in the urban management process. This is the most frequently cited variable in the analysis of the city management function (Table 2.1). In order to ensure this holistic perspective (the second most important variable), it is necessary to identify the costs of all proposals (all modes of intervention), allocate them to agencies, and illustrate the percentage funding responsibility of local government, compared to the other players. The higher the percentage score (i.e. the greater the funding responsibility of agencies other than local government), the greater is the need for integration.

Thus, an urban intervention matrix can be introduced. It can illustrate the percentage score of the extent of integration required, according to the pattern of funding. This is a dynamic conceptual framework in that any changes in value will alter the extent of integration required. The first institutional development imperative for third world city management is therefore *the integration of all the players in the city-building process*. An integration test is offered in the Appendix at the end of this volume.

In essence, one seeks to integrate the functions (or process) of city management. Institutional development therefore has to create the planning systems and monitoring procedures to encourage the integration of organisations in the city management process; the necessary policy and planning capability.

Decentralisation

In terms of the strategic aspects of institutional development, the second most salient point seems to be the fundamental importance of decentralising the urban management process to a strengthened local government system. This is the most frequently cited variable in the analysis of the city management form (Table 3.1). In order to achieve this and ensure a creative inter-agency arrangement, as a consequence of the decentralisation (the second most important variable), it is necessary to set the urban management function against the structuring criteria. By allocating values to the levels of decentralisation, and with local government seen as the mid-point, it is possible to quantify its level. The higher the percentage score, the greater the level of decentralisation, away from central government.

Thus, an urban management matrix can be introduced. It illustrates the percentage score of and rating for the level of decentralisation, according to the organisational distribution of the urban management functions. This is a dynamic conceptual framework in that any changes in value will alter the level, and therefore the category, of decentralisation. The second institutional development imperative for third world city management is therefore *the decentralisation of the urban management process*. A decentralisation test is offered in the Appendix at the end of this volume.

In essence, one seeks to decentralise the organisation (or structure) of city management. Institutional development therefore has to create the urban management regulations to encourage the decentralisation of power and resources, so that local government is capable of ensuring the provision and maintenance of infrastructure and services for its growing cities: the necessary regulatory and procedural reform.

Sustainability

The third, by its nature, is more concerned with the normative characteristics of institutional development (ID), rather than the substantive nature of third world city management. However, its ID imperative applies equally to itself as it does to the substantive area of intervention. Thus, the third ID imperative, applied to the third world city management process, is presented below.

In terms of the strategic aspects of institutional development, the third most salient point seems to be the fundamental importance of sustaining the functions of the urban management process. This is the most frequently cited variable in the analysis of institutional development (Table 1.1). In order to achieve this, through an iterative, learning and experimental approach to ID (the second most important variable), it is necessary to identify the activities being strengthened. This must follow the functions being analysed. Observations have to be presented. They can then be scored and rated. The higher the score, the higher the chance of sustainability and self-development. This is a dynamic conceptual framework in that any changes in value will alter the probability rating for sustainability. The third institutional development imperative for third world city management is therefore *the sustainability of the urban management process*. A sustainability test is offered in the Appendix at the end of this volume.

In essence, one seeks to sustain the institutional development for third world city management. Institutional development therefore has to create the structures and capabilities to allow local government to play a sustained, central role in the urban management process; the necessary organisational restructuring and strengthening (where the organisational structures are functionally determined).

The institutional development imperatives for urban management are illustrated as an urban intervention matrix (Figure A.1), an urban management matrix (Figure A.2) and a sustainability test (Figure A.3). These are presented in the Appendix to this text.

What remains is a summary and conclusion.

Summary and Conclusion

Parts I to III considered in some detail the recent theoretical material on institutional development and urban management in the third world. The essence of their initial conclusions are summarised in their respective Tables 1.1 to 3.1.

Parts IV and V looked at two related cases of institutional development in practice. The first focused on the importance of the organisation-environment relationship. The second highlighted the importance of testing sustainability.

Part VI reviewed the process of ID and its strategic imperatives, in relation to third world city management.

The ID process

In the first case, the institutional development project was implemented. The council's performance targets were stated. Its organisational and financial strategies were implemented to satisfy these targets. A counterpart chief executive was recruited and trained. However, early on in the project, it also became clear that to confine the project to a traditional concept of institution building would be only half the task. The institution (the city council) needed to know what was happening in its environment (the city). It needed to understand the dynamics of change in the city. It needed to organise itself to plan for and cope with that change. In short, it needed to develop a city-building capability.

The heart of the institution building was the development of simultaneous thinking about infrastructure and services provision (to support the economic development of the city) and organisational and financial arrangements (to ensure the council's ability to do the providing). This wider concept of urban management, to which the city council was advised to aspire, was considerably in excess of the traditional notion of institutional development contained in the project's terms of reference. This wider concept was central to the second case; the lessons had been learnt.

In this experience, institution building started at the bottom. In the first case, it was essential to get things moving as quickly as possible. Quick personnel matters were addressed. Logistical questions like transport and equipment were acted upon. Financial problems were tackled.

While this was happening, a wider and deeper understanding of the organisation was taking place. This was essential for the strategic nature of the next stage. Equally, in the second case, a quick first development strategy was prepared by the three councils with no previous experience in preparing such documents. While this was happening, a wider and deeper understanding of each city's development needs was taking place. This was essential to allow for the full picture to be grasped, through additional housing and financial analysis.

Every organisation should have a clear vision of what it is attempting to perform. By doing so, it should have a central concern for the environment within which it operates; it is in two parts. First is the policy environment; in the council's case, national government policy. Secondly, is the operating environment in which the organisation seeks to have an impact. In both cases, it was to build capacity to provide and maintain infrastructure and services in the city.

The standard practice is to leave a project with some documents. These are intended to encapsulate the systems and procedures resulting from the project. In the first case, a management manual was prepared. It focused on all the central administrative and financial procedures, to allow the council to function. In the event of a dramatic turnover in staff, at least there would be a document to offer rudimentary guidance to newcomers. Also, the outline of an annual report was submitted. It included explicit operational performance targets for the council. These centred on the management processes and the idea of reviewing performance. The component, additional to those standard texts, was an integrated development strategy. This was conceived and prepared as part of the additional concern for the council to tackle its environment. It became the first part of the triumvirate of policy development (strategy), implementation (management manual) and review (annual report). In the second case, an urban management manual was prepared. Also, an urban infrastructure policy paper was developed, to allow government departments to understand the enormity of the task facing the urban management system (of both central and local government).

Thus, institution building requires patience. In the first case, it required progress from firm, practical foundations. A clear strategic vision was developed. The traditional notions of efficiency and financial surplus were subsumed to the wider notion of an organisation, with a dynamic and responsive relationship with its environment. That process was captured in its integrated development strategy. In the second case, each council's development strategy was the central (but not exclusive) focus for the test of sustainability. Institutions must have a positive impact on their environments. That impact must be sustainable through enhanced organisational capacity.

Strategic characteristics of ID in relation to third world city management

All three institutional development imperatives are concerned with the outcomes of ID: the extent of integration, the level of decentralisation and the degree of sustainability. When these concepts are combined, they offer a layered set of related ideas to guide the process of institutional development for third world city management.

- First, is the core of urban interventions; providing the infrastructure and services. This highlights the modes of intervention by urban management in the city. This is the first holistic characteristic of urban management, concerning the *integration* of all the players in the city-building process, irrespective of organisation.
- Secondly, is the extent of urban management; ensuring an organisation's ability (a) to plan for, provide and maintain its city's infrastructure and services and (b) to be in a fit condition, organisationally and financially, to do so. This highlights the scope and style of urban management, with its more general concerns for intervening in both the city and its governing organisation (as the central co-ordinating force for the process). This is the second holistic characteristic of urban management, concerning *decentralisation* to ensure a symbiotic relationship between the city and its governing institution.
- Finally, is the test of institutional development; the organisation's ability to prepare the strategy for urban management to provide the infrastructure and services. This highlights not only the scope and style of, but also the guidelines for urban management (through the checklist for the development strategy) and, therefore, the required functional focus for institution building (through strengthening, training and skills transfer). This is the third holistic characteristic of urban management, concerning the *sustainability* of all elements of the urban management process.

Institutional development (ID) for third world city management must be prepared to embrace the holistic nature of the urban management challenge. It may then have a chance to give a meaningful address to the challenge facing the cities of today and tomorrow, in the developing world.

In so doing, this book has arrived at a point where it can answer a question in the literature from an author who is central to the urban management debate. It is argued by Stren (1993) that 'while comparative and conceptual work has taken place within the (UN Habitat – Urban Management) Programme sectors, the overall concept of urban management has not been addressed head on. Is it an objective, a process or a structure?'[1] The response from this book is that urban management has an objective, is a process, with a clear structure. In reverse order; first, the *structure* governs:

- the function and integration of the process,
- the organisation and decentralisation of the process, and
- the ID and sustainability for the process.

Secondly, the *process* seeks to embrace the holistic nature of the urban management challenge.

Finally, the structure and process of urban management seek to achieve the simple but fundamental twin *objectives* of:

- planning for, providing and maintaining a city's infrastructure and services, and
- making sure that the city's local government is in a fit state, organisationally and financially, to do so.

Thus, urban management is the building of cities and their local governments. In this context, institutional development is the building of capacity to conduct the urban management process. Therefore, because of the pervading weakness of urban management practice in the developing world, institutional development becomes an integral part of that process. So, the implication for practitioners is that ideally, third world city managers will become institutional development experts.

In conclusion, this volume has attempted to achieve five things. First, it offered three conceptual frameworks, for institutional development (Table 1.1), the city management function (Table 2.1) and the city management form (Table 3.1). Secondly, it highlighted the fundamental importance of the organisation–environment relationship in institutional development. This was in terms of both going beyond a traditional, organisation-focused, terms of reference (Part IV) and measuring the impact of urban management in its development environment

(Part V). Thirdly, it presented a practical framework for testing the sustainability of ID; in this case, the transfer of an urban management capability to counterpart urban chief executives in Malawi (Table 4.1). Fourthly, it offered operating checklists for both the institutional development process (Table 5.1) and the preparation of integrated development strategies (Table 6.1). Finally, it highlighted the institutional development imperatives for third world city management (Part VI), along with their testing frameworks (Appendix: Figures A.1 to A.3).

This text has therefore attempted to develop a set of conceptual frameworks, operating checklists and testing frameworks to guide future interventions in the urban management systems of developing countries. The hope is that these frameworks and checklists will encourage both theorists and practitioners to discover solutions to the urban management challenge in their parts of the third world.

Appendix: Institutional Development Imperatives

The following three figures offer a basis for testing the institutional development imperatives for third world city management.

Figure A.1 is the urban intervention matrix. It is designed to highlight the extent of integration required by the co-ordinating agency for the urban management process – in the normal course of events, assumed to be local government. The matrix offers the core infrastructure interventions. It sets them against the range of possible organisations within a decentralisation spectrum. The importance is to identify not only the extent of integration required but also the nature and location of the organisations (outside the co-ordinating agency) responsible for funding the infrastructure.

Figure A.2 is the urban management matrix. It is designed to illustrate the level of decentralisation of the urban management process, defined by the functional checklist of the integrated development strategy. The elements of the development strategy (the function) are set against the possible organisations (the form). The importance is to gain an understanding of the organisational pattern for the urban management process.

Figure A.3 is the sustainability test for institutional development. It is designed to illustrate the chance of sustainability and self-development. The focus for institutional development is the functional checklist for the integrated development strategy. Each function is given a percentage weighting, according to relative importance. It is given a percentage score according to its probability of sustainability and self-development. The importance is to present observations about the host organisation's ability to produce the strategy; the core of the urban management process.

None of these figures is meant to offer an absolute determination of the extent of integration, level of decentralisation and chance of sustainability of the urban management process in developing countries. However, they are meant to offer an approach to thinking about urban management that gives hard pressed practitioners a chance to offer a structure to their thinking. The functional and organisational variables must obviously be modified according to local circumstances. The figures presented here are taken from Malawi's urban sector.

Figure A.1 Urban intervention matrix: integrating all the players

Decentralisation Sector Sub-sector	FORM					
	Delegation Private		Devolution Local govern't		Deconcentration Central govern't	
	NGO	Bus/Para	One tier	Two tiers	Regional	HQ
FUNCTION						
Network infrastructure:						
– water	2	116				
– sewerage			60			
– solid waste			5			
– flood control			0			
– power supply		0				
– trunk roads			117			135
– road reconstruction			63			
Serviced land (general)						
– housing						297
– commerce						0
– industry						5
– other						0
Serviced land (traditional)						
– site & service			129			
– squatter upgrading			53			
– (official) area upgrading			27			

	Cost	%			
Buildings					
– government			24		
– council					
Services					
– health					
– education			72		
– others (by the council)			438		
Total infrastructure costs by sector	2	116	526	0	0	461
Total services costs by sector			438		438
Total infrastructure provision	1,105	100			
Private sector provision	118	11			
Local government provision	526	48			
Central government provision	461	42			

EXTENT OF INTEGRATION REQUIRED — 52%

Figure A.2   Urban management matrix: form according to function

	Decentralisation Sector Sub-sector	FORM Delegation		Devolution		Deconcentration	
FUNCTION	Funding source (Tax/user Charge) # Economies of scale*	Private NGO	Bus/Para	Local govern't One tier*	Two tiers*	Central govern't Reg'l	HQ
	Score #	5	4	3	3	2	1
CITY BUILDING							
Context:							
population; economics; land-use; networks;	T			3			
environment; projections; poverty; city government.	T			3			
Network infrastructure:							
– water	C		4				
– sewerage	C			3			
– solid waste	C			3			
– flood control	T			3			
– power supply	C		4				
– trunk roads	T						1
road reconstruction	T			3		1	–
Serviced land (general)							
– housing	C						1

– commerce	C		1
– industry	C		1
– other	C		1
Serviced land (traditional)			
– site & service	C	3	
– squatter upgrading	C	3	
– (official) area upgrading	C	3	
Buildings			
– government	T	3	
– council	T		1
Services			
– health	C		1
– education	C		1
– others (by the council)	T	3	
Financing			
total cost by agency; council shortfall; SPBC1;	T	3	
SPBC2; the compromise and its justification.	T	3	
COUNCIL BUILDING			
Organisational:			
structures & personnel; planning processes;	T	3	
contextual reforms.	T		1
Financial:			
cost saving; revenue increasing;	T	3	
long term asset creation.	T	3	

Figure A.2 continued

Policy:
budget development; policy development;   T   3
integration of policy & budget planning.   T   3

Maximum delegation to the trading sector = 145 (100%). Minimum deconcentration within central govern't = 29 (20%). Over 73% = delegated model; 73–47% = devolved model; Under 47% = deconcentrated model.

LEVEL OF DECENTRALISATION   **49% DEVOLUTION**

Figure A.3 Institutional development: sustainability for third world city management

VARIABLES and COMPONENTS (S = scope; M = mode of intervention)		OBSERVATIONS	% Score	% weight	Weighted % score
CITY BUILDING					
Context: population; economics; land use; networks; environment; projections; poverty; city government.	S	Each of these components is within the comfortable grasp of the planning departments of the two larger cities' planning departments. The smaller councils' will have more difficulty.	75	15	11
Network infrastructure: water; sewerage; solid waste; flood control; power supply, trunk roads; road reconstruction.	M	Project proposals for each component is still dependent on the support of outside agencies. Additional strengthening is still required.	60	15	9
Serviced land (general): housing (according to type); commerce; industry; others (such as institutions or government).	M	Project proposals for each component is a developing competence in the two larger city councils. The smaller two cities especially, need additional assistance.	75	10	8
Serviced land (traditional): site & service; squatter upgrade; existing (official) area upgrading.	M	Project proposals for each component is a developing competence in the two larger city councils. The smaller two cities especially, need additional assistance.	75	10	8
Buildings: government proposals; council initiatives; council projects; small scale projects.	M	There seems to be no shortage of technical proposals for specific buildings.	90	5	5

Figure A.3 continued

Services: health; education; other council services with a direct impact on the community	M	Analysis of services needs and development is in its infancy, for all councils. Additional help is required to develop competence in this topic.	40	10	4
Financing: total cost, by agency; council shortfall; SPBC1; SPBC2; the compromise and its justification.	S	Strategy, programme, budget and consequence (SPBC) analysis was only conceived and attempted in late 1993. It requires refinement and further TA before it is consolidated.	60	15	9
COUNCIL BUILDING					
Organisational: structures & personnel; planning processes; contextual reforms.	M	Structures and personnel issues are well understood and competently acted upon. Planning processes are becoming stronger. Contextual reforms are dependent on central government.	95	6	6
Financial: cost saving; revenue increasing; long term asset creation.	M	The councils are presenting a variety of cost saving and revenue increasing measures. All councils have a minimum of five year capital programmes.	90	6	5
Policy: budget development; policy development; integration of polilcy & budget planning.	S	Each council's annual budget cycle is mature. The policy development cycle has been established. Integrating policy and budget is the means to sustain the planning competence.	100	8	8
Rating for sustainability scores; e.g, VG = very good chance of sustainability & self-development. Over 89% = VG; 70–89% = Good; 50–69% = Modest; 30–49% = Poor; Under 30% = VP.			na	100	72

CHANCE OF SUSTAINABILITY AND SELF-DEVELOPMENT — 72% GOOD

Notes and References

Preface

1. R. McGill (1994) 'Integrated urban management: an operational model for Third World city managers', *Cities*, Vol. 11, No. 1, pp. 35–47.
2. R. McGill (1995) 'Urban management performance: an operational guide for Third World city managers', *Cities*, Vol. 12, No. 5, pp. 337–51.

1 Defining Institutional Development

1. M. Blase (1986) *Institution building: a source book* (Columbia: University of Missouri Press), p. 329.
2. P. Blunt and P. Collins (eds) (1994) 'Institution building in developing countries', Special issue of *Public Administration and Development*, Vol. 14, No. 2, p. 111.
3. L. Adamolekun (1990) 'Institutional perspectives on Africa's development crisis', *Public Sector Management*, Vol. 3, No. 2, p. 5.
4. L. Graham (1993) 'The dilemmas of managing transitions in weak states: the case of Mozambique', *Public Administration and Development*, Vol. 13, No. 4, p. 417.
5. L. Salman (1992) 'Reducing poverty: an institutional perspective', Poverty and Social Policy Series, Paper No. 1 (Washington, DC: World Bank), p. 11.
6. M. Kiggundu, J. Jorgensen and T. Hafsi (1983) 'Administrative theory and practice in developing countries: a synthesis', *Administrative Science Quarterly*, Vol. 28, p. 66.
7. Blase, *Institution building*, p. 321.
8. G. Shabbir Cheema (1987) 'Strengthening urban institutional capabilities: issues and responses', in Asian Development Bank (1987b) *Urban policy issues* (Manila: Asian Development Bank), p. 149.
9. G. Shabbir Cheema (1993) 'The challenge of urban management: some issues', in Shabbir Cheema (ed.) (1993) *Urban management: policies and innovations in developing countries* (Westport, Conn.: Greenwood Praeger Press), p. 13.
10. N. Uphoff (1986) *Local institutional development: an analytical sourcebook with cases* (West Hartford, Conn.: Kumarian Press), p. 8.
11. H. Colebatch and P. Degeling (1986) 'Talking and doing in the work of administration', *Public Administration and Development*, Vol. 6, No. 4, p. 339.
12. Blase, *Institution building*, p. 329.
13. Uphoff, *Local Institutional development*, p. 9.
14. Adamolekun, 'Institutional perspectives on Africa's development crisis', p. 6.
15. Blase, *Institution building*, p. 329.

16. Ibid., p. 330.
17. Further Education Unit (1986) *Preparing for change: the management of curriculum-led institutional development* (Laxa: Longman), p. 4.
18. Colebatch and Degeling, 'Talking and doing in the work of administration', p. 344.
19. Ibid., p. 350.
20. Ibid., p. 351.
21. Ibid.
22. D. Brown (1989) 'Bureaucracy as an issue in Third World management: an African case study', *Public Administration and Development*, Vol. 9, No. 3, p. 380.
23. Uphoff, *Local institutional development*, p. 8.
24. P. Blunt (1990) 'Strategies for enhancing organisational effectiveness in the Third World', *Public Administration and Development*, Vol. 10, No. 3, p. 310.
25. Ibid., p. 303.
26. Ibid., p. 304.
27. Ibid., p. 305.
28. Ibid., p. 306
29. H. Werlin (1991b) 'Understanding administrative bottlenecks', *Public Administration and Development*, Vol. 11, No. 3, pp. 194–206.
30. G. Honandle (1982) 'Development administration in the eighties: new agendas or old perspectives', *Public Administration Review*, No. 42, p. 176.
31. Ibid.
32. Adamolekun, 'Institutional perspectives on Africa's development crisis', p. 14.
33. O.P. Dwivedi and J. Nef (1982) 'Crisis and continuities in development theory and administration: First and Third World perspectives', *Public Administration and Development*, Vol. 2, No. 1, p. 60.
34. Ibid., p. 62.
35. Ibid., p. 64.
36. Ibid., p. 65.
37. Adamolekun, 'Institutional perspectives on Africa's development crisis'.
38. M. Alveson (1987) *Organisational theory and technocratic consciousness; rationality, ideology and quality of work* (Berlin and New York: Walter de Gruyter), p. 16.
39. Ibid., p. 245.
40. Ibid., p. 258.
41. Ibid., p. 249.
42. Ibid., p. 253.
43. Werlin 'Understanding administrative bottlenecks', p. 196.
44. Honandle, 'Development administration in the eighties', p. 178.
45. Dwivedi and Net, op. cit., p. 74.
46. Ibid.
47. Brown, 'Bureaucracy as an issue in Third World management', p. 371.
48. T. Franks (1989) 'Bureaucracy, organisation and development', *Public Administration and Development*, Vol. 9, No. 3, p. 368.
49. G. Hyden (1990) 'Creating an enabling environment', in World Bank

(1990) *The long-term perspective study of Sub-Saharan Africa. Vol. 3, Institutional and Socio-political issues* (Washington, DC: World Bank), p. 80.

50. D. Hirschmann (1993) 'Institutional development in the era of economic policy reform', *Public Administration and Development*, Vol. 13, No. 2, pp. 116–17.
51. A. Israel (1987) *Institutional development: incentives to performance* (Washington, DC: World Bank and Baltimore: The Johns Hopkins University Press), p. 1.
52. Ibid.
53. B. Buyck (1991) 'The bank's use of technical assistance for institutional development', World Bank Working Paper No. 578 (Washington, DC: World Bank), p. 5.
54. C. Gray, L. Khadiagala and R. Moore (1990) 'Institutional development work in the bank: a review of 84 bank projects', World Bank Working Paper, No. 437 (Washington, DC: World Bank), p. 2.
55. S. Paul (1990a) 'Institutional development in World Bank projects', World Bank Working Paper No. 392 (Washington, DC: World Bank), p. 7.
56. UNDP (1991) *UNDP assistance in the Third World: a thematic assessment* (New York: UNDP), pp. 51–2.
57. J. Horberry and M. Le Marchant (1991) 'Institutional strengthening in international environmental consulting', *Public Administration and Development*, Vol. 11, No. 4, p. 385.
58. Blase, *Institution building*, p. 332.
59. Ibid., p. 335.
60. Ibid., p. 337.
61. Ibid., p. 338.
62. Ibid., p. 339.
63. Ibid., p. 340.
64. D. Brinkerhoff (1994) 'Institutional development in World Bank projects: analytic approaches and intervention designs', *Public Administration and Development*, Vol. 14, No. 2, p. 147.
65. Blase, *Institution building*, p. 340.
66. Ibid., p. 401.
67. Uphoff, *Local institutional development*, p. 192.
68. Ibid., p. 196.
69. H. Werlin (1991a) 'Editorial: Bottlenecks to developments: studies from the World Bank's economic development institute', *Public Administration and Development*, Vol. 11, No. 3, p. 190.
70. B. Nunberg and J. Nellis (1990) 'Civil service reform and the World Bank', World Bank Working Paper No. 422 (Washington, DC: World Bank), p. i.
71. Ibid., p. 24.
72. Ibid., p. 31.
73. Gray, Khadiagala and Moore, 'Institutional development work in the bank', p. 11.
74. Ibid., p. 13.
75. A. Churchill (1991) 'Implementing reform: strategy and tactics'. Paper presented at the ministers' conference, Mexico, September, 1991. In-

dustry and Energy Department (Washington, DC: World Bank), p. 1.

76. Ibid., p. 2.
77. Ibid., p. 3.
78. Ibid., p. 4.
79. Ibid.
80. Ibid., p. 5.
81. Ibid., p. 7.
82. Ibid.
83. Ibid.
84. Paul, 'Institutional developments in World Bank projects', p. iii.
85. S. Paul (1991) 'The [World] Bank's work on institutional development in sectors: emerging tasks and challenges', Country Economics Department, Public Sector Management and Private Sector Development Division, November 1 (Washington, DC: World Bank), p. 1.
86. Brinkerhoff, 'Institutional development' p. 151.
87. V. Moharir (1991) 'Capacity building initiative for Sub-Saharan Africa', *Public Enterprise*, Vol. 11, No. 4, pp. 234–45.
88. Ibid., p. 237.
89. Gray, Khadiagada and Moore, 'Institutional development work in the land' p. 26.
90. World Bank (1993c) *Getting results: the World Bank's agenda for improving development effectiveness* (Washington, DC: World Bank), p. 2.
91. Ibid., p. 7.
92. UNDP (1989) *Urban transition in developing countries: policy issues and implications for technical co-operation in the 1990s. Programme Advisory Note* (New York: United Nations Development Programme), p. 35.
93. Paul, 'Institutional developments in World Bank projects', p. 2.
94. U. Locher and R. McGill (1994) *Municipal development programme for Sub-Saharan Africa. Final evaluation of MDP* (Phase 1); Eastern and *Southern Africa module. Final Report*, June (Ottawa: Federation of Canadian Municipalities), pp. 58–9.
95. C. Madavo (1989) 'Strengthening local governments in Sub-Saharan Africa' opening paper in World Bank (1989b) *Strengthening local governments in Sub-Saharan Africa: proceedings of two workshops* (Washington, DC: World Bank). Republished as an EDI policy seminar report, No. 21, in 1990, p. 65.
96. Blunt and Collins (eds), 'Institution building in developing countries', p. 116.
97. Paul, 'Institutional developments in World Bank project', p. 11 and Paul (1990b) 'Institutional reforms in sector adjustment operations: the World Bank's experience', World Bank Discussion Paper No. 92 (Washington, DC: World Bank), pp. v–vi.
98. Blase, *Institution building: a source book*, p. 330.
99. Honandle, 'Development administration in the eighties', p. 178.
100. Uphoff, *Local institutional development*, p. 192.

2 Applying ID in the Third World

1. B. Buyck (1991) 'The bank's use of technical assistance for institutional development', World Bank Working Paper No. 578 (Washington, DC: World Bank), p. 25.
2. Asian Development Bank (1986) *Environmental planning and management: a regional symposium* (Manila: Asian Development Bank), p. 46; Asian Development Bank (1987a) *Environmental planning and management, and the project cycle* (Manila: Asian Development Bank), p. 16; World Bank (1993c) *Getting results: the World Bank's agenda for improving development effectiveness* (Washington, DC: The World Bank), p. 19.
3. G. Honandle and J. Rosengard (1983) 'Putting projectised development in perspective', *Public Administration and Development*, Vol. 3, No. 4, p. 299.
4. D. Rondinelli (1983) 'Projects as instruments of development administration', *Public Administration and Development*, Vol. 3, No. 4, p. 308.
5. Ibid., p. 317.
6. D. Hulme (1992) 'Enhancing organisational effectiveness in developing countries: the training and visit system revisited', *Public Administration and Development*, Vol. 12, No. 5, p. 433.
7. D. Brinkerhoff and M. Ingle (1989) 'Integrating blueprint and process: a structured approach to development management', *Public Administration and Development*, Vol. 9, No. 5, p. 488.
8. T. Dichter (1989) 'Development management: plain or fancy? Sorting out some muddles', *Public Administration and Development*, Vol. 9, No. 3, p. 383.
9. L. Salman (1992) 'Reducing poverty: an institutional perspective', Poverty and Social Policy Series, Paper No. 1 (Washington, DC: World Bank), p. 5.
10. G. Baldwin (1990) 'Nongovernmental organisations and African development: an inquiry', in World Bank (1990), p. 92.
11. World Bank (1983) *World Development Report* (Washington, DC: World Bank), p. 126.
12. D. Conyers and M. Kaul (1990a) 'Strategic issues in development management: learning from successful experience, Part I', *Public Administration and Development*, Vol. 10, No. 2, p. 128.
13. Ibid., p. 130.
14. Ibid., p. 131.
15. Ibid., p. 132.
16. Ibid., p. 133.
17. Ibid., p. 134.
18. Ibid., p. 135.
19. Ibid., p. 136.
20. Ibid., p. 137.
21. M. Kaul (1988) 'Strategic issues in development management: learning from successful experiences', *Public Sector Management*, Vol. 1, No. 3, p. 15.
22. Ibid., p. 17.

23. Ibid., p. 18.
24. Ibid., p. 19.
25. Ibid., p. 20.
26. Ibid., p. 21.
27. Ibid.
28. A. Israel (1987) *Institutional development: incentives to performance* (Washington, DC: World Bank and Baltimore: The Johns Hopkins University Press), p. 31.
29. Ibid., p. 32.
30. Ibid., p. 34.
31. Ibid., p. 36.
32. Ibid., p. 37.
33. Ibid., p. 39.
34. Ibid., p. 40.
35. Ibid., p. 132.
36. G. Shabbir Cheema (1987) 'Strengthening urban institutional capabilities: issues and responses', in Asian Development Bank (1987b) *Urban policy issues* (Manila: Asian Development Bank), p. 178.
37. Honandle and Rosengard, 'Putting projectised development in practice', p. 304.
38. Brinkerhoff and Ingle, 'Integrating blueprint and process', pp. 488–9.
39. UNDP (1990a) *Cities, people and poverty, urban development cooperation for the 1990s* UNDP strategy paper (New York: UNDP), p. viii.
40. Dichter, 'Development management: plain or fancy? Sorting out some muddles', p. 398.
41. C. Kinder (1988) 'Total resource management in the Third World', *Public Sector Management*, Vol. 1, No. 1, p. 40.
42. C. Turner (1983) 'Curriculum-led institutional development: the management model'. Coombe Lodge Working Paper, No. 1849 (Bristol: Further Education Staff College).
43. Blase, *Institution building: a source book*, p. 350.
44. Israel, *Institutional development: incentives to performance*, p. 28.
45. Blase, *Institution building: a source book*, p. 404.
46. Buyck, 'The bank's use of technical assistance for institutional development', p. 14.
47. Ibid., p. 17.
48. Ibid., p. 26.
49. M. Bamberger and E. Hewitt (1987) 'A manager's guide to monitoring and evaluating urban development programmes: a handbook for programme managers and researcher', World Bank Technical Paper No. 54 (Washington, DC: World Bank), p. 4.
50. Buyck, 'The land's use of technical assistance for institutional development', p. 25.
51. D.F. Luke (1986) 'Trends in development administration: the continuing challenge to the efficacy of the post-colonial state in the Third World', *Public Administration and Development*, Vol. 6, No. 1, p. 81.
52. J. Wunsch (1991a) 'Institutional analysis and decentralisation: developing an analytical framework for effective Third World administrative reform', *Public Administration and Development*, Vol. 11, No. 5, p. 436.

53. Israel, *Institutional development: incentive to performance*, p. 48.
54. Ibid., p. 200.
55. T. Pike (1988) 'The experience of British aid in the urban field – possible future directions', *Habitat International*, Vol. 12, No. 3, p. 167.
56. Buyck, 'The land's use of technical assistance for institutional development', pp. 30–1.
57. Ibid., p. 34.
58. Asian Development Bank (1991) *Guidelines for integrated regional economic-cum-environmental development planning* (Manila: Asian Development Bank), p. 30.
59. N. Harris (1990) 'Urbanisation, economic development and policy in developing countries', Working Paper No. 19 (London: Development Planning Unit, University College), p. 29.
60. World Bank (1989b) *Sub-Saharan Africa: from crisis to sustainable growth* (Washington, DC: World Bank).
61. Ibid., p. 58.
62. UNCHS (1984b) *Human settlements policies and institutions: issues, options, trends and guidelines* (Nairobi: United Nations Centre for Human Settlements (Habitat)), p. 130.
63. Conyers and Kaul, 'Strategic issues in development management', p. 294.
64. A. Laquian (1979) 'Human resource development for human settlement policies', *Habitat International*, Vol. 3, No. 3/4, p. 399.
65. M. Juppenlatz (1979) 'A comprehensive approach to the training of human settlements', *Third World Planning Review*, Vol. 1, No. 1, p. 94.
66. Ibid., p. 99.
67. Laquian, 'Human resource development', p. 398.
68. T. Blair (1985) 'Education for habitat', in T. Blair (ed.), *Strengthening urban management* (New York: Plenum), p. 198.
69. Shabbir Cheema, 'Strengthening urban institutional capabilities', pp. 176–7.
70. R. Gunesekera (1988) 'Training urban development managers: an example from the technical co-operation training programme for India', *Habitat International*, Vol. 12, No. 3, p. 154.
71. H.D. Kopardekar (1989) 'Training and developing skills for urban management', *Urban Affairs Quarterly*, Centre for Urban Studies (Nagarlok: The Indian Institute of Public Administration), Vol. 21, No. 4, p. 134.
72. M. Sanwal (1990) 'Revitalising organisations in developing countries: the case of an administrative training unit', *Public Sector Management*, Vol. 3, No. 3, p. 59.
73. M. Mattingly (1989) 'Implementing planning with teaching: using training to make it happen', *Third World Planning Review*, Vol. 11, No. 4, p. 417.
74. Ibid., p. 418.
75. U. Locher and R. McGill (1994) *Municipal development programme for Sub-Saharan Africa. Final evaluation of MDP (Phase 1); Eastern and Southern Africa module. Final Report*, June (Ottawa: Federation of Canadian Municipalities).
76. C. Benninger (1987) 'Training for the improvement of human settlements', *Habitat International*, Vol. 11, No. 1, p. 156.
77. P. Sidabutar, N. Rukmana, R. van den Hoff and F. Steinberg (1991)

'Development of urban management capacities: training for integrated urban infrastructure development in Indonesia', *Cities*, Vol. 8, May, p. 145.
78. Ibid., p. 146.
79. D. Pasteur (1992) 'Training for urban local government in Sri Lanka', *Papers in the Administration and Development*, No. 42 (Birmingham: Institute of Local Government Studies), pp. 2–3.
80. Mattingly, 'Implementing planning with teaching', p. 102.
81. F. Steinberg (1991) 'Urban infrastructure development in Indonesia', *Habitat International*, Vol. 15, No. 4, p. 18.
82. L. Roberts (1990) 'The policy environment of management development institutions in Anglophone Africa', Economic Development Institute Policy Seminar Report, No. 26 (Washington, DC: World Bank), p. 33.
83. M. Qadeer (1993) 'Planning education in less developed countries of the Commonwealth: an assessment', *Habitat International*, Vol. 17, No. 1, pp. 69–84, table 2.
84. Brinkerhoff and Ingle, 'Integrating blueprint and process', pp. 488–9.
85. Israel, *Institutional development*, p. 48.
86. Mattingly, 'Implementing planning with teaching', p. 418.

Summary to Part I

1. D.F. Luke (1986) 'Trends in development administration: the continuing challenge to the efficacy of the post-colonial state in the Third World', *Public Administration and Development*, Vol. 6, No. 1, p. 82.
2. M. Esman (1988) 'The maturing of development administration', *Public Administration and Development*, Vol. 8, No. 2, p. 129.
3. World Bank (1991e) 'The reform of public sector management: lessons from experience', Policy and Research Series, No. 18, Country Economics Department (Washington, DC: World Bank), p. 37.
4. M. Blase (1986) *Institution building: a source book* (Columbia: University of Missouri Press), p. 330.
5. G. Honandle (1982) 'Development administration in the eighties: new agendas or old perspectives', *Public Administration Review*, No. 42, p. 178.
6. N. Uphoff (1986) *Local institutional development: an analytical sourcebook with cases* (West Hartford, Conn.: Kumarian Press), p. 192.
7. D. Brinkerhoff and M. Ingle (1989) 'Integrating blueprint and process: a structured approach to development management', *Public Administration and Development*, Vol. 9, No. 5, pp. 488–9.
8. A. Israel (1987) *Institutional development: incentives to performance* (Washington, DC: World Bank and Baltimore: The Johns Hopkins University Press), p. 48.
9. M. Mattingly (1989) 'Implementing planning with teaching: using training to make it happen', *Third World Planning Review*, Vol. 11, No. 4, p. 418.
10. Uphoff, *Local institutional development*, p. 8.

3 Planning Perspectives

1. UNCHS (1987c) *Global report on human settlements* (Nairobi: United Nations Centre for Human Settlements (Habitat)), p. 98.
2. UNCHS (1984a) *An approach to the analysis of national human settlements: institutional arrangements* (Nairobi: United Nations Centre for Human Settlements (Habitat)), p. 1.
3. UNCHS (1989c) *Urbanisation and sustainable development in the Third World: an unrecognised global issue* (Nairobi: United Nations Centre for Human Settlements (Habitat)), p. 6; J.E. Hardoy and D. Satterthwaite (1991) 'Environmental problems of Third World cities: a global issue ignored?' *Public Administration and Development*, Vol. 11, No. 4, pp. 341–61.
4. R. Stren and P. McCarney (1992) 'Urban research in the developing world: towards an agenda for the 1990s', Major Report No. 26. Centre for Urban and Community Studies, University of Toronto, p. 2.
5. D. Lee-Smith and R.E. Stren (1991) 'New perspectives on African urban management', *Environment and Urbanization*, Vol. 3, No. 1, p. 27.
6. E. Mills (1991) 'Urban efficiency, productivity and economic development', *World Bank Annual Conference on Development Economics: Report of proceedings* (Washington, DC: World Bank), p. 21.
7. E. Wegelin (1990) 'New approaches in urban services delivery: a comparison of emerging experience in selected Asian countries', *Cities*, Vol. 7, August, p. 245.
8. UNCHS (1987b) *Executive summary of the global report on human settlements* (Nairobi: United Nations Centre for Human Settlements (Habitat)), p. 8.
9. R.E. Stren (1993) 'Urban management in development assistance: an elusive concept', *Cities*, Vol. 10, May, p. 127.
10. J. Leitmann, C. Bartone and J. Bernstein (1992) 'Environmental management and urban development: issues and options for Third World cities', *Environment and Urbanisation*, Vol. 4, No. 2, p. 132.
11. J.E. Hardoy and D. Satterthwaite (1990) 'The future city', in J.E. Hardoy, S. Cairncross and D. Satterthwaite (eds) (1990) *The poor die young: housing and health in Third World cities* (London: Earthscan), pp. 228–44; D. Rondinelli (1988a) 'Giant and secondary city growth in Africa', in M. Dogan and J.D. Kasarda (1988) *The metropolis era: Vol. 1, a world of giant cities* (London: Sage Publications), pp. 291–321.
12. G. Clarke (1991) 'Urban management in developing countries: a critical role', *Cities*, Vol. 8, May, p. 107.
13. R. White (1989) 'The influence of environmental and economic factors on the urban crisis', in R.E. Stren and R. White (eds) (1989) *African cities in crisis: managing rapid urban growth* (Boulder: Westview Press), p. 19.
14. S.K. Sharma (1989) 'Municipal management', *Urban Affairs Quarterly – India*, Vol. 21, No. 4, p. 47.
15. J.M. Lusagga Kironde (1992) 'Received concepts and theories in African urbanisation and management strategies: the struggle continues', *Urban Studies*, Vol. 29, No. 8, p. 1289.

16. P. Knox and C. Masilela (1989) 'Attitudes to Third World urban planning: practitioners versus outside experts', *Habitat International*, Vol. 13, No. 3, p. 69.
17. C. Rogerson (1989a) 'Managing urban growth in South Africa: learning from international experience', *South African Geographical Journal*, No. 71, p. 129.
18. D. Okpala (1987) 'Received concepts and theories on African urbanisation studies and urban management strategies: a critique', *Urban Studies*, Vol. 24, p. 141.
19. Institute of Development Studies (1978) *Development Research Digest*, No. 1, Spring, pp. 11–14, on J. Collins, I. Muller and M. Safier (1975) *Planned urban growth: the Lusaka experience 1957–1973* (London: Development Planning Unit, University College).
20. C.S. Chandrasekhara (1989) 'Improving municipal management', *Urban Affairs Quarterly*, Centre for Urban Studies (Nagarlok: The Indian Institute of Public Administration), Vol. 21, No. 4, p. 66.
21. E.M. Pernia (1991) 'Some aspects of urbanisation and the environment in South East Asia', Report No. 54 (Manila: Asian Development Bank), p. 20.
22. Ibid., p. 21.
23. Ibid., p. 23.
24. C. Rakodi (1987) 'Urban plan preparation in Lusaka', *Habitat International*, Vol. 11, No. 4, p. 95.
25. A. Lakshmanan and E. Rotner (1985) 'Madras, India: low cost approaches to managing development', in J.P. Lea and J.M. Courtney (eds) *Cities in conflict: planning and management of Asian cities* (Washington, DC: World Bank), p. 85.
26. A. Sinou (1988) 'From planning to management', *RISED Bulletin*, No. 8 (Brussels: European Environmental Bureau), p. 25.
27. UNCHS (1987a) *Environmental guidelines for settlements planning and management. Vol. 1, Institutionalising environmental planning and management of settlements development* (Nairobi: United Nations Centre for Human Settlements (Habitat)), p. 2.
28. H. Richardson (1993) 'Problems of metropolitan management in Asia', in G. Shabbir Cheema (ed.) *Urban management: policies and innovations in developing countries* (Westport, Conn.: Greenwood Praeger Press), p. 61.
29. C. Farvacque and P. McAuslan (1992) 'Reforming urban land policies and institutions in developing countries', Urban Management Programme Policy Paper No. 5 (Washington, DC: World Bank), p. 63.
30. G. Clarke (1992) 'Towards appropriate forms of urban spatial planning', *Habitat International*, Vol. 16, No. 2, pp. 149–50.
31. UNCHS (1987c) *Global report on human settlements*, pp. 98–9.
32. A. Turner (1992) 'Urban planning in the developing world: lessons from experience', *Habitat International*, Vol. 16, No. 2, p. 124.
33. K. Davey (1983) 'Development administration revisited', *Papers in Administration and Development*, No. 20 (Birmingham: Institute of Local Government Studies), pp. 16–17.
34. D. McNeill (1983) 'The changing practice of urban planning: the World Bank and other influences', Working Paper No. 15 (London: Develop-

ment Planning Unit, University College), p. 5.

35. N. Devas (1989) 'New directions for urban planning and management', *Papers in Administration and Development*, No. 34 (Birmingham: Institute of Local Government Studies), pp. 13–14.

36. M. Safier (1992) 'Urban development: policy planning and management. Practitioners' perspectives on public learning over three decades', *Habitat International*, Vol. 16, No. 2, p. 11.

37. K.C. Sivaramakrishnan and I. Green (1986) *Metropolitan management: the Asian experience* (Oxford University Press for the World Bank).

38. F. Halla (1985) 'Changing the theoretical basis of urban planning from "procedures" to "political economy"', Working Paper No. 16 (London: Development Planning Unit, University College), pp. 36–7.

39. Ibid.

40. D. Rondinelli (1984) 'Small towns in developing countries: potential centres for growth, transformation and integration', in H. Detlef Kammeier and P.J. Swan (eds) *Equity with growth: planning perspectives for small towns in developing countries* (Bangkok: Asian Institute for Technology), p. 42.

41. UNCHS (1987b) *Executive summary of the global report on human settlements* (Nairobi: United Nations Centre for Human Settlements (Habitat)), pp. 11–12.

42. K. Davey (1993) 'Elements of urban management', Urban Management Programme, Working Paper No. 11 (Washington, DC: World Bank), p. 36.

43. H.R. Espinoza (1985) 'Planning and national development', *Planning and Administration*, Vol. 12, No. 2, p. 29.

44. B.O. De Albornoz (1985) 'The municipalities and local planning', *Planning and Administration*, Vol. 12, No. 2, p. 32.

45. A. Illaramendi (1985) 'Integral plans: an experience with public participation and housing in Venezuela', in T. Blair (ed.) *Strengthening urban management* (New York: Plenum), p. 40.

46. M. Wallis (1987) 'Local government and development in Southern African states: Botswana and Lesotho compared', *Planning and Administration*, Vol. 14, No.1, p. 72.

47. C.P. Rees (1987) 'Urban development: the environmental dimension', in Asian Development Bank (1987a) *Urban policy issues* (Manila: Asian Development Bank), p. 231.

48. E. Dawson (1992) 'District planning with community participation in Peru: the work of the institute of local democracy – IPADEL', *Environment and Urbanisation*, Vol. 4, No. 2, p. 96.

49. P.H. Hector (1985) 'The participation of local governments in the planning process of Panama', *Planning and Administration*, Vol. 12, No. 2, p. 41.

50. T.A. Aina (1990) 'The politics of sustainable Third World urban development', in D. Cadman and G. Payne (eds) (1990) *The living city: towards a sustainable future* (London and New York: Routledge), pp. 202–3.

51. S. Domicelj (1988) 'International assistance in the urban sector', in Asian Development Bank (1987a) *Urban policy issues* (Manila: Asian Development Bank), p. 252.

52. G. Clarke (1985) 'Jakarta, Indonesia: planning to solve urban conflicts', in J.P. Lea and J.M. Courtney (eds) (1985) *Cities in conflict: planning and management of Asian cities* (Washington, DC: World Bank), p. 44.

53. R. Allport and N. Einsiedel (1986) 'An innovative approach to metropolitan management in the Philippines', *Public Administration and Development*, Vol. 6, No. 1, p. 27.

54. Ibid., p. 28

55. J. Courtney and J. Lea (1985) 'Lessons in resolving the conflicts (of managing Asian cities)', in J.P. Lea and J.M. Courtney (eds) (1985) *Cities in conflict: planning and management of Asian cities* (Washington, DC: World Bank), p. 106.

56. F. Amos (1989) 'Strengthening municipal government', *Cities*, Vol. 6, No. 3, p. 206.

57. F. Davidson (1991) 'Gearing up for effective management of urban development', *Cities*, Vol. 8, No. 2, p. 122.

58. Ibid., p. 126.

59. B.K. Lee, (1987) 'Major urban development issues: an overview', in Asian Development Bank (1987a) *Urban policy issues* (Manila: Asian Development Bank), p. 30.

60. UNCHS (1987c) *Global report on human settlements*, p. 108.

61. J. Linn (1983) *Cities in the developing world; policies for their equitable and efficient growth* (New York: Oxford University Press), pp. 57–8.

62. Institute of Development Studies (1978) *Development Research Digest*, No. 1, Spring, p. 13.

63. Stren and McCarney (1992) 'Urban research', p. 47.

64. J. Perlman (1993) 'Mega-cities: global urbanisation and innovation', in G. Shabbir Cheema (ed.) (1993) *Urban management: policies and innovations in developing countries* (Westport, Conn.: Greenwood Praeger Press), p. 47.

65. D. Bhadra and A. Brandao (1993) 'Urbanisation, agricultural development and land allocation', World Bank Discussion Paper No. 201 (Washington, DC: World Bank), p. 4.

66. G. Shabbir Cheema (1993) 'The challenge of urban management: some issues', in G. Shabbir Cheema (ed.) (1993) *Urban management: policies and innovations in developing countries* (Westport, Conn.: Greenwood Praeger Press), p. 12.

67. J.E. Hardoy and D. Satterthwaite (1989) *Squatter citizen: life in the urban Third World* (London: Earthscan), p. 12.

68. UNCHS (1990a) *Financing human settlements development and management in developing countries* (Nairobi: United Nations Centre for Human Settlements (Habitat)), p. 51.

69. J.E. Hardoy and D. Satterthwaite (1990) 'The future city', in J.E. Hardoy, S. Cairncross and D. Satterthwaite (eds) (1990) *The poor die young: housing and health in Third World cities* (London: Earthscan), pp. 232–3.

70. R.E. Stren with V. Bhatt *et al.* (1992) 'An urban problematique: the challenge of urbanisation for development assistance', Centre for Urban and Community Studies (University of Toronto), p. 29.

71. J.D. Montgomery (1988) 'The informal service sector as an administrative resource', in D. Rondinelli and G. Shabbir Cheema (eds) (1988) *Ur-*

ban services in developing countries: public and private roles in urban government (Houndmills: Macmillan), p. 91.

72. Hardoy and Satterthwaite, 'The future city', p. 236.
73. Institute of Development Studies, *Development Research Digest*, p. 12.
74. Sinou, 'From planning to management', p. 25.
75. Ibid., p. 26.
76. A.L. Mabogunje (1992) 'Perspective on urban land and urban management policies in Sub-Saharan Africa', Africa Technical Department Series No. 196 (Washington, DC: World Bank), p. x.
77. G. Ayittey (1990) 'Indigenous African settlements: an assessment', in World Bank (1990) *The long-term perspective study of Sub-Saharan Africa. Vol. 3, Institutional and Socio-political issues* (Washington, DC: World Bank), p. 28.
78. Sinou, 'From planning to management'.
79. W.E. Rees (1992) 'Ecological footprints and appropriated carrying capacity: what urban economics leaves out', *Environment and Urbanisation*, Vol. 4, No. 2, p. 129.
80. J. Kolo (1991) 'Environmental planning in the Third World: dilemmas and possibilities', *Habitat International*, Vol. 15, Nos 1/2, p. 213.
81. L. Tacconi and C. Tisdell (1993) 'Holistic sustainable development: implications for planning processes, foreign aid and support for research', *Third World Planning Review*, Vol. 15, No. 4, p. 411.
82. T. Johnson (1990) 'Development impact exactions: an alternative method of financing urban development', *Third World Planning Review*, Vol. 12, pp. 144–5.

4   Scope of Intervention

1. R.E. Stren (1993) 'Urban management in development assistance: an elusive concept', *Cities*, Vol. 10, May, p. 131.
2. Ibid., p. 137.
3. K. Davey (1993) 'Elements of urban management', Urban Management Programme Working Paper No. 11 (Washington, DC: World Bank), pp. 19–20.
4. P. Williams (1978) 'Urban managerialism: a concept of relevance?', *Area*, Vol. 10, No. 3, p. 236.
5. Ibid., p. 237.
6. Ibid., p. 239.
7. Ibid., p. 240.
8. S. Leonard (1982) 'Urban managerialism: a period of transition', *Progress in Human Geography*, Vol. V, No. 2, p. 210.
9. S.K. Sharma (1989) 'Municipal management', *Urban Affairs Quarterly – India*, Vol. 21, No. 4, p. 48.
10. C. Rakodi (1991) 'Cities and people: towards a gender-aware urban planning process?', *Public Administration and Development*, Vol. 11, p. 542.
11. K.C. Sivaramakrishnan and L. Green (1986) *Metropolitan management: the Asian experience* (Oxford University Press for the World Bank), p. 12.

12. C. Marbach (1986) 'A review of ten years of *Habitat International'*, *Habitat International*, Vol. 10, No. 4, p. 196.
13. A. Ramachandran (1993) 'Improvement of municipal management', *Habitat International*, Vol. 17, No. 1, p. 12.
14. Ibid., p. 13.
15. F. Amos (1993) 'Comment on Ramachandran (1993)', *Habitat International*, Vol. 17, No. 4, p. 93.
16. F. Steinberg (1991) 'Urban infrastructure development in Indonesia', *Habitat International*, Vol. 15, No. 4, p. 7.
17. A. Cotton and R. Franceys (1988) 'Urban infrastructure: trends, needs and the role of aid', *Habitat International*, Vol. 12, No. 3, p. 142.
18. H. Richardson (1993) 'Problems of metropolitan management in Asia', in G. Shabbir Cheema (ed.) *Urban management: policies and innovations in developing countries* (Westport, Conn.: Greenwood/Praeger Press), p. 66. E. Brennan and H. Richardson (1989) 'Asian megacity characteristics, problems and policies', *International Regional Science Review*, Vol. 12, No. 2, pp. 117–29.
19. Steinberg, 'Urban infrastructure development in Indonesia'.
20. J. Linn (1983) *Cities in the developing world: policies for their equitable and efficient growth* (New York: Oxford University Press), pp. 56–7.
21. World Bank (1993a) *Developing the occupied territories: an investment in peace*. No. 1, Overview (Washington, DC: World Bank), pp. 9–10.
22. C.S. Chandrasekhara (1989) 'Improving municipal management', *Urban Affairs Quarterly*, Centre for Urban Studies (Nagarlok: The Indian Institute of Public Administration), Vol. 21, No. 4, p. 55.
23. Ibid., p. 56.
24. UNDP (1990b) *Human development report* (New York: Oxford University Press), p. 90.
25. F. Amos (1989) 'Strengthening municipal government', *Cities*, Vol. 6, No. 3, p. 208.
26. B. Thomson (1989) 'ODA workshop on urbanisation and British aid: a note for discussion', *Cities*, Vol. 6, No. 3, p. 172.
27. R.E. Stren (1991) 'Old wine in new bottles? An overview of Africa's urban problems and the "urban management" approach to dealing with them', *Environment and Urbanization*, Vol. 3, No. 1, p. 10.
28. Amos, 'Strengthening municipal government', p. 202.
29. A. Churchill (1985) 'Foreword', to J.P. Lea and J.M. Courtney (eds) *Cities in conflict: planning and management of Asian cities* (Washington, DC: World Bank), p. v.
30. Richardson, 'Problems of metropolitan management in Asia', p. 63.
31. Ibid., p. 64.
32. Ibid., p. 65.
33. G. Clarke (1991) 'Urban management in developing countries: a critical role', *Cities*, Vol. 8, May, p. 95.
34. Ibid., p. 96.
35. Ibid., p. 97.
36. J.P. Lea and J.M. Courtney (1985) 'Conflict resolution in the Asian city: an overview', in J.P. Lea and J.M. Courtney (eds) *Cities in conflict:*

planning and management of Asian cities (Washington, DC: World Bank), p. 6.

37. Ibid.
38. UNDP (1989) *Urban transition in developing countries: policy issues and implications for technical co-operation in the 1990s. Programme Advisory Note* (New York: United Nations Development Programme), p. 60.
39. G. Shabbir Cheema (1993) 'The challenge of urban management: some issues', in G. Shabbir Cheema (ed.) *Urban management: policies and innovations in developing countries* (Westport, Conn.: Greenwood Praeger Press), p. 7.
40. R.E. Stren with V. Bhatt *et al.* (1992) 'An urban problematique: the challenge of urbanisation for development assistance', Centre for Urban and Community Studies (University of Toronto), p. xiii.
41. Ibid., p. xiv.
42. Ibid., p. xxi.
43. Ibid., p. 4.
44. Ibid., p. 10.
45. Ibid., p. 67.
46. Ibid., pp. 68–9.
47. Ibid., p. 76.
48. J. Doyen (1990) 'The management of urban growth in Sub-Saharan Africa: an operational perspective from the World Bank', Internal paper from the Infrastructure Division, Africa Technical Department, March 16. Presented at the launch of the Municipal Development Programme (Washington, DC: World Bank), p. 2.
49. World Bank (1991c) *Urban policy and economic development: an agenda for the 1990s*, A World Bank Policy Paper (Washington, DC: World Bank), p. 36.
50. Ibid., p. 37.
51. A.L. Mabogunje (1993) 'Infrastructure: the crux of modern urban development', *Urban Edge*, Vol. 1, No. 3, p. 3 (Washington, DC: World Bank), p. 3.
52. D. Rondinelli (1990a) *'Decentralising urban development programs: a framework for analysis* (Washington, DC: US Agency for International Development), p. 3, citing J. Jacobs (1984) *Cities and the wealth of nations: principles of economic life* (New York: Random House).
53. Rondinelli, op. cit.
54. A. van Huyck (1987) 'Defining the roles of the private and public sectors in urban development', in Asian Development Bank (1987b) *Urban policy issues* (Manila: Asian Development Bank), p. 109.
55. Ibid.
56. J.E. Hardoy and D. Satterthwaite (1987) 'Housing and health: do architects and planners have a role?', *Cities*, Vol. 4, No. 3, pp. 226–7.
57. J. Cains (1988) 'Urbanisation and urban policy in the Third World', *Habitat International*, Vol. 12, No. 3, p. 95.
58. V. Gnaneshwar (1990) 'Basic services approach to urban development: Indian experience', *Cities*, Vol. 7, No. 4, p. 337.
59. E. Cheetham (1991) 'Comment on E. Mills (1991) *Urban efficiency, productivity and economic development, World Bank Annual Confer-*

ence on Development Economics: Report of proceedings' (Washington, DC: World Bank), p. 237.

60. G. Roth (1987) *The private provision of public services in developing countries* (Washington, DC: Oxford University Press for the World Bank), p. 230.

61. Ibid., p. 264.

62. M. Cohen (1988) 'Replicating urban shelter programmes: problems and challenges', in D. Rondinelli and G. Shabbir Cheema (eds) *Urban services in developing countries: public and private roles in urban government* (Houndmills: Macmillan), p. 123.

63. E. Mills and C. Becker (1986) *Studies in Indian urban development* (Oxford University Press), p. 207.

64. D. Rondinelli (1988b) 'Increasing the access of the urban poor to urban services: problems, policy alternatives and organisational choices', in D. Rondinelli and G. Shabbir Cheema (eds) (1988) *Urban services in developing countries: public and private roles in urban government* (Houndmills: Macmillan), p. 19.

65. R. Stren and P. McCarney (1992) 'Urban research in the developing world: towards an agenda for the 1990s', Major Report No. 26 (Centre for Urban and Community Studies, University of Toronto), p. 19.

66. B.K. Lee (1987) 'Major urban development issues: an overview', in Asian Development Bank (1987b) *Urban policy issues* (Manila: Asian Development Bank), p. 38.

67. C. Rogerson (1989b) 'Successful urban management in Seoul, South Korea: policy lessons for South Africa', *South African Geographical Journal*, No. 71, p. 171.

68. E. Wegelin (1990) 'New approaches in urban services delivery: a comparison of emerging experience in selected Asian countries', *Cities*, Vol. 7, August, p. 248.

69. Ibid., pp. 249–50.

70. Ibid., p. 247.

71. Ibid., pp. 250–1.

72. J. Courtney and J. Lea (1985) 'Lessons in resolving the conflicts (of managing Asian cities)', in J.P. Lea and J.M. Courtney (eds) *Cities in conflict: planning and management of Asian cities* (Washington, DC: World Bank), p. 106.

73. H. Henward, Jr. (1985) 'Metro Manila: conflicts and illusions in planning urban development', in J.P. Lea and J.M. Courtney (eds) *Cities in conflict: planning and management of Asian cities* (Washington, DC: World Bank), p. 21.

74. *The Economist* (1994) 'Infrastructure in Asia: the trillion-dollar dream', February 26, London, p. 86.

75. World Bank and UNCHS (1989) *Urban management programme: overview of programme activities* (Washington, DC: World Bank and Nairobi: UNCHS), p. 2.

76. Ibid., p. 4.

77. Ibid., p. 6.

78. Ibid., p. 7.

79. Ibid., p. 11.

80. World Bank and UNCHS (1990) *Urban management programme: phase 2* (Washington, DC: World Bank and Nairobi: UNCHS), p. 1.
81. World Bank and UNCHS (1991) *Urban management programme: revised prospectus* (Washington, DC: World Bank and Nairobi: UNCHS), p. 13.
82. R.E. Stren (1993) 'Urban management in development assistance: an elusive concept', *Cities*, Vol. 10, May, p. 131.
83. UNCHS (1990c) *The sustainable cities programme* (Nairobi: United Nations Centre for Human Settlements (Habitat)), p. 1.
84. UNCHS (1991) *Sustainable city demonstrations* (Nairobi: United Nations Centre for Human Settlements (Habitat)), p. 5.
85. Ibid., p. 7.
86. F. Amos (1989) 'Strengthening municipal government', *Cities*, Vol. 6, No. 3, p. 206.
87. Asian Development Bank (1987b) *Urban policy issues* (Manila: Asian Development Bank), p. 10.
88. D. Rondinelli (1987) 'National objectives and strategies for urban development in Asia', in Asian Development Bank (1987b) *Urban policy issues* (Manila: Asian Development Bank), p. 79.
89. UNDP (1990a) *Cities, people and poverty, urban development cooperation for the 1990s*, UNDP strategy paper (New York: UNDP), p. 3.
90. Ibid., p. 4.
91. Ibid., p. 5.
92. Ibid., p. 21.
93. Ibid., p. 53.
94. E. Caputo (1989) 'Enabling local economic growth', in World Bank (1989b) *Strengthening local governments in Sub-Saharan Africa: proceedings of two workshops* (Washington, DC: World Bank). Republished as an EDI policy seminar report, No. 21, in 1990, p. 111.
95. D. Hart and C. Rogerson (1989) 'Urban management in Kenya: South African policy issues', *South African Geographical Journal*, No. 71, p. 198.
96. T.L. Bertone (1992) 'Improving local government in Sri Lanka', *International Review of Administrative Sciences*, Vol. 58, No. 1, p. 72.
97. Sivaramakrishnan and Green, *Metropolitan management: the Asian experience*, p. 90.
98. Shabbir Cheema (1993), 'The challenge of urban management: some issues', p. 14.
99. Stren with Bhatt *et al.*, 'An urban problematique: the challenge of urbanisation for development assistance'.
100. N. Harris (ed.) (1992) *Cities in the 1990s: the challenge for developing countries* (London: UCL Press), p. xxi.

Summary to Part II

1. J. Linn (1983) *Cities in the developing world; policies for their equitable and efficient growth* (New York: Oxford University Press), pp. 57–8.
2. F. Davidson (1991) 'Gearing up for effective management of urban development', *Cities*, Vol. 8, No. 2, p. 132.

5 Organisational Dilemmas

1. World Bank (1993a) *Developing the occupied territories: an investment in peace. No. 1, Overview* (Washington, DC: World Bank).
2. G. Shabbir Cheema (1993) 'The challenge of urban management: some issues', in G. Shabbir Cheema (ed.) *Urban management: policies and innovations in developing countries* (Westport, Conn.: Greenwood Praeger Press), p. 13.
3. D. Rondinelli (1988b) 'Increasing the access of the urban poor to urban services: problems, policy alternatives and organisational choices', in D. Rondinelli and G. Shabbir Cheema (eds) (1988) *Urban services in developing countries: public and private roles in urban government* (Houndmills: Macmillan), p. 51.
4. UNCHS (1984b) *Human settlements policies and institutions: issues, options, trends and guidelines* (Nairobi: United Nations Centre for Human Settlements (Habitat)), p. 105.
5. P. Mawhood (1987) 'Decentralisation and the Third World in the 1980s', *Planning and Administration*, Vol. 14, No. 1, p. 14.
6. H. Richardson (1993) 'Problems of metropolitan management in Asia', in G. Shabbir Cheema (ed.) (1993) *Urban management: policies and innovations in developing countries* (Westport, Conn.: Greenwood Praeger Press), p. 67.
7. H.J. Allen (1987) 'Decentralisation for development: a point of view', *Planning and Administration*, Vol. 14, No. 1, pp. 23–30; P.S. Nooi (1987) 'Local self-government reform: a comparative study of selected countries in Africa and Southeast Asia', *Planning and Administration*, Vol. 14, No. 1, pp. 31–8; G.O. Orewa (1987) 'Local self-government: developments in Anglophone Africa', *Planning and Administration*, Vol. 14, No. 1, pp. 39–47.
8. C. Rakodi (1987) 'Urban plan preparation in Lusaka', *Habitat International*, Vol. 11, No. 4, p. 95.
9. R. Baker (1989) 'Institutional innovation, development and environmental management: an "administrative trap" revisited. Part 1', *Public Administration and Development*, Vol. 9, No. 1, p. 33.
10. *Environment and Urbanisation* (1991) 'Editor's introduction. Rethinking local government: views from the Third World', *Environment and Urbanization*, Vol. 3, No. 1, p. 3.
11. Ibid., p. 5.
12. Ibid.
13. B.K. Lee (1987) 'Major urban development issues: an overview', in Asian Development Bank (1987b) *Urban policy issues* (Manila: Asian Development Bank), p. 42.
14. J.D. Montgomery (1988) 'The informal service sector as an administrative resource', in D. Rondinelli and G. Shabbir Cheema (eds) *Urban services in developing countries: public and private roles in urban government* (Houndmills: Macmillan), p. 105.
15. N. Devas (1989) 'New directions for urban planning and management', *Papers in the administration of development*, No. 34 (Birmingham: Institute of Local Government Studies), p. 16.

16. C. Rakodi (1990) 'Can third world cities be managed?', in D. Cadman and G. Payne (eds) *The living city: towards a sustainable future* (London and New York: Routledge), p. 112.
17. R.E. Stren and R. White (1989) 'Conclusion', in R.E. Stren and R. White (eds) (1989) *African cities in crisis: managing rapid urban growth* (Boulder: Westview Press), p. 309.
18. R.E. Stren (1991) 'Old wine in new bottles? An overview of Africa's urban problems and the "urban management" approach to dealing with them', *Environment and Urbanization*, Vol. 3, No. 1, p. 22.
19. UNCHS (1987c) *Global report on human settlements* (Nairobi: United Nations Centre for Human Settlements (Habitat)), p. 106.
20. Ibid., pp. 110–11.
21. UNCHS (1989a) *Institutional arrangements for regional (subnational) development planning* (Nairobi: United Nations Centre for Human Settlements (Habitat)), p. 67.
22. Stockholm (1985) *Rethinking the Third World city*. Report from round table meeting in Stockholm, May, 1985. Sponsored by the Swedish Ministry of Housing and Physical Planning, Stockholm, p. 25.
23. A. Ramachandran (1985) 'Large cities and human settlement administration', in T. Blair (ed.) *Strengthening urban management* (New York: Plenum), p. 276.
24. N. Harris (1990) 'Urbanisation, economic development and policy in developing countries', Working Paper, No. 19, Development Planning Unit, University College, London, p. 27.
25. L.H. Hai (1988) 'Urban service provision in a plural society: approaches in Malaysia', in D. Rondinelli and G. Shabbir Cheema (eds) Urban *services in developing countries: public and private roles in urban government* (Houndmills: Macmillan), p. 144.
26. N. Bubba and D. Lamba (1991) 'Urban management in Kenya', *Environment and Urbanization*, Vol. 3, No. 1, p. 58.
27. Asian Development Bank, Halcrow Fox and Associates and INLOGOV (1992) *Botabek institutional development study; interim report* (Manila: Asian Development Bank), summary.
28. D. Olowu and P. Smoke (1992) 'Determinants of success in African local governments: an overview', *Public Administration and Development*, Vol. 12, No. 2, pp. 14–15.
29. J. Wunsch (1990a) 'Beyond the failure of the centralised state: toward self-governance and an alternative institutional paradigm', in J. Wunsch and D. Olowu (eds) (1990) *The failure of the centralised state: institutions and self-governance in Africa* (Boulder: Westview Press), pp. 286–8.
30. H. Werlin (1992) 'Linking decentralisation and centralisation: a critique of the new development administration', *Public Administration and Development*, Vol. 12, No. 3, p. 224.
31. J. Wunsch (1990b) 'Centralisation and development in post-independence Africa', in J. Wunsch and D. Olowu (eds) (1990) *The failure of the centralised state: institutions and self-governance in Africa* (Boulder: Westview Press), p. 60.
32. J. Wunsch and D. Olowu (1990) 'The failure of the centralised African state', in J. Wunsch and D. Olowu (eds) *The failure of the centralised*

state: institutions and self-governance in Africa (Boulder: Westview Press), p. 11.

33. D. Olowu and J. Wunsch (1990) 'Conclusion: self-governance and African development', in J. Wunsch and D. Olowu (eds), p. 305.
34. *Environment and Urbanisation*, op. cit., p. 5.
35. D. Oluwa (1987) 'The study of African local government since 1960', *Planning and Administration*, Vol. 14, No. 1, p. 56.
36. D. Olowu (1990) 'The failure of current decentralisation programmes in Africa', in J. Wunsch and D. Olowu (eds).
37. C. Ake (1990) 'Sustaining development on the indigenous', in World Bank (1990a) *The long-term perspective study of Sub-Saharan Africa. Vol. 3, Institutional and Socio-political issues* (Washington, DC: World Bank), p. 11.
38. Olowu, 'The failure of current decentralisation programmes in Africa', pp. 91–2.
39. Oluwu and Smoke (1992) 'Determinants of success in African local governments: an overview', *Public Administration and Development*, pp. 2–3.
40. A. Israel (1992) 'Issues for infrastructure management in the 1990s', World Bank Discussion Paper No. 171 (Washington, DC: World Bank), p. 77.
41. F. Uribe-Echevarria (1985) 'The decentralisation debate in Columbia: lessons from the experience', *Planning and Administration*, Vol. 12, No. 2, p. 12.
42. T.E. Blas (1985) 'The reason for and feasibility of participation in development in Latin America', *Planning and Administration*, Vol. 12, No. 2, p. 24.
43. Ibid., p. 25.
44. R. Prud'homme (1989) 'Main issues in decentralisation', in World Bank (1989b) *Strengthening local governments in Sub-Saharan Africa: proceedings of two workshops* (Washington, DC: World Bank). Republished as an EDI policy seminar report, No. 21, in 1990, p. 71.
45. J. Kolo (1987) 'The institutional dimension of participatory and decentralised planning in Nigeria. A challenge to planners', *Habitat International*, Vol. 11, No. 2, p. 9.
46. P. Ceccarelli (1989) 'The territorial aspects of decentralisation', in World Bank (1989b), p. 75.
47. Olowu (1990) 'The failure of decentralisation programmes in Africa', p. 91.
48. Werlin (1992) 'Linking decentralisation and centralisation', p. 228.
49. Ibid.
50. Wunsch (1991b) 'Sustaining Third World infrastructure investment', *Public Administration and Development*, Vol. 11, No. 1, p. 5.
51. Werlin (1992) 'Linking decentralisation and centralisation: a critique of the new development administration', *Public Administration and Development*, Vol. 12, No. 3, p. 234.
52. UNCHS (1984b) *Human settlements policies and institutions: issues, options, trends and guidelines* (Nairobi: United Nations Centre for Human Settlements (Habitat)), p. 106.
53. UNCHS (1990b) *Roles, responsibilities and capabilities for the management of human settlements: recent trends and future prospects* (Nairobi:

United Nations Centre for Human Settlements (Habitat)), p. 49.

54. M. Malo and P.J. Nas (1991) 'Local autonomy: urban management in Indonesia', *Sojourn: Social Issues in Southeast Asia* (Singapore: Institute of Southeast Asian Studies), Vol. 6, No. 2, p. 182.
55. G. Shabbir Cheema (1988) 'Services for the urban poor: policy responses in developing countries', in D. Rondinelli and G. Shabbir Cheema (eds) *Urban services in developing countries: public and private roles in urban government* (Houndmills: Macmillan), p. 247.
56. Ibid., p. 250.
57. UNCHS (1990b) *Roles, responsibilities and capabilities for the management of human settlements*, pp. 49–50.
58. K.C. Sivaramakrishnan and L. Green (1986) *Metropolitan management: the Asian experience* (Oxford University Press for the World Bank), p. 49.
59. UNCHS (1990b) *Roles, responsibilities and capabilities for the management of human settlements*, pp. 8–9.
60. Ibid., p. 65.
61. D. Rondinelli (1986) 'Extending urban services in developing countries: policy options and organisational choices', *Public Administration and Development*, Vol. 6, No. 1, p. 5.
62. Shabbir Cheema, 'Services for the urban poor', p. 250.
63. D. Rondinelli (1990a) *Decentralising urban development programs: a framework for analysis* (Washington, DC: US Agency for International Development), p. 1.
64. Ibid., p. 10.
65. Ibid.
66. Ibid., p. 11.
67. Ibid.
68. A.L. Mabogunje (1991) 'Local government issues in Africa', Paper presented at the launch of the Municipal Development Programme in Harare in May, 1991 (Ibadan, Nigeria: University of Ibadan), p. 9.
69. J.E. Hardoy and D. Satterthwaite (1992) *Environmental problems in Third World cities: an agenda for the poor and the planet* (London: International Institute for Environment and Development), p. 64.
70. Rondinelli, *Decentralising urban development programs*, p. 76.
71. P. Ljung and J. Zhang (1989) 'The World Bank support for institutional and policy reform in the metropolitan areas: the case of Calcutta', *Habitat International*, Vol. 13, No. 2, p. 13.
72. D.S. Meshram and R.P. Bansal (1989) 'Structure of municipal bodies: some basic issues', *Urban Affairs Quarterly* (Nagarlok: The Indian Institute of Public Administration), Vol. 21, No. 4, p. 34.

6 Structuring Criteria

1. K.C. Sivaramakrishnan and L. Green (1986) *Metropolitan management: the Asian experience* (Oxford University Press for the World Bank), pp. 54–5.
2. M. Faizullah (1989) 'Urban local government and urban development in Bangladesh', *Planning and Administration*, Vol. 16, No. 2, p. 64.
3. Ibid., p. 65.

4. T. Ngom (1989) 'Appropriate standards for infrastructure in Dakar', in R.E. Stren and R. White (eds) *African cities in crisis: managing rapid urban growth* (Boulder, Colo.: Westview Press), p. 198.

5. Ibid., pp. 200–1.

6. J. Moyo (1989) 'The demand for urban services in Africa', in World Bank (1989b) *Strengthening local governments in Sub-Saharan Africa: proceedings of two workshops* (Washington, DC: The World Bank). Republished as an EDI policy seminar report, No. 21, in 1990, p. 88.

7. Ibid.

8. G. Shabbir Cheema (1987) 'Strengthening urban institutional capabilities: issues and responses', in Asian Development Bank (1987b) *Urban policy issues* (Manila: Asian Development Bank), pp. 174–5.

9. R. Batley and N. Devas (1988) 'The management of urban development', *Habitat International*, Vol. 12, No. 3, p. 181.

10. E. Brennan and H. Richardson (1989) 'Asian megacity characteristics, problems and policies', *International Regional Science Review*, Vol. 12, No. 2, p. 126.

11. Moyo, 'The demand for urban services in Africa', p. 88.

12. R.E. Stren (1989b) 'Institutional arrangements (for local government)', in World Bank (1989b). Republished as an EDI policy seminar report, No. 21, in 1990, pp. 94–5.

13. I. Blore, S. Dutta and M. Willson (1992) 'Sustaining city services', *Papers in Administration and Development*, No. 44 (Birmingham: Institute of Local Government Studies), p. 13.

14. Ibid., p. 15.

15. Ibid., p. 17.

16. Ibid.

17. G. Roth (1987) *The private provision of public services in developing countries* (Oxford University Press for the World Bank).

18. Moyo, 'The demand for urban services in Africa', p. 89.

19. R.E. Stren (1989c) 'Urban local government in Africa', in R.E. Stren and R. White (eds) (1989) *African cities in crisis: managing rapid urban growth* (Boulder: Westview Press), p. 25.

20. Sivaramakrishnan and Green, *Metropolitan management: the Asian experience*, p. 57.

21. Ibid., pp. 58–9.

22. UNCHS (1984b) *Human settlements policies and institutions: issues, options, trends and guidelines* (Nairobi: United Nations Centre for Human Settlements (Habitat)), p. 117.

23. UNCHS (1984a) *An approach to the analysis of national human settlements institutional arrangements* (Nairobi: United Nations Centre for Human Settlements (Habitat)), p. 30.

24. L. Egunjobi and A. Oladoja (1987) 'Administrative constraints in urban planning and development', *Habitat International*, Vol. 11, No. 4, p. 93.

25. N. Harris (ed.) (1992) *Cities in the 1990s; the challenge for developing countries* (London: UCL Press), p. 44.

26. R. Bahl and J. Linn (1992) *Urban public finance in developing countries* (New York: Oxford University Press for the World Bank), p. 404.

27. Ibid., p. 407.

28. Ibid., p. 409.
29. UNCHS (1989b) *Methods for the allocation of investments in infrastructure within integrated development planning* (Nairobi: United Nations Centre for Human Settlements (Habitat)), p. 15.
30. G. Clarke (1992) 'Towards appropriate forms of urban spatial planning', *Habitat International*, Vol. 16, No. 2, p. 162.
31. Shabbir Cheema (1987) 'Strengthening urban institutional capabilities', p. 154.
32. Ibid., p. 155.
33. Ibid.
34. Ibid.
35. S.K. Sharma (1989) 'Municipal management', *Urban Affairs Quarterly – India*, Vol. 21, No. 4, p. 50.
36. T. Banergee (1989) 'Issues in financial structure and management: the case of the Calcutta metropolitan area', *Regional Development Dialogue*, Vol. 10, No. 1, p. 75.
37. K. Dhiratayakinant (1989) 'Issues in financial structure and management: the case of Bangkok metropolis', *Regional Development Dialogue*, Vol. 10, No. 1, p. 129.
38. Ibid., p. 130.
39. H. Franz (1986) 'Interorganisational arrangements and co-ordination at policy level', in F.X. Kaufmann, B. Majone and V. Ostrom (1986) *Guidance control and evaluation in the public sector* (Berlin and New York: Walter de Gruyter), p. 491.
40. Sharma, 'Municipal Management', p. 50.
41. S. Pearsall (1984) 'Multi-agency planning for natural areas in Tennessee', *Public Administration Review*, Vol. 44, No. 1, p. 47.
42. R. Allport and N. Einsiedel (1986) 'An innovative approach to metropolitan management in the Philippines', *Public Administration and Development*, Vol. 6, No. 1, p. 34.
43. E. Ostrom (1983) 'A public service industry approach to the study of local government structure and performance', *Policy and Politics*, Vol. 11, No. 3, p. 335.
44. Ibid.
45. Ibid., p. 337.
46. Bahl and Linn, *Urban public finance in developing countries,* p. 418.
47. Sivaramakrishnan and Green, *Metropolitan Management*, p. 83.
48. Ibid., p. 82.
49. Ibid.
50. Bahl and Linn, *Urban public finance*, p. 412.
51. Ibid., p. 415.
52. H. Fuhr (1994) 'Municipal institutional strengthening and donor coordination: the case of Ecuador', *Public Administration and Development*, Vol. 14, No. 2, p. 182.
53. Bahl and Linn, *Urban public finance*, p. 415.
54. L. Adamolekun (1989) 'Issues in development management in Sub-Saharan Africa', Policy Seminar Report No. 19, Economic Development Institute (Washington, DC: World Bank), p. 14.
55. G. Cochrane (1983) 'Policies for strengthening local government in de-

veloping countries', World Bank Staff Working Paper No. 582 (Washington, DC: World Bank), p. 47.

56. R.E. Stren (1993) 'Urban management in development assistance: an elusive concept', *Cities*, Vol. 10, May, p. 137.

57. D. Hart (1989) 'Mismanaged urbanisation in Africa: the examples of Cairo and Lagos', *South African Geographical Journal*, No. 71, p. 191.

58. O.P. Mathur (1987) 'The financing of urban development', in Asian Development Bank (1987b) *Urban policy issues* (Manila: Asian Development Bank), p. 142.

59. R. Prud'homme (1989) 'Main issues in decentralisation', in World Bank (1989b) *Strengthening local governments in Sub-Saharan Africa: proceedings of two workshops* (Washington, DC: World Bank). Republished as an EDI policy seminar report, No. 21, in 1990, p. 69.

60. Ibid., p. 70.

61. Ibid., p. 71.

62. V. Prakash (1988) 'Financing urban services in developing countries', in D. Rondinelli and G. Shabbir Cheema (eds) *Urban services in developing countries: public and private roles in urban government* (Houndmills: Macmillan), p. 77.

63. Ibid., p. 82.

64. Bahl and Linn, *Urban public finance*, p. 418.

65. R.E. Stren (1989a) 'The administration of urban services', in R.E. Stren and R. White (eds) (1989) *African cities in crisis: managing rapid urban growth* (Boulder: Westview Press), pp. 37–8.

66. B. Menezes (1985) 'Calcutta, India: conflict or consistency', in J.P. Lea and J.M. Courtney (eds) (1985) *Cities in conflict: planning and management of Asian cities* (Washington, DC: World Bank), p. 68.

67. Ibid., p. 69.

68. Bahl and Linn, *Urban public finance*, p. 386.

69. D. Rondinelli (1990b) 'Financing the decentralisation of urban services: administrative requirements for fiscal improvements', *Studies in Comparative International Development*, Vol. 25, No. 2, p. 44.

70. Stren (1989a) 'The administration of urban services', p. 66.

71. P. Sidabutar, N. Rukmana, R. van den Hoff and F. Steinberg (1991) 'Development of urban management capacities: training for integrated urban infrastructure development in Indonesia', *Cities*, Vol. 8, May, p. 142.

72. Ibid.

73. R. Martin (1989) 'Developing the capacity for urban management in Africa', *Cities*, Vol. 8, May, p. 139.

74. J. Fyfe (1988) 'Manpower planning and development in an organisation', *Public Administration and Development*, Vol. 8, No. 3, p. 312.

75. Ibid.

76. Sivaramakrishnan and Green, *Metropolitan management*, p. 75.

77. Rondinelli, 'Financing the decentralisation of urban service', p. 54.

78. IULA (1987), 'World wide declaration on local self-government', *Planning and Administration*, Vol. 14, No. 1, pp. 125–7.

79. J.E. Hardoy and D. Satterthwaite (1986) 'Shelter, infrastructure and services in Third World cities', *Habitat International*, Vol. 10, No. 3, pp. 245–84.

80. N. Harris (1989) 'Aid and urbanisation: an overview', *Cities*, Vol. 6, No. 3, p. 182.
81. R.E. Stren with V. Bhatt *et al.* (1992) 'An urban problematique: the challenge of urbanisation for development assistance', Centre for Urban and Community Studies (University of Toronto), p. 126.

7 Project Development

1. Malawi Government (1987) *Statement of development policies 1987–1996* (Zomba, Malawi: GOM).
2. Malawi Government (1986) *Lilongwe outline zoning scheme* (Lilongwe, Malawi: GOM).
3. Malawi Government (1987), op. cit., para 18.9.
4. Ibid., para 21.18.
5. R. Jones and M. Pendlebury (1988) *Public Sector Accounting* (London: Pitman).

8 Institutional Development Performance

1. Lilongwe City Council (1991): (a) *Annual report (draft)*, August; (b) *Integrated development strategy (3rd edition)*, August; (c) *Management manual*, August.

Summary and Conclusion

1. R.E. Stren (1993) 'Urban management in development assistance: an elusive concept', *Cities*, Vol. 10, May, p. 137.

Bibliography

Adamolekun, L. (1989) 'Issues in development management in Sub-Saharan Africa', Policy Seminar Report No. 19, Economic Development Institute (Washington, DC: World Bank).

Adamolekun, L. (1990) 'Institutional perspectives on Africa's development crisis', *Public Sector Management*, Vol. 3, No. 2, pp. 5–15.

Aina, T.A. (1990) 'The politics of sustainable Third World urban development', in Cadman and Payne (eds).

Ake, C. (1990) 'Sustaining development on the indigenous', in World Bank (1990), pp. 7–21.

Allen, H.J. (1987) 'Decentralisation for development: a point of view', *Planning and Administration*, Vol. 14, No. 1, pp. 23–30.

Allport, R. and N. Einsiedel (1986) 'An innovative approach to metropolitan management in the Philippines', *Public Administration and Development*, Vol. 6, No. 1, pp. 23–48.

Alveson, M. (1987) *Organisational theory and technocratic consciousness; rationality, ideology and quality of work* (Berlin and New York: Walter de Gruyter).

Amos, F. (1989) 'Strengthening municipal government', *Cities*, Vol. 6, No. 3, pp. 202–8.

Amos, F. (1993) 'Comment on Ramachandran (1993)', *Habitat International*, Vol. 17, No. 4, pp. 93–4.

Asian Development Bank (1986) *Environmental planning and management: a regional symposium* (Manila: Asian Development Bank).

Asian Development Bank (1987a) *Environmental planning and management: a regional symposium* (Manila: Asian Development Bank).

Asian Development Bank (1987b) *Urban policy issues* (Manila: Asian Development Bank).

Asian Development Bank (1991) *Guidelines for integrated regional economic-cum-environmental development planning* (Manila: Asian Development Bank).

Asian Development Bank, Halcrow Fox and Associates and INLOGOV (1992) *Botabek institutional development study: interim report* (Manila: Asian Development Bank).

Ayittey, G. (1990) 'Indigenous African settlements: an assessment', in World Bank (1990), pp. 22–31.

Bahl, R. and J. Linn (1992) *Urban public finance in developing countries* (New York: Oxford University Press for the World Bank).

Baker, R. (1989) 'Institutional innovation, development and environmental management: an "administrative trap" revisited. Part 1', *Public Administration and Development*, Vol. 9, No. 1, pp. 29–47.

Baldwin, G. (1990) 'Nongovernmental organisations and African development: an inquiry', in World Bank (1990), pp. 91–101.

Bamberger, M. and E. Hewitt (1987) 'A manager's guide to monitoring and evaluating urban development programmes: a handbook for programme managers and researchers', World Bank Technical Paper No. 54 (Washington, DC: World Bank).

Banergee, T. (1989) 'Issues in financial structure and management: the case of the Calcutta metropolitan area', *Regional Development Dialogue*, Vol. 10, No. 1, pp. 61–80.

Bartone, C., J. Bernstein, J. Leitmann and J. Eigan (1994) 'Toward environmental strategies for cities: policy considerations for urban environmental management in developing countries', Urban Management Programme, Policy Paper No. 18 (Nairobi: UNCHS).

Batley, R. and N. Devas (1988) 'The management of urban development', *Habitat International*, Vol. 12, No. 3, pp. 173–86.

Benninger, C. (1987) 'Training for the improvement of human settlements', *Habitat International*, Vol. 11, No. 1, pp. 145–60.

Bertone, T.L. (1992) 'Improving local government in Sri Lanka', *International Review of Administrative Sciences*, Vol. 58, No. 1, pp. 71–7.

Bhadra, D. and A. Brandao (1993) 'Urbanisation, agricultural development and land allocation', World Bank Discussion Paper No. 201 (Washington, DC: World Bank).

Blair, T. (1985) 'Education for habitat' in T. Blair (ed.) (1985), pp. 194–215.

Blair, T. (ed.) (1985) *Strengthening urban management* (New York: Plenum).

Blase, M. (1986) *Institution building: a source book* (Columbia: University of Missouri Press).

Blas, T.E. (1985) 'The reason for and feasibility of participation in development in Latin America', *Planning and Administration*, Vol. 12, No. 2, pp. 22–6.

Blore, I., S. Dutta and M. Willson 1992) 'Sustaining city services', *Papers in Administration and Development*, No. 44 (Birmingham: Institute of Local Government Studies).

Blunt, P. (1990) 'Strategies for enhancing organisational effectiveness in the Third World', *Public Administration and Development*, Vol. 10, No. 3, pp. 299–314.

Blunt, P. and P. Collins (1994) 'Introduction' in Blunt and Collins (eds) (1994), pp. 111–20.

Blunt, P. and P. Collins (eds) (1994) 'Institution building in developing countries', Special issue of *Public Administration and Development*, Vol. 14, No. 2.

Brennan, E. and H. Richardson (1989) 'Asian megacity characteristics, problems and policies', *International Regional Science Review*, Vol. 12, No. 2, pp. 117–29.

Brinkerhoff, D. (1994) 'Institutional development in World Bank projects: analytic approaches and intervention designs', *Public Administration and Development*, Vol. 14, No. 2, pp. 135–52.

Brinkerhoff, D. and M. Ingle (1989) 'Integrating blueprint and process: a structured approach to development management', *Public Administration and Development*, Vol. 9, No. 5, pp. 487–504.

Brown, D. (1989) 'Bureaucracy as an issue in Third World management: an African case study', *Public Administration and Development*, Vol. 9, No. 3, pp. 369–80.

Bubba, N. and D. Lamba (1991) 'Urban management in Kenya', *Environment and Urbanization*, Vol. 3, No. 1, pp. 37–59.

Buyck, B. (1991) 'The bank's use of technical assistance for institutional development', World Bank Working Paper No. 578 (Washington, DC: World Bank).

Cadman, D. and G. Payne (eds) (1990) *The living city: towards a sustainable future* (London and New York: Routledge).

Cains, J. (1988) 'Urbanisation and urban policy in the Third World', *Habitat International*, Vol. 12, No. 3, pp. 93–7.

Campbell, T. (1991) 'Decentralisation to local government in Latin American countries: national strategies and local responses in planning, spending and management', Latin America and the Caribbean Technical Department, Report No. 5 (Washington, DC: World Bank).

Caputo, E. (1989) 'Enabling local economic growth', in World Bank (1989b), pp. 107–12.

Ceccarelli, P. (1989) 'The territorial aspects of decentralisation', in World Bank (1989b), pp. 73–5.

Chandrasekhara, C.S. (1989) 'Improving municipal management', *Urban Affairs Quarterly*, Centre for Urban Studies (Nagarlok: The Indian Institute of Public Administration), Vol. 21, No. 4, pp. 54–67.

Cheetham, E. (1991) 'Comment on Mills, E. (1991) *Urban efficiency, productivity and economic development, World Bank Annual Conference on Development Economics: Report of proceedings*' (Washington, DC: World Bank), pp. 221–35; pp. 237–9.

Churchill, A. (1985) 'Foreword', to Lea and Courtney (eds) (1985), p. v.

Churchill, A. (1991) 'Implementing reform: strategy and tactics'. Paper presented at the Ministers' Conference, Mexico, September, 1991, Industry and Energy Department (Washington, DC: World Bank).

Clarke, G. (1985) 'Jakarta, Indonesia: planning to solve urban conflicts', in Lea and Courtney (eds) (1985), pp. 35–58.

Clarke, G. (1991) 'Urban management in developing countries: a critical role', *Cities*, Vol. 8, May, pp. 93–107.

Clarke, G. (1992) 'Towards appropriate forms of urban spatial planning', *Habitat International*, Vol. 16, No. 2, pp. 149–66.

Cochrane, G. (1983) 'Policies for strengthening local government in developing countries', World Bank Staff Working Paper No. 582 (Washington, DC: World Bank).

Cohen, M. (1988) 'Replicating urban shelter programmes: problems and challenges', in Rondinelli and Shabbir Cheema (eds), pp. 113–24.

Colebatch, H. and P. Degeling (1986) 'Talking and doing in the work of administration', *Public Administration and Development*, Vol. 6, No. 4, pp. 339–56.

Collins, J., I. Muller and M. Safier (1975) *Planned urban growth: the Lusaka experience 1957–1973* (London: Development Planning Unit, University College).

Conyers, D. and M. Kaul (1990) 'Strategic issues in development management: learning from successful experience. Part I', *Public Administration and Development*, Vol. 10, No. 2, pp. 127–40.

Cotton, A. and R. Franceys (1988) 'Urban infrastructure: trends, needs and the role of aid', *Habitat International*, Vol. 12, No. 3, pp. 139–47.

Courtney, J. and J. Lea (1985) 'Lessons in resolving the conflicts (of managing Asian cities)', in Lea and Courtney (eds) (1985), pp. 101–8.

Davey, K. (1983) 'Development administration revisited', *Papers in Administration and Development*, No. 20 (Birmingham: Institute of Local Government Studies).

Davey, K. (1993) 'Elements of urban management', Urban Management Programme Working Paper No. 11 (Washington, DC: World Bank).

Davidson, F. (1991) 'Gearing up for effective management of urban development', *Cities*, Vol. 8, No. 2, pp. 120–33.

Dawson, E. (1992) 'District planning with community participation in Peru: the work of the institute of local democracy – IPADEL', *Environment and Urbanisation*, Vol. 4, No. 2, p. 96.

de Albornoz, B.O. (1985) 'The municipalities and local planning', *Planning and Administration*, Vol. 12, No. 2, pp. 32–5.

Detlef Kammeier, H. and P.J. Swan (eds) (1984). *Equity with growth: planning perspectives for small towns in developing countries* (Bangkok: Asian Institute for Technology).

Devas, N. (1989) 'New directions for urban planning and management', *Papers in Administration and Development*, No. 34 (Birmingham: Institute of Local Government Studies).

Devas, N. and C. Rakodi (eds) (1993) *Managing fast growing cities: new approaches to urban planning and management in the developing world* (London: Longman Scientific and Technical).

Dhiratayakinant, K. (1989) 'Issues in financial structure and management: the case of Bangkok metropolis', *Regional Development Dialogue*, Vol. 10, No. 1, pp. 111–44.

Dillinger, W. (1994) 'Decentralisation and its implications for urban service delivery,' Urban Management Programme Discussion Paper, No. 16 (Nairobi: UNCHS).

Dichter, T. (1989) 'Development management: plain or fancy? Sorting out some muddles', *Public Administration and Development*, Vol. 9, No. 3, pp. 381–94.

Dogan, M. and J.D. Kasarda (1988) *The metropolis era, Vol. 1: a world of giant cities* (London: Sage Publications).

Domicelj, S. (1988) 'International assistance in the urban sector', in Asian Development Bank (1987b), pp. 247–68.

Doyen, J. (1990) 'The management of urban growth in Sub-Saharan Africa: an operational perspective from the World Bank', internal paper from the Infrastructure Division, Africa Technical Department, March 16. Presented at the launch of the Municipal Development Programme (Washington, DC: World Bank).

Dwivedi, O.P. and J. Nef (1982) 'Crisis and continuities in development theory and administration: First and Third World perspectives', *Public Administration and Development*, Vol. 2, No. 1, pp. 59–77.

The Economist (1994) 'Infrastructure in Asia: the trillion-dollar dream', February 26, p. 86 (London: Economist Publications).

Egunjobi, L. and A. Oladoja (1987) 'Administrative constraints in urban planning and development', *Habitat International*, Vol. 11, No. 4, pp. 87–94.

Environment and Urbanisation (1991) 'Editor's introduction. Rethinking local government: views from the Third World', *Environment and Urbanization*, Vol. 3, No. 1, pp. 3–8.

Esman, M. (1988) 'The maturing of development administration', *Public Administration and Development*, Vol. 8, No. 2, pp. 125–34.

Espinoza, H.R. (1985) 'Planning and national development', *Planning and Administration*, Vol. 12, No. 2, pp. 28–31.

Faizullah, M. (1989) 'Urban local government and urban development in Bangladesh', *Planning and Administration*, Vol. 16, No. 2, pp. 59–69.

Farvacque, C. and P. McAuslan (1992) 'Reforming urban land policies and institutions in developing countries', Urban Management Programme Policy Paper No. 5 (Washington, DC: World Bank).

Fox, W. (1994) *Strategic options for urban infrastructure management*, Urban Management Programme, Policy Paper No. 17 (Nairobi: UNCHS).

Franks, T. (1989) 'Bureaucracy, organisation and development', *Public Administration and Development*, Vol. 9, No. 3, pp. 357–68.

Franz, H. (1986) 'Interorganisational arrangements and co-ordination at policy level', in Kaufmann *et al.* (1986), pp. 479–94.

Fuhr, H. (1994) 'Municipal institutional strengthening and donor coordination: the case of Ecuador', *Public Administration and Development*, Vol. 14, No. 2, pp. 169–86.

Further Education Unit (1986) *Preparing for change: the management of curriculum-led institutional development* (Laya: Longman).

Fyfe, J. (1988) 'Manpower planning and development in an organisation', *Public Administration and Development*, Vol. 8, No. 3, pp. 305–16.

Galal, A. and M. Shirley (eds) (1994) 'Does privatisation deliver?: highlights from a World Bank conference,' EDI Development Studies (Washington DC: World Bank).

Gnaneshwar, V. (1990) 'Basic services approach to urban development: the Indian experience', *Cities*, Vol. 7, No. 4, pp. 333–40.

Graham, L. (1993) 'The dilemmas of managing transitions in weak states: the case of Mozambique', *Public Administration and Development*, Vol. 13, No. 4, pp. 409–22.

Gray, C., L. Khadiagala and R. Moore (1990) 'Institutional development work in the bank: a review of 84 bank projects', World Bank Working Paper No. 437 (Washington, DC: World Bank).

Gunesekera, R. (1988) 'Training urban development managers: an example from the technical co-operation training programme for India', *Habitat International*, Vol. 12, No. 3, pp. 149–61.

Hai, L.H. (1988) 'Urban service provision in a plural society: approaches in Malaysia', in Rondinelli and Shabbir Cheema (eds) (1988), pp. 125–46.

Halla, F. (1985) 'Changing the theoretical basis of urban planning from "procedures" to "political economy"', Working Paper No. 16, Development Planning Unit (London: University College).

Hardoy, J.E. and D. Satterthwaite (1986) 'Shelter, infrastructure and services in Third World cities', *Habitat International*, Vol. 10, No. 3, pp. 245–84.

Hardoy, J.E. and D. Satterthwaite (1987) 'Housing and health: do architects and planners have a role?', *Cities*, Vol. 4, No. 3, pp. 221–35.

Hardoy, J.E. and D. Satterthwaite (1989) *Squatter citizen: life in the urban Third World* (London: Earthscan).

Hardoy, J.E. and D. Satterthwaite (1990) 'The future city', in Hardoy *et al.* (eds) (1990), pp. 228–44.

Hardoy, J.E. and D. Satterthwaite (1991) 'Environmental problems of Third World cities: a global issue ignored?', *Public Administration and Development*, Vol. 11, No. 4, pp. 341–61.

Hardoy, J.E. and D. Satterthwaite (1992) *Environmental problems in Third World cities: an agenda for the poor and the planet* (London: International Institute for Environment and Development).

Hardoy, J.E., S. Cairncross and D. Satterthwaite (eds) (1990) *The poor die young: housing and health in Third World cities* (London: Earthscan).

Harris, N. (1989) 'Aid and urbanisation: an overview', *Cities*, Vol. 6, No. 3, pp. 174–85.

Harris, N. (1990) 'Urbanisation, economic development and policy in developing countries', Working Paper, No. 19, Development Planning Unit (London: University College).

Harris, N. (ed.) (1992) *Cities in the 1990s; the challenge for developing countries* (London: UCL Press).

Hart, D. (1989) 'Mismanaged urbanisation in Africa: the examples of Cairo and Lagos', *South African Geographical Journal*, No. 71, pp. 182–92.

Hart, D. and C. Rogerson (1989) 'Urban management in Kenya: South African policy issues', *South African Geographical Journal*, No. 71, pp. 192–200.

Hector, P.H. (1985) 'The participation of local governments in the planning process of Panama', *Planning and Administration*, Vol. 12, No. 2, pp. 37–42.

Henward, Jr., H. (1985) 'Metro Manila: conflicts and illusions in planning urban development', in Lea and Courtney (1985), pp. 19–33.

Hirschmann, D. (1993) 'Institutional development in the era of economic policy reform', *Public Administration and Development*, Vol. 13, No. 2, pp. 113–28.

v.d. Hoff, R. and Steinberg, F. (eds) (1992) *Innovative approaches to urban management* (Aldershot: Avebury).

Honandle, G. (1982) 'Development administration in the eighties: new agendas or old perspectives', *Public Administration Review*, No. 42, pp. 174–9.

Honandle, G. and J. Rosengard (1983) 'Putting projectised development in perspective', *Public Administration and Development*, Vol. 3, No. 4, pp. 299–305.

Horberry, J. and M. Le Marchant (1991) 'Institutional strengthening in international environmental consulting', *Public Administration and Development*, Vol. 11, No. 4, pp. 381–99.

Hulme, D. (1992) 'Enhancing organisational effectiveness in developing countries: the training and visit system revisited', *Public Administration and Development*, Vol. 12, No. 5, pp. 433–46.

Hyden, G. (1990) 'Creating an enabling environment', in World Bank (1990).

Illaramendi, A. (1985) 'Integral plans: an experience with public participation and housing in Venezuela', in T. Blair (1985), pp. 37–48.

Institute of Development Studies (1978) *Development Research Digest*, No. 1, Spring, pp. 11–14, in Collins *et al.* (1975) (Brighton: IDS).

Israel, A. (1987) *Institutional development: incentives to performance* (Washington, DC: World Bank and Baltimore: The Johns Hopkins University Press).

Israel, A. (1992) 'Issues for infrastructure management in the 1990s', World Bank Discussion Paper No. 171 (Washington, DC: World Bank).

IULA (1987) 'World wide declaration on local self-government', *Planning and Administration*, Vol. 14, No. 1, pp. 125–7.

Jacobs, J. (1984) *Cities and the wealth of nations: principles of economic life* (New York: Random House).

Johnson, T. (1990) 'Development impact exactions: an alternative method of financing urban development', *Third World Planning Review*, Vol. 12, pp. 131–46.

Jones, R. and M. Pendlebury (1988) *Public Sector Accounting* (London: Pitman).

Juppenlatz, M. (1979) 'A comprehensive approach to the training of human settlements', *Third World Planning Review*, Vol. 1, No. 1, pp. 86–99.

Kaufmann, F.X., B. Majone and V. Ostrom (1986) *Guidance control and evaluation in the public sector* (Berlin and New York: Walter de Gruyter).

Kaul, M. (1988) 'Strategic issues in development management: learning from successful experiences', *Public Sector Management*, Vol. 1, No. 3, pp. 12–25.

Kessides, C. (1993) 'Institutional options for the provision of infrastructure', World Bank Discussion Paper No. 212 (Washington, DC: World Bank).

Kessides, C. (1993) 'The contributions of infrastructure to economic development', World Bank Discussion Paper No. 213 (Washington, DC: World Bank).

Kiggundu, M., J. Jorgensen and T. Hafsi (1983) 'Administrative theory and practice in developing countries: a synthesis', *Administrative Science Quarterly*, Vol. 28, pp. 66–84.

Kinder, C. (1988) 'Total resource management in the Third World', *Public Sector Management*, Vol. 1, No. 1, pp. 27–41.

Knox, P. and C. Masilela (1989) 'Attitudes to Third World urban planning: practitioners versus outside experts', *Habitat International*, Vol. 13, No. 3, pp. 67–81.

Kolo, J. (1987) 'The institutional dimension of participatory and decentralised planning in Nigeria. A challenge to planners', *Habitat International*, Vol. 11, No. 2, pp. 5–10.

Kopardekar, H.D. (1989) 'Training and developing skills for urban management', *Urban Affairs Quarterly*, Centre for Urban Studies (Nagarlok: The Indian Institute of Public Administration), Vol. 21, No. 4, pp. 130–42.

Lakshmanan, A. and E. Rotner (1985) 'Madras, India: low cost approaches to managing development', in Lea and Courtney (1985), pp. 81–94.

Laquian, A. (1979) 'Human resource development for human settlement policies', *Habitat International*, Vol. 3, Nos 3/4, pp. 393–401.

Lea, J.P. and J.M. Courtney (1985) Conflict resolution in the Asian city: an overview', in Lea and Courtney (eds) (1985), pp. 3–15.

Lea, J.P. and J.M. Courtney (eds) (1985) *Cities in conflict: planning and management of Asian cities* (Washington, DC: World Bank).

Lee, B.K. (1987) 'Major urban development issues: an overview', in Asian Development Bank (1987b), pp. 15–60.

Lee-Smith, D. and Stren, R.E. (1991) 'New perspectives on African urban management', *Environment and Urbanization*, Vol. 3, No. 1, pp. 23–36.

Leitmann, J., C. Bartone and J. Bernstein (1992) 'Environmental management and urban development: issues and options for Third World cities', *Environment and Urbanisation*, Vol. 4, No. 2, pp. 131–40.

Leonard, S. (1982) 'Urban managerialism: a period of transition', *Progress in Human Geography*, Vol. V, No. 2, pp. 190–215.

Lilongwe City Council (1991a) *Annual report (draft)*, August (Lilongwe, Malawi: Lilongwe City Council).

Lilongwe City Council (1991b) *Integrated development strategy: 3rd edition*, August (Lilongwe, Malawi: Lilongwe City Council).

Lilongwe City Council (1991c) *Management manual*, August (Lilongwe, Malawi: Lilongwe City Council).

Linn, J. (1983) *Cities in the developing world; policies for their equitable and efficient growth* (New York: Oxford University Press).

Locher, U. and R. McGill (1994) *Municipal development programme for Sub-Saharan Africa. Final evaluation of MDP (Phase 1); Eastern and Southern Africa module. Final Report*, June (Ottawa: Federation of Canadian Municipalities).

Ljung, P. and J. Zhang (1989) 'The World Bank support for institutional and policy reform in the metropolitan areas: the case of Calcutta', *Habitat International*, Vol. 13, No. 2, pp. 5–13.

Luke, D.F. (1986) 'Trends in development administration: the continuing challenge to the efficacy of the post-colonial state in the Third World', *Public Administration and Development*, Vol. 6, No. 1, pp. 73–86.

Lusagga Kironde, J.M. (1992) 'Received concepts and theories in African urbanisation and management strategies: the struggle continues', *Urban Studies*, Vol. 29, No. 8, pp. 1277–92.

Mabogunje, A.L. (1991) 'Local government issues in Africa'. Paper presented at the launch of the Municipal Development Programme in Harare in May, 1991 (Ibadan, Nigeria: University of Ibadan).

Mabogunje, A.L. (1992) 'Perspective on urban land and urban management policies in Sub-Saharan Africa', Africa Technical Department Series No. 196 (Washington, DC: World Bank).

Mabogunje, A.L. (1993) 'Infrastructure: the crux of modern urban development', *Urban Edge*, Vol. 1, No. 3 (Washington, DC: World Bank) p. 3.

Madavo, C. (1989) 'Strengthening local governments in Sub-Saharan Africa: opening paper', in World Bank (1989b), pp. 62–6.

Malawi Government (1986) *Lilongwe outline zoning scheme* (Lilongwe, Malawi: GOM).

Malawi Government (1987) *Statement of development policies, 1987–1996* (Zomba, Malawi: GOM).

Malo, M. and P.J. Nas (1991) 'Local autonomy: urban management in Indonesia', *Sojourn: Social Issues in Southeast Asia*, Vol. 6, No. 2, pp. 175–202 (Singapore: Institute of Southeast Asian Studies).

Marbach, C. (1986) 'A review of ten years of *Habitat International*', *Habitat International*, Vol. 10, No. 4, pp. 167–205.

Martin, R. (1989) 'Developing the capacity for urban management in Africa', *Cities*, Vol. 8, May, pp. 134–41.

Mathur, O.P. (1987) 'The financing of urban development', in Asian Development Bank (1987), pp. 115–146.

Mattingly, M. (1988) 'From town planning to development planning: a transition through training', *Habitat International*, Vol. 12, No. 2, pp. 97–109.

Mattingly, M. (1989) 'Implementing planning with teaching: using training to make it happen', *Third World Planning Review*, Vol. 11, No. 4, pp. 417–28.

Mawhood, P. (1987) 'Decentralisation and the Third World in the 1980s', *Planning and Administration*, Vol. 14, No. 1, pp. 10–22.

McGill, R. (1984) 'Evaluating organisational performance in public administration', *Public Administration Bulletin*, No. 43, pp. 27–41.

McNeill, D. (1983) 'The changing practice of urban planning: the World Bank and other influences', Working Paper No. 15, Development Planning Unit (London: University College).

Menezes, B. (1985) 'Calcutta, India: conflict or consistency', in Lea and Courtney (eds) (1985), pp. 61–78.

Meshram, D.S. and R.P. Bansal (1989) 'Structure of municipal bodies: some basic issues', *Urban Affairs Quarterly* (Nagarlok: The Indian Institute of Public Administration), Vol. 21, No. 4, pp. 30–6.

Mills, E. and C. Becker (1986) *Studies in Indian urban development* (Oxford: Oxford University Press).

Mills, E. (1991) 'Urban efficiency, productivity and economic development', *World Bank Annual Conference on Development Economics: Report of proceedings* (Washington, DC: World Bank) pp. 221–36.

Moharir, V. (1991) 'Capacity building initiative for Sub-Saharan Africa', *Public Enterprise*, Vol. 11, No. 4, pp. 234–45.

Montgomery, J.D. (1988) 'The informal service sector as an administrative resource', in Rondinelli and Shabbir Cheema (eds) (1988), pp. 89–112.

Moyo, J. (1989) 'The demand for urban services in Africa', in World Bank (1989b), pp. 83–8.

Ngom, T. (1989) 'Appropriate standards for infrastructure in Dakar', in Stren, and White (1989), pp. 177–202.

Nooi, P.S. (1987) 'Local self-government reform: a comparative study of selected countries in Africa and Southeast Asia', *Planning and Administration*, Vol. 14, No. 1, pp. 31–8.

Nunberg, B. and J. Nellis (1990) 'Civil service reform and the World Bank', World Bank Working Paper No. 422 (Washington, DC: World Bank).

OECD (1991) *Urban infrastructure: finance and management* (Paris: Organisation for Economic Co-operation and Development).

Okpala, D. (1987) 'Received concepts and theories on African urbanisation studies and urban management strategies: a critique', *Urban Studies*, Vol. 24, pp. 137–50.

Olowu, D. (1990) 'The failure of current decentralisation programmes in Africa', in J. Wunsch *et al.* (eds) (1990), pp. 74–99.

Olowu, D. and P. Smoke (1992) 'Determinants of success in African local governments: an overview', *Public Administration and Development*, Vol. 12, No. 2, pp. 1–18.

Olowu, D. and J. Wunsch (1990) 'Conclusion: self-governance and African development', in Wunsch *et al.* (eds) (1990), pp. 293–318.

Oluwa, D. (1987) 'The study of African local government since 1960', *Planning and Administration*, Vol. 14, No. 1, pp. 48–59.

Orewa, G.O. (1987) 'Local self-government: developments in Anglophone Africa', *Planning and Administration*, Vol. 14, No. 1, pp. 39–47.

Ostrom, E. (1983) 'A public service industry approach to the study of local government structure and performance', *Policy and Politics*, Vol. 11, No. 3, pp. 313–41.

Pasteur, D. (1992) 'Training for urban local government in Sri Lanka', *Papers in Administration and Development*, No. 42 (Birmingham: Institute of Local Government Studies).

Paul, S. (1990a) 'Institutional development in World Bank projects', World Bank Working Paper No. 392 (Washington, DC: World Bank).

Paul, S. (1990b) 'Institutional reforms in sector adjustment operations: the World Bank's experience', World Bank Discussion Paper No. 92 (Washington, DC: World Bank).

Paul, S. (1991) 'The (World) Bank's work on institutional development in sectors: emerging tasks and challenges'. Country Economics Department, Public Sector Management and Private Sector Development Division, November 1 (Washington, DC: World Bank).

Pearsall, S. (1984) 'Multi-agency planning for natural areas in Tennessee', *Public Administration Review*, Vol. 44, No. 1, pp. 43–8.

Perlman, J. (1993) 'Mega-cities: global urbanisation and innovation', in Shabbir Cheema (1993b), pp. 19–50.

Pernia, E.M. (1991) 'Some aspects of urbanisation and the environment in South East Asia', Report No. 54 (Manila: Asian Development Bank).

Peterson, G., G.T. Kingsley and J. Telgarsky (1994) 'Multi sectoral investment planning', Urban Management Programme, Working Paper No. 3 (Nairobi: UNCHS).

Pike, T. (1988) 'The experience of British aid in the urban field – possible future directions', *Habitat International*, Vol. 12, No. 3, pp. 163–8.

Prakash, V. (1988) 'Financing urban services in developing countries', in Rondinelli and Shabbir Cheema (eds) (1988), pp. 59–88.

Prud'homme, R. (1989) 'Main issues in decentralisation', in World Bank (1989b), pp. 67–71.

Qadeer, M. (1993) 'Planning education in less developed countries of the Commonwealth: an assessment', *Habitat International*, Vol. 17, No. 1, pp. 69–84.

Rakodi, C. (1987) 'Urban plan preparation in Lusaka', *Habitat International*, Vol. 11, No. 4, pp. 95–111.

Rakodi, C. (1990) 'Can third world cities be managed?', in Cadman, D. and Payne, G. (eds) (1990), pp. 111–24.

Rakodi, C. (1991) 'Cities and people: towards a gender-aware urban planning process?', *Public Administration and Development*, Vol. 11, pp. 541–59.

Ramachandran, A. (1985) 'Large cities and human settlement administration', in Blair, T. (ed.) (1985), pp. 272–9.

Ramachandran, A. (1993) 'Improvement of municipal management', *Habitat International*, Vol. 17, No. 1, pp. 3–31.

Rees, C.P. (1987) 'Urban development: the environmental dimension', in Asian Development Bank (1987a), pp. 227–46.

Rees, W.E. (1992) 'Ecological footprints and appropriate carrying capacity: what urban economics leaves out', *Environment and Urbanisation*, Vol. 4, No. 2, pp. 121–30.

Richardson, H. (1993) 'Problems of metropolitan management in Asia', in Shabbir Cheema (ed.) (1993), pp. 51–75.

Roberts, L. (1990) 'The policy environment of management development institutions in Anglophone Africa', Economic Development Institute Policy Seminar Report, No. 26 (Washington, DC: World Bank).

Rogerson, C. (1989a) 'Managing urban growth in South Africa: learning from international experience', *South African Geographical Journal*, No. 71, pp. 129–33.

Rogerson, C. (1989b) 'Successful urban management in Seoul, South Korea: policy lessons for South Africa', *South African Geographical Journal*, No. 71, pp. 166–73.

Rondinelli, D. (1983) 'Projects as instruments of development administration', *Public Administration and Development*, Vol. 3, No. 4, pp. 307–27.

Rondinelli, D. (1984) 'Small towns in developing countries: potential centres for growth, transformation and integration', in Detlef Kammeier *et al.* (eds) (1984), pp. 10–48.

Rondinelli, D. (1986) 'Extending urban services in developing countries: policy options and organisational choices', *Public Administration and Development*, Vol. 6, No. 1, pp. 1–22.

Rondinelli, D. (1987) 'National objectives and strategies for urban development in Asia', in Asian Development Bank (1987b), pp. 61–88.

Rondinelli, D. (1988a) 'Giant and secondary city growth in Africa', in Dogan *et al.*, pp. 291–321.

Rondinelli, D. (1988b) 'Increasing the access of the urban poor to urban services: problems, policy alternatives and organisational choices', in Rondinelli and Shabbir Cheema (eds) (1988), pp. 19–58.

Rondinelli, D. (1990a) *Decentralising urban development programs: a framework for analysis* (Washington, DC: US Agency for International Development).

Rondinelli, D. (1990b) 'Financing the decentralisation of urban services: administrative requirements for fiscal improvements', *Studies in Comparative International Development*, Vol. 25, No. 2, pp. 43–59.

Rondinelli, D. and G. Shabbir Cheema (eds) (1988) *Urban services in developing countries: public and private roles in urban government* (Houndmills: Macmillan).

Roth, G. (1987) *The private provision of public services in developing countries* (Washington, DC: Oxford University Press for the World Bank).

Safier, M. (1992) 'Urban development: policy planning and management. Practitioners' perspectives on public learning over three decades', *Habitat International*, Vol. 16, No. 2, pp. 5–12.

Salman, L. (1992) 'Reducing poverty: an institutional perspective', Poverty and Social Policy Series, Paper No. 1 (Washington, DC: World Bank).

Sanwal, M. (1990) 'Revitalising organisations in developing countries: the case of an administrative training unit', *Public Sector Management*, Vol. 3, No. 3, pp. 53–63.

Schiavo-Campo, S. (1994) 'Institutional change and the public sector in transitional economies', World Bank Discussion Paper No. 241 (Washington DC: World Bank).

Shabbir Cheema, G. (1987) 'Strengthening urban institutional capabilities: issues and responses', in Asian Development Bank (1987b), pp. 147–84.

Shabbir Cheema, G. (1988) 'Services for the urban poor: policy responses in developing countries', in Rondinelli and Shabbir Cheema (eds) (1988), pp. 243–62.

Shabbir Cheema, G. (1993) 'The challenge of urban management: some issues', in Shabbir Cheema, G. (ed.), pp. 1–16.

Shabbir Cheema, G. (ed.) (1993) *Urban management: policies and innovations in developing countries* (Westport, Conn: Greenwood Praeger Press).

Shah, A. (1994) 'The reform of intergovernmental fiscal relations in developing and emerging market economies', World Bank Policy and Research Series, No. 23 (Washington, DC: World Bank).

Sharma, S.K. (1989) 'Municipal management', *Urban Affairs Quarterly – India*, Vol. 21, No. 4, pp. 47–53.

Sidabutar, P., N. Rukmana, R. van den Hoff and F. Steinberg (1991) 'Development of urban management capacities: training for integrated urban infrastructure development in Indonesia', *Cities*, Vol. 8, May, pp. 142–50.

Sinou, A. (1988) 'From planning to management', *RISED Bulletin*, No. 8 (Brussels: European Environmental Bureau) pp. 25–6.

Sivaramakrishnan, K.C. and L. Green (1986) *Metropolitan management: the Asian experience* (Oxford University Press for the World Bank).

Steinberg, F. (1991) 'Urban infrastructure development in Indonesia', *Habitat International*, Vol. 15, No. 4, pp. 3–26.

Stockholm (1985) *Rethinking the Third World City.* Report from round table meeting in Stockholm, May, 1985. Sponsored by the Swedish Ministry of Housing and Physical Planning, Stockholm.

Stren, R.E. (1989a) 'The administration of urban services', in Stren and White (eds) (1989), pp. 37–68.

Stren, R.E. (1989b) 'Institutional arrangements (for local government)', in World Bank (1989b), pp. 88–94.

Stren, R.E. (1989c) 'Urban local government in Africa', in Stren and White (eds) (1989), pp. 20–36.

Stren, R.E. (1991) 'Old wine in new bottles? An overview of Africa's urban problems and the "urban management" approach to dealing with them', *Environment and Urbanization*, Vol. 3, No. 1, pp. 9–22.

Stren, R.E. (1993) 'Urban management in development assistance: an elusive concept', *Cities*, Vol. 10, May, pp. 120–38.

Stren, R.E. with V. Bhatt *et al.* (1992) 'An urban problematique: the challenge of urbanisation for development assistance', Centre for Urban and Community Studies (University of Toronto).

Stren, R. and P. McCarney (1992) 'Urban research in the developing world: towards an agenda for the 1990s', Major Report No. 26, Centre for Urban and Community Studies (University of Toronto).

Stren, R.E. and R. White (1989) 'Conclusion', in Stren *et al.* (eds) (1989), pp. 305–12.

Stren, R.E. and R. White (eds) (1989) *African cities in crisis: managing rapid urban growth* (Boulder, Colo.: Westview Press).

Tacconi, L. and C. Tisdell (1993) 'Holistic sustainable development: implications for planning processes, foreign aid and support for research', *Third World Planning Review*, Vol. 15, No. 4, pp. 411–28.

Thomson, B. (1989) 'ODA workshop on urbanisation and British aid: a note for discussion', *Cities*, Vol. 6, No. 3, pp. 171–3.

Turner, A. (1992) 'Urban planning in the developing world: lessons from experience', *Habitat International*, Vol. 16, No. 2, pp. 113–25.

Turner, C. (1983) 'Curriculum-led institutional development: the management model', Coombe Lodge Working Paper No. 1849 (Bristol: Further Education Staff College).

UNCHS (1984a) *An approach to the analysis of national human settlements: institutional arrangements* (Nairobi: United Nations Centre for Human Settlements (Habitat)).

UNCHS (1984b) *Human settlements policies and institutions: issues, options, trends and guidelines* (Nairobi: United Nations Centre for Human Settlements (Habitat)).

UNCHS (1987a) *Environmental guidelines for settlements planning and management. Vol. 1, Institutionalising environmental planning and management of settlements development* (Nairobi: United Nations Centre for Human Settlements (Habitat)).

UNCHS (1987b) *Executive summary of the global report on human settlements* (Nairobi: United Nations Centre for Human Settlements (Habitat)).

UNCHS (1987c) *Global report on human settlements* (Nairobi: United Nations Centre for Human Settlements (Habitat)).

UNCHS (1989a) *Institutional arrangements for regional (subnational) development planning* (Nairobi: United Nations Centre for Human Settlements (Habitat)).

UNCHS (1989b) *Methods for the allocation of investments in infrastructure within integrated development planning* (Nairobi: United Nations Centre for Human Settlements (Habitat)).

UNCHS (1989c) *Urbanisation and sustainable development in the Third World: an unrecognised global issue* (Nairobi: United Nations Centre for Human Settlements (Habitat)).

UNCHS (1990a) *Financing human settlements development and management in developing countries* (Nairobi: United Nations Centre for Human Settlements (Habitat)).

UNCHS (1990b) *Roles, responsibilities and capabilities for the management of human settlements: recent trends and future prospects* (Nairobi: United Nations Centre for Human Settlements (Habitat)).

UNCHS (1990c) *The sustainable cities programme* (Nairobi: United Nations Centre for Human Settlements (Habitat)).

UNCHS (1991) *Sustainable city demonstrations* (Nairobi: United Nations Centre for Human Settlements (Habitat)).

UNDP (1989) *Urban transition in developing countries: policy issues and implications for technical co-operation in the 1990s. Programme Advisory Note* (New York: United Nations Development Programme).

UNDP (1990a) *Cities, people and poverty, urban development cooperation for the 1990s*. UNDP strategy paper (New York: UNDP).

UNDP (1990b) *Human development report* (New York: Oxford University Press).

UNDP (1991) *UNDP assistance in the Third World: a thematic assessment* (New York: UNDP).

Uphoff, N. (1986) *Local institutional development: an analytical sourcebook with cases* (West Hartford, Conn.: Kumarian Press).

Uribe-Echevarria, F. (1985) 'The decentralisation debate in Columbia: lessons from the experience', *Planning and Administration*, Vol. 12, No. 2, pp. 10–20.

van Huyck, A. (1987) 'Defining the roles of the private and public sectors in urban development', in Asian Development Bank (1987b), pp. 89–114.

Wallis, M. (1987) 'Local government and development in Southern African states: Botswana and Lesotho compared', *Planning and Administration*, Vol. 14, No. 1, pp. 68–76.

Wegelin, E. (1990) 'New approaches in urban services delivery: a comparison of emerging experience in selected Asian countries', *Cities*, Vol. 7, August, pp. 224–58.

Werlin, H. (1991a) 'Editorial. Bottlenecks to developments: studies from the World Bank's economic development institute', *Public Administration and Development*, Vol. 11, No. 3, pp. 189–92.

Werlin, H. (1991b) 'Understanding administrative bottlenecks', *Public Administration and Development*, Vol. 11, No. 3, pp. 193–206.

Werlin, H. (1992) 'Linking decentralisation and centralisation: a critique of the new development administration', *Public Administration and Development*, Vol. 12, No. 3, pp. 223–36.

White, R. (1989) 'The influence of environmental and economic factors on the urban crisis', in Stren and White (eds), pp. 1–19.

Williams, P. (1978) 'Urban managerialism: a concept of relevance?', *Area*, Vol. 10, No. 3, pp. 236–40.

World Bank (1983) *World Development Report* (Washington, DC: World Bank).

World Bank (1989a) *Strengthening local governments in Sub-Saharan Africa: proceedings of two workshops* (Washington, DC: World Bank). Republished as an EDI policy seminar report, No. 21, in 1990.

World Bank (1989b) *Sub-Saharan Africa: from crisis to sustainable growth* (Washington, DC: World Bank).

World Bank (1990) *The long-term perspective study of Sub-Saharan Africa. Vol. 3, Institutional and Socio-political issues* (Washington, DC: World Bank).

World Bank (1991a) *The municipal development programme for Sub-Saharan Africa: a partnership for developing local government capacity* (Washington, DC: World Bank).

World Bank (1991b) *The reform of public sector management: lessons from experience*, Policy and Research Series, No. 18. Country Economics Department (Washington, DC: World Bank).

World Bank (1991c) *Urban policy and economic development: an agenda for the 1990s*, A World Bank Policy Paper (Washington, DC: World Bank).

World Bank (1993a) *Developing the occupied territories: an investment in peace. No. 1, Overview* (Washington, DC: World Bank).

World Bank (1993b) *Developing the occupied territories: an investment in peace. No. 5, Infrastructure* (Washington, DC: World Bank).

World Bank (1993c) *Getting results: the World Bank's agenda for improving development effectiveness* (Washington, DC: World Bank).

World Bank and UNCHS (1989) *Urban management programme: overview of programme activities* (Washington, DC: World Bank and Nairobi: UNCHS).

World Bank and UNCHS (1990) *Urban management programme: phase 2* (Washington, DC: World Bank and Nairobi: UNCHS).

World Bank and UNCHS (1991) *Urban management programme: revised prospectus* (Washington, DC: World Bank and Nairobi: UNCHS).

World Bank (1994) *Development report: infrastructure for development* (Washington, DC: World Bank).

Wunsch, J. (1990a) 'Beyond the failure of the centralised state: toward self-governance and an alternative institutional paradigm', in Wunsch *et al.* (eds) (1990), pp. 270–92.

Wunsch, J. (1990b) 'Centralisation and development in post-independence Africa', in Wunsch *et al.* (eds) (1990), pp. 43–73.

Wunsch, J. (1991a) 'Institutional analysis and decentralisation: developing an analytical framework for effective Third World administrative reform', *Public Administration and Development*, Vol. 11, No. 5, pp. 431–51.

Wunsch, J. (1991b) 'Sustaining Third World infrastructure investments: decentralisation and other strategies', *Public Administration and Development*, Vol. 11, No. 1, pp. 5–24.

Wunsch, J. and D. Olowu (1990) 'The failure of the centralised African state', in Wunsch *et al.* (eds) (1990), pp. 1–22.

Wunsch, J. and D. Olowu (eds) (1990) *The failure of the centralised state: institutions and self-governance in Africa* (Boulder, Colo.: Westview Press).

Index